# New and Improved

## The Transformation of American Women's Emotional Culture

*John C. Spurlock*

and

*Cynthia A. Magistro*

NEW YORK UNIVERSITY PRESS

*New York and London*

NEW YORK UNIVERSITY PRESS
New York and London

Library of Congress Cataloging-in-Publication Data
Spurlock, John C., 1954–
    New and improved : the transformation of American women's
emotional culture / John C. Spurlock and Cynthia A. Magistro.
    p.   cm. — (The history of emotions series)
    Includes bibliographical references and index.
    ISBN 0-8147-8045-8 (cloth : alk. paper)
    1. Women—United States—History—20th century. 2. Women—United
States—Psychology—History—20th century. 3. Emotions—Social
aspects—United States—History—20th century. 4. United
States—Social life and customs—20th century—Psychological
aspects. 5. Emotions in literature. I. Magistro, Cynthia A., 1956–
II. Title. III. Series: History of emotion series.
    HQ1420 .S68 1998
    305.4'0973'0904—ddc21                98-9050
                                              CIP

New York University Press books are printed on acid-free paper,
and their binding materials are chosen for strength and durability.

Manufactured in the United States of America
10  9  8  7  6  5  4  3  2  1

*To Lucille Spurlock*
*and the memory of Lawton M. Spurlock*
JCS

*To Rhoda Louise Kraft Magistro*
*and Philip John Magistro*
CAM

en's writings have given us the best sources available for un-
ng the lived experience of emotion. Women may have written
t gender imbalances or to claim their distinctive voice, but they
te to understand and shape their feelings.[1] Their writings allow
xplore the culture of the first decades of this century from the
tive of emotionally engaged participants.

men's words make clear the turning away from the Victorian past
d modern culture. Women worked to adopt the emotional styles
new century. Yet we have found, in every stage of their lives, that
en frequently failed to live out the emotional images they had taken
eir own. A persistent tension underlay the emotional lives of early
ntieth-century women. Although embracing the new emotional style,
men struggled with lingering messages from Victorian sources and
h their own failure to successfully manage emotions or to navigate
e century's new emotional demands.

Of course, claims about the experience of women must come with
nany caveats. This study deals with white, middle-class women. Even
within this narrow category, the women we have studied are largely
Protestant, better educated, and more articulate than women in the population at large. These women came from all parts of the United States,
but they tended to live in the middle Atlantic and New England states.
Although we do not claim to have found a representative sample, we
have worked to provide generalizations about our diarists that resonate
with the experience of a much wider range of American women in the
1920s and 1930s.

We found unpublished diaries most useful for providing insights into
the complex and vivid emotional lives of women. Among the unpublished diaries eight stand out as particularly detailed and extensive. These
diaries, with their lengthy descriptions of emotional experiences and
comments on cultural materials, allowed us to enter the emotional
worlds of the writers. The long entries of these diaries also lent themselves to textual analysis of the meanings that women gave to their experiences.[2] These women kept diaries over many years and through a
number of important life transitions. Thus for each one we saw consistency in personal style across a variety of developmental tasks, including
courtship, career decisions, and marriage or motherhood or both.

While diary-keeping seems to have been fairly common in the early
twentieth century, the women who wrote frequently in their diaries for
decades may have differed from their contemporaries in important ways.

# Contents

ond, wom
derstandi
to protes
also wro
us to e
perspe

Wo
towar
of the
wom
as tl
twe
wo
wi
th

# Preface

This is a study of the emotional lives of adolescent ar
the United States in the early twentieth century. We as
plays an important role in shaping the emotions of ina
quently, we have relied on the work of cultural and so
especially works in the relatively new field of history of
Following a long tradition in the periodization of the twent
we see the 1910s through the early 1930s as a time of tran
Victorian to modern culture, and in the chapters that follow v
the major cultural changes that shaped the lives of American
Yet our approach has been to write cultural history as personal
Although we have read widely in the cultural materials of our 1
we have also closely studied the writings of women coming of ag
living through their adult lives in the 1910s through the early 19
Through their writings, we have attempted to understand how individ
women appropriated the cultural messages of this period and used the
to understand and to shape their experiences of friendship, love, moth
erhood, loss, and loneliness.

Relying on the personal writings of women has shaped our work in
two ways. First, the diaries, letters, and reminiscences of approximately
fifty women, born between 1887 and 1916, have helped set the agenda
for our research. Although we began reading primary documents with a
set of questions and topics to consider, the self-writings of women often
led us to new questions. Most of the emotional issues that we explore in
the chapters that follow emerged not from the cultural materials that we
read but from the concerns of women experiencing these emotions. Sec-

The persistent diarists may have been more introspective, more sensitive to emotional experiences. On the other hand, recent theories of women's development stress the importance of both feelings and relationships for women generally. Our diarists, who wrote about these things in detail, seem only to have more consistently verbalized than other women the entangled and ineffable female experiences of relatedness and desire.[3]

The use of diaries also raises the issue of deception. All diarists construct, to varying degrees, the pictures they would like to have of themselves from cultural scripts. One of our diarists, now in her early eighties, added an annotation to a statement she had made in her 1920s diaries: "Lies!"[4] Still, the sensitivity of these women to cultural scripts means that, as we became better acquainted with both their diaries and their cultural contexts, we could fairly accurately identify where they found images and ideals. This same familiarity also made it abundantly clear when scripts, images, and ideals failed to match the emotions of the moment.

We have attempted to correct for possible blind spots among persistent diarists by setting their experiences within contexts provided by other kinds of self-writing. A second group of approximately twenty women wrote diaries or letters that, although less extensive than those described above, serve as important sources of information about the cultural forces shaping women's emotional experiences. These women wrote close to the time that they experienced the emotions they described, and in this sense they share with the first group an immediacy that often vividly portrays the emotional conflicts and rewards that they experienced. However, the usefulness of these writings was limited by three considerations. (1) Many of these diaries or collections had been edited for publication and omitted details of everyday life or private matters or both. (2) Some of these works had limited discussions of emotional issues. (3) Some dealt with limited time periods or dimensions of women's lives. Edythe Weiner's diary from her sophomore year in high school, for instance, is a rich source for understanding the emotional trials of adolescent girls, but it deals with only one year.

Women in our third group wrote letters, reminiscences, memoirs, and autobiographies more distant from the lived experience of emotion than the works in either of the first two groups. These works are inevitably mediated by concerns for self-presentation different from those of women writing only for themselves or their most intimate friends. These works primarily served to provide examples and verification of themes identified in the writings of our core of persistent diarists. The works in this third group generally provided less detail, less emotional emphasis, and less candor than the work of women in the two other groups.

By matching the concerns and experiences of persistent diarists to those expressed in other self-writings, we see patterns of consistency in women's lives. Often we can further extend the applicability of this pattern through the use of contemporary social science or popular culture. The tension created by the new heterosexual freedom, for instance, appears repeatedly in the cinema of the early decades of the century, in the comments of people interviewed in Muncie, Indiana, and in the writings of women. Although the culture beckoned women to greater sexual pleasure, that pleasure often seemed difficult to achieve.

Taken together, the experiences of the women in this study illustrate the range of emotional possibilities available to most middle-class women living in the 1920s and 1930s. In the chapters that follow, we explore that range through the stories of individual women. The chapters reflect the stages of life that these women would have recognized: adolescence, young adulthood or singlehood, marriage, motherhood. Not all of these women participated equally in these culturally prescribed stages, and we attempt to do some justice to the variety of their life experiences. Each chapter provides a summary of the major cultural messages about emotional life for women at particular stages of life and shows how these women appropriated those messages and ideals. In addition, each chapter describes the difficulties that women encountered when culture proved an inadequate guide to emotional life.

Although any book requires a great deal of work, from the beginning we have been pleasantly aware of the good luck that made writing this book possible, especially the help of friends and colleagues. Peter Stearns extended his support and his good advice at the very beginning of our venture into the history of emotions. He later helped move our work from its early stages to the prospectus for the present book, and he gave helpful suggestions for revising an early draft of the book. Jan Lewis also read and commented on portions of this manuscript. Our editor at New York University, Jennifer Hammer, proved an invaluable guide prior to and during the publication process. New York University Press also made a wise choice in the anonymous reviewer for this work, whose comments helped and encouraged our revisions.

We relied on the competence and friendliness of staff at the Schlesin-

# Contents

# *Preface*

This is a study of the emotional lives of adolescent and adult women in the United States in the early twentieth century. We assume that culture plays an important role in shaping the emotions of individuals. Consequently, we have relied on the work of cultural and social historians, especially works in the relatively new field of history of the emotions. Following a long tradition in the periodization of the twentieth century, we see the 1910s through the early 1930s as a time of transition from Victorian to modern culture, and in the chapters that follow we describe the major cultural changes that shaped the lives of American women. Yet our approach has been to write cultural history as personal history. Although we have read widely in the cultural materials of our period, we have also closely studied the writings of women coming of age and living through their adult lives in the 1910s through the early 1920s. Through their writings, we have attempted to understand how individual women appropriated the cultural messages of this period and used them to understand and to shape their experiences of friendship, love, motherhood, loss, and loneliness.

Relying on the personal writings of women has shaped our work in two ways. First, the diaries, letters, and reminiscences of approximately fifty women, born between 1887 and 1916, have helped set the agenda for our research. Although we began reading primary documents with a set of questions and topics to consider, the self-writings of women often led us to new questions. Most of the emotional issues that we explore in the chapters that follow emerged not from the cultural materials that we read but from the concerns of women experiencing these emotions. Second, women's writings have given us the best sources available for understanding the lived experience of emotion. Women may have written to protest gender imbalances or to claim their distinctive voice, but they also wrote to understand and shape their feelings.[1] Their writings allow us to explore the culture of the first decades of this century from the perspective of emotionally engaged participants.

Women's words make clear the turning away from the Victorian past toward modern culture. Women worked to adopt the emotional styles of the new century. Yet we have found, in every stage of their lives, that women frequently failed to live out the emotional images they had taken as their own. A persistent tension underlay the emotional lives of early twentieth-century women. Although embracing the new emotional style, women struggled with lingering messages from Victorian sources and with their own failure to successfully manage emotions or to navigate the century's new emotional demands.

Of course, claims about the experience of women must come with many caveats. This study deals with white, middle-class women. Even within this narrow category, the women we have studied are largely Protestant, better educated, and more articulate than women in the population at large. These women came from all parts of the United States, but they tended to live in the middle Atlantic and New England states. Although we do not claim to have found a representative sample, we have worked to provide generalizations about our diarists that resonate with the experience of a much wider range of American women in the 1920s and 1930s.

We found unpublished diaries most useful for providing insights into the complex and vivid emotional lives of women. Among the unpublished diaries eight stand out as particularly detailed and extensive. These diaries, with their lengthy descriptions of emotional experiences and comments on cultural materials, allowed us to enter the emotional worlds of the writers. The long entries of these diaries also lent themselves to textual analysis of the meanings that women gave to their experiences.[2] These women kept diaries over many years and through a number of important life transitions. Thus for each one we saw consistency in personal style across a variety of developmental tasks, including courtship, career decisions, and marriage or motherhood or both.

While diary-keeping seems to have been fairly common in the early twentieth century, the women who wrote frequently in their diaries for decades may have differed from their contemporaries in important ways.

ger Library, Radcliffe College, where most of our research was conducted, and at the Huntington Library in San Marino, California, and the Vassar College Library. The staff at the Sophia Smith Collection, Smith College, readily extended their help, especially Amy Hague who guided us during our early visits to the papers of some of our most important diarists. The use of the papers of Gladys Bell Penrod was possible because of the generosity of Ivan McGee, Director of the Indiana County Historical and Genealogical Society. We also wish to thank Suzanne Ohl of the Tyrone Historical Society. The papers were identified by the Gender Studies survey at Seton Hill College under the direction of Chris Mueseler.

Our home base was the Reeves Memorial Library, Seton Hill College, where Denise Sticha and other staff took our unending interlibrary loan requests in stride and seemed capable of finding virtually everything we asked for. The Faculty Development Committee at Seton Hill College, under the leadership of Bernadette Fondy, helped our project from the beginning, with support for travel to conferences, released time, and sabbatical leave. Students at Seton Hill also had a hand in our work, especially Mary Ciccoccioppo, Alison Mahany, and Tanya Scalzitti.

Friends and colleagues read portions of the work and provided insights into the arcana of past times or special disciplines, including Jim Reed, John Gillis, Foster Jones, Jill Kelly, Kurt Piehler, Bonnie Gorscak, Alvaro Barriga, Philip Cushman, and Constance Fischer. Lynore Banchoff and others contributed during the morning study group discussions at the annual meetings of the Society for Values in Higher Education. We also benefitted from comments and discussions of our work at the Lewis and Clark Gender Studies Symposium and the encouragement of the symposium's chair, Jane Hunter.

Beth Twiggar Goff gave us her candid and useful comments about our reading of her diary. Mr. and Mrs. DeLane Penrod encouraged our project and also provided telling details about the life of Mr. Penrod's mother, the first diarist we studied, Gladys Bell Penrod.

We owe an immeasurable debt to our families. Charles and Pauline Arneson, Donna and Rick Bimeal, Louise and Ron Bennett, and Dani and Phil Magistro provided logistical support. Most important, we could not have written this book without the support and encouragement of our spouses, Rebecca Spurlock and David Mente, and our children, Ruth and Esther, and Emily and Julia.

## I

# Self and Emotion in
# the Early Twentieth Century

In February 1918 Viola White, a graduate of Wellesley College working as a clerk typist in New York City, attended a revival given by the evangelist William Biedernolf. An Episcopalian and a socialist, White probably attended out of curiosity. Her journal entry on the event mixes sarcasm and exasperation. "There was considerable old-fashioned emotionalism both in audience and speaker," she wrote, "the usual front-seat bore who snorts 'praise the Lord' whenever the speaker makes a point you might have liked to hear, a good deal about white-haired mother waiting on the other side, and little children at the gate of the St. Louis Exposition (White City) for heaven, and the glassy eyes of the dying infidel."[1]

While White dismissed the revival with a literary turn of phrase— "the sort of thing you can't sneer at if you are a decent human being, and can't respect if you're a thinking one"—she may have felt drawn to the "old-fashioned emotionalism" she disdained. Her passage also shows a clear consciousness of what Congregationalist minister J. H. Denison in 1928 called "emotional culture." According to Denison, "every successful civilization has owed its success to an elaborate system by which certain emotions were cultivated." He believed that every society required common emotional experiences to maintain its "inner coherence" and that both custom and religion cultivated socially valuable emotions.[2] His concept of emotional culture resonates with some areas of emotional research in sociology, psychology, and history during the last thirty years. A shift in the metaphorical understanding of emotion has taken place over several centuries in western Europe and America. The passions, which acted on Achilles in the *Iliad*, seemed to come from outside, a gift or curse from the gods. In more recent centuries, emotion appeared as the property of the individual, as it still does in day-to-day discussion. Some contemporary psychologists, however, have shifted the metaphor again, seeing emotion as a product of "reflective thought" or of role playing.[3]

Culture becomes far more important in understanding the expression of emotion as the metaphorical understanding shifts away from internal processes toward social roles. For middle-class women in the nineteenth century, feelings grew in the context of distinctively female spheres. Warm relations with mothers, other female relatives, and female friends formed the bedrock of social connection and emotional experience. The single most important bridge between the separate spheres was courtship. Through the conventions of calling and long acquaintance, courtship allowed young women and men slowly to open to one another their inmost and secret selves and to understand members of the opposite sex as they never had before. Courting couples held to a standard of premarital chastity, because of moral scruples and fear of accidental pregnancy. This undoubtedly increased the intensity of feelings of the couple for one another. Women also had to take special pains to assure themselves of their lover's commitment because of the limits of economic alternatives to marriage for women. Marriage exercised an extraordinary influence on women's lives. The status of their husbands became their own status. Yet the network of friends that women built up during their youth continued and provided continuity in their lives. The woman's sphere often took on greater importance as Victorian women aged and the passions of romance faded somewhat while the duties of wife and husband took more and more of the couple's time. The great experience of the woman's life could be expected with the birth of children and the transformation of wife into mother.[4]

Every culture elaborates its own emotionology or set of evaluations of emotion. Romantics and Victorians alike prized sentiment, yet by the early twentieth century "sentimental" would become a pejorative description of the Victorian era. One of the large trends within American emotionology has been the shift since the nineteenth century from a positive regard for most intense emotional experiences toward a suspicion of emotional intensity. At the same time, new evaluations of some emotions entered American culture. Emotions such as grief and anger, which Victorians embraced, came to seem mainly negative. Like Bob Cratchit, in Dickens's *A Christmas Carol*, who urged his family never to forget Tiny Tim, Victorian Americans held on to their grief as a living connection to departed loved ones. By 1919 John Watson, the founder of behaviorism, called grief "a maladjustment period" that normally "disappears as soon as new objects are found or new conditioned reflexes have been entrained."[5]

The changing emotionology signaled a shift in every part of women's lives. The separate spheres of the nineteenth century declined in importance with the growth of an adolescent peer culture and greater work opportunities for women. Women grew up in a world that prized socializing between the sexes, and they rejected the sentimental and repressive courtship practices of the nineteenth century. They dated many men and exchanged caresses with many of those dates. With so many men to choose from, modern women expected to find the right man, the match who would change their lives and make possible a marriage of companionship and good sex. Motherhood, once considered the purest and highest of the passions, lost some of its importance and much of its intensity. Modern women expected fulfillment in marriage, companionship, or career. Like the stereotypical flapper who took up smoking and necking with gusto, modern women took up new emotional experiences with blithe courage, actively seeking up-to-date versions of love and happiness and were relieved that they lived in an age free from taboo and prudery.

Yet emotional experiences rarely matched expectations. Women often found their dreams and desires frustrated, even when they worked to meet the cultural prescriptions for fulfillment and happiness. The tension between emotional culture and emotional experience had many sources. Living in a period of transition during the early establishment of the new emotional norms, many women found that they harbored conflicting values—Victorian and modern points of view might seem equally compelling at different times and in different situations. Yet the pervasiveness and persuasiveness of new emotional formulas sometimes led women to embrace standards and ideals that failed to match their own needs or their lived reality. Although modern culture provided the tools for understanding and managing feelings, it also set up expectations that left women disappointed or ambivalent about their own experience.

Commentators during the 1920s and historians since then have agreed that the culture changed more rapidly and profoundly for women than for men. The "new woman," "the new freedom," and the "sexual revolution" all referred to cultural changes that moved young women out of the Victorian home and into the public realm that men had long claimed as their own. The women whose journals, letters, reminiscences, and autobiographies provide the sources for this study were at the center of this transformation of American emotional culture. White, middle class, and well educated, these women studied and adopted the new culture through magazines and movies and practiced it in parked cars, dorm rooms, offices, and suburban homes. The diarists among these women also reflected on this new culture and their experience of life in it. They poured out their feelings in lines written close to the experience of passion and in some ways performed their feelings and passion in their writing.

Our collection of diarists, memoirists, and autobiographers offers insights into the experiences that middle-class women had of American culture and into the ways that culture shaped women's emotional lives. The range of the middle class, even in the 1920s, was extraordinary, as women from farms and working-class families claimed cultural ideals in common with much wealthier women from old New England families. Although dating and companionate marriage may have spread unevenly across the country, by the mid-1920s the values supporting modern courtship and marriage appeared in strikingly similar terms in the journals of a rural schoolteacher in Pennsylvania and the daughter of a partner in the Morgan bank. Both women suffered from feelings of inadequacy and emptiness, and both hoped for a passionate experience of life. Whether these longings came from their culture or from their psyche (if the two can be separated), the shared feelings point toward general developments and experiences among middle-class women in the United States.

## Education of the Senses

Although the trends that would make American culture modern and put the impress of American culture on modern culture throughout the world originated in the late nineteenth century, those trends became powerfully evident only after the end of World War I and the adoption of the Prohibition Amendment. According to varying accounts, Americans either gleefully or nervously abandoned the comforting verities of nineteenth-century Victorianism and embraced a culture of "terrible honesty." "I'd as soon live in a scummy pond as in the atmosphere of 1921," wrote Viola White at the dawning of the modern era in American life, "unemployment all about, hopelessness on park benches."[6] She saw around her the tattered remains of the Victorian era as the postwar depression strangled economic activity. The boom that followed in 1922 would empty Manhattan's park benches and bolster the emerging culture of material abundance. The desires of the individual in the new century became framed as a problem to be solved through new possessions, thus creating an opportunity for those with goods to sell. Department stores and advertising joined with the mass media of magazines and movies to show modern women and men the shape of passion. The culture of abundance and consumption reshaped the emotions and expectations that constitute individual identity.

The Victorian home had been the central feature of an emotional culture supported by liberal Protestantism and sentimental literature. As a contrast to and a haven from the world, the home stood as one of the important divisions within Victorian society, separating the spheres of men and women. In the world, men labored within a dynamic and often amoral economy that transformed everything in its path. Within the home, other values applied. The warmth of the home, and especially the love of mothers, sheltered young lives from the rigors of the world. Within a sphere defined by close, affectionate ties, mothers and female relatives and friends shaped the lives of children and brought them to adulthood with religious convictions and scrupulous morality.[7]

Whether in the home or the world middle-class Victorians held up a standard of restraint for their emotional lives. Early in the nineteenth century antislavery orator Theodore Weld had expressed his own struggle to maintain an outwardly calm and dignified bearing: "I am *constitutionally,* as far as *emotions* are concerned, a quivering mass of intensities kept in subjection only by the *rod of iron* in the strong hand of conscience and reason." Strategies such as assuming the appearance of calm to control anger or other passions, and directing stern commands to oneself, could augment reason and conscience. Even mothers had to guard their emotions to save impressionable children from distress. The Victorian devotion to decorum also appeared in the demand for conformity to public morality.[8] For men, scrupulous adherence to moral standards might be waived—especially if powerful sexual drives had to be vented—as long as they maintained public standards. Women had no such loopholes in their social contract. The purity of wife and mother stood as a warrant for the Victorian home and, by extension, of the Victorian social ideal.

The division between home and world had already begun to break down by the end of the nineteenth century. The separate spheres and the double standard came under attack, initially from the supporters of the morality of the home. Reformers demanded a single standard of behavior, and intellectuals demanded a new standard of "honesty" that meant a willingness to consider facts and accept conclusions that Victorians would have deemed unfit for discussion. Contemporary observers offered a variety of causes for the transformation of Victorian culture, including war, Prohibition, jazz, and racial devolution. A conservative psychologist at the end of the 1920s called the decade "the great age of freedom; the age of glory for him who can find another idol to smash and another taboo to kill by bold defiance." The most usual suspect, however, was the economic system, which had remained outside the home and outside its moral compass.[9] And even though reformers at the end of the nineteenth century hoped to impose the home's moral imperatives in the world, it was the world that prevailed.

Rather than moral uplift, the modern world valued consumption. The mass production techniques introduced into major American industries in the last decades of the nineteenth century transformed the livelihood and the living conditions of virtually all Americans. Viola Goode Liddell, born in 1902, remembered the changes that the new industrial age brought to her small town in Alabama following the World War—the railroad, the mail order catalog, the gramophone, ragtime and Broadway music, bicycles, then cars, and then electricity and the telephone. Ann Marie Low chronicled the appearance of the telephone in rural North Dakota in 1924 with its party line that allowed all the neighbors to listen to everyone's calls. Her father resisted the purchase of a radio until the 1930s and then wouldn't allow a loudspeaker in the house. But talking movies had reached the area by 1929.[10]

New technology, as Liddell and Low reveal, meant new possessions. By the 1920s advertising pictured a democracy of commodities in which the bounty of mass production became available to ever greater numbers. The middle class grew as the economy created more white-collar jobs and as labor-saving devices eliminated some of the need for servants. The rapid change in makes and models of all kinds of new goods demanded an expertise that young people seemed to acquire more readily than their parents. Advertisements showed individuals improving their lives and gaining happiness by buying the latest goods. "It is all so silly," a social worker wrote in the early years of the Depression of the advertisements she saw, "nothing but sham. Back of it, of course, is the whole system of competition," she added. She might have noted further that back of it stood new values that rejected struggle and self-control in favor of what one of her contemporaries called "consumptionism," a life of abundance without pain or conflict.[11]

A psychologist and educator writing in the 1930s lamented the "artificial character of life induced by machine production. It has cast us adrift from our elemental bearings, distorted our perspective, and too often destroyed the sincerity of our lives." Along with the growing separation of individuals from the fruits of their labor, Melvin Haggerty lamented the loss of the "unity of art and life," which could satisfy the natural human desire for color, light, motion, and craft.[12] For a growing proportion of Americans, however, the satisfactions of color, light, and motion (at least) thrived in America's department stores. The department store became the school of the consumer society, enticing customers with its displays and vast array of dry goods and educating shoppers' senses through colorful spectacles. The stores also provided shoppers with restaurants, music, and child care, drawing middle-class women into a world of comfort and even leisure.[13]

Travel could show young women the importance and peculiarity of the American department store. Jessamyn West noted that every town in England had a Woolworth's, but only the biggest English emporia "can compare with any shop in Los Angeles." Foreign correspondent Dorothy Thompson, who spent more of her adult life in Europe than in middle America, thought that the chain stores contributed to the shoddiness of American life. She wrote to Sinclair Lewis of the many stores vying for attention—not only Woolworth's, but Kresge's, McCrory's, Marshall Fields, Piggly Wiggly, and "innumerable" five, ten, and twenty-five cent stores.[14]

"What I want the store to be is a little piece of the modern world *at its best*," says the fictional owner of a small-town department store in Dorothy Canfield Fisher's *The Homemaker*. "It is my ambition to make every trip to our store as educative as an afternoon tea-party for the women-folk on a farm," he tells an admiring new employee. "I want to select for them the *right things*, the things they never could select for themselves for lack of training."[15] The first trip to a department store could become a major life event for young women from rural areas. Viola Liddell went shopping in Selma for the first time as a teenager. Believing that dress sizes corresponded to ages, she asked for a size sixteen. The clerk provided a rapid and probably scornful lesson on shopping and clothing, much to Viola's future benefit. Edythe Weiner, living in Glens Falls, New York, in the mid-1920s, knew department stores at age fourteen much better than Viola Liddell did at sixteen. Edythe delighted in her periodic trips to New York City to buy shoes and clothes.[16] Clara Savage, a hardworking journalist, had little time to record her life in detail in her prewar diary, but she often noted shopping trips. "Spent half the day working and half the day shopping," she wrote of one Saturday. "Mother and I put in hours of searching the stores." On one of her trips to Wanamakers she began to feel unwell. "I had to lie down in their hospital but did the shopping."

Savage would later write for *Good Housekeeping* that "one of the chief pleasures of many a woman's life is in collecting possessions" and that "lifeless things" such as furniture and clothing could inspire "a strong emotional attachment."[17] A dynamic capitalism had created a world of abundance, and advertising and department stores sought to enhance the allure of goods with appeals to fundamental drives or emotions. The culture of consumptionism not only encouraged desire for commodities, it also stressed the emotional valence of commodities. Advertising agencies and department stores recognized that women spent most of the household's income. Advertisements appealed primarily to women, and department stores catered to the presumed needs and desires of women. Together they gave objects charisma that could make shopping an emotional catharsis. Mt. Holyoke College student Ruth Raymond read French until her eyes tired and then bought an expensive Japanese scarf "as a consolation for my weariness." Years later she still used shopping for consolation, although this time the dress, shoes, rouge, and tap slippers were to lighten her mood after learning of the need for major dental work.[18] Raymond lived in Massachusetts, but the value of shopping for emotional adjustment reached into the South. Emily Tapscott Clark suffered from heat, loneliness, and an irritating stepmother until "quite suddenly I bought a perfectly darling new dress," which met with "gratifying appreciation."[19]

Sometimes women found their desires worrisome. "I would love to believe, and I can't help thinking that clothes shouldn't matter," wrote a sensitive midwestern college student; "but I can't keep them from mattering."[20] Winifred Willis, a writer living in New York, wanted money for only two things—"ravishing clothes & self-improvement." She then corrected herself for putting clothes first before her desire for reading, study, and travel. "But I have a pagan worship of clothes. I would array me resplendently anew each three or four hours of the day." She wrote of one shopping trip, "Yesterday I bought a stunning new sport suit," and then described the "soft, white gown with a brilliant orange and black jacket." She concluded, "O, I am so happy!"[21]

## The Modern Self

The consumer culture conspired with industrial society to reshape the modern self. By self we mean the constellation of experiences and expectations that an individual recognizes as integral to her identity, that give meaning to her life, and that shape her relationships with her society and culture. Americans from the early nineteenth century had faced the demands of adjusting behavior and appearance for diverse groups in a fluid social system. Etiquette books became advice manuals for managing social and geographic mobility. Yet, even though Victorians recognized the mutability of public appearances, they clung to an ideal of self as a hard core of inner qualities and desires to be kept secret from all but the most intimate of friends. For early twentieth-century Americans, the self seemed far more fluid and public.[22]

Several trends contributed to the changes in self-understanding. As commodities proliferated, so did the anxieties and desires invented by advertisers. This commodification of emotion probably flattened emotional intensity. During these same decades the expansion and transformation of work and society placed a premium on an individual's ability to understand and fit into rapidly changing social settings. The Columbia philosopher and educator John Dewey lamented that in the modern world individuals failed to find "support and commitment" as participants in "a social whole."[23] By the 1920s psychologists and sociologists tended toward the view of Harvard psychologist William McDougall that "if a man belongs to several groups, each having a distinct code, he will . . . be liable to develop as many distinct selves." John Watson, the behaviorist psychologist and advertising executive, disagreed energetically with McDougall on most issues, but he defined personality in ways that accorded with McDougall's view as "an individual's total assets . . . and liabilities . . . on the reaction side," or more economically as "the end product of our habit system." Watson stressed the adaptive response of the individual to the environment. The personality changes constantly, he wrote, "the only adjusted person is a dead person." For Victorians the ideal of character mediated between the genuine self and the demands of society. For moderns, the demands of society became more diverse and character more malleable, while self seemed either to wither away or became conflated with the mix of demands and responses in social interaction.[24]

"I'm just beginning to realize how many different personalities one has," wrote college student Martha Lavell as she reflected on the different responses she made to letters from different friends.[25] The perceived multiplicity of the self could call into question the genuineness of any particular experience of self. Anne Morrow, the daughter of the ambassador to Mexico, keenly felt the plasticity of life in diplomatic social circles: "This life is so unreal—I don't know what my real smile is and what [is] my party one, what my real feelings are and what [are] the superficial ones."[26] Women often felt that there was "no one ready-made self behind activities," as John Dewey put it.[27] This cast doubt on the emotional experiences of the varying selves in their many social settings. Without the certainty of a genuine self, emotional experience required confirmation other than its self-evident existence.

Middle-class women tried to pin down the chimera of self. They watched for experiences that carried their own manifest of authenticity. Moments of reflective self-awareness and intense emotion might appear to fit extraordinarily well into an assumed scheme, or they might nudge a young woman into a new and unexpected realization. They experienced these moments as intense and unmistakable epiphanies. In writing of a new plane that she and her husband were testing, Anne Morrow Lindbergh wrote, "It was one of those few moments in life when you are absorbed and overcome by the utter perfection of a thing, like seeing a perfect rider swing a perfect polo pony, or watching the Panama Canal locks open, or hearing Harold Samuel play Bach."[28] Dorothy Smith Dushkin, a musician living in Chicago, felt moved by the vitality of African Americans in a movie. "If we only had more of it—or perhaps any—& were willing to express it what a falling off the offices of nerve doctors & psychiatrists would have!"[29] Virtually every diarist included in this study reported moments of similar emotional insight and self-awareness. Such moments allowed diarists to affirm or to refine their self-understandings.

If some emotional experiences carried their own proof of authenticity, most of emotional life depended on social and cultural cues. Movies, plays, popular music, and fiction, along with the ever-present popular advice literature in newspapers and magazines, formed as well as reflected the emotional landscape of modern America. Like the railroad and the mail-order catalog, modern culture might appear in the lives of young women piecemeal, as not always welcome novelties. Gladys Hasty, who grew up in rural Maine, decided against attending the University of Maine because it had "supplied us with a substitute teacher who came in lipstick and a black silk dress."[30] In rural Pennsylvania, Gladys Bell found the jazz she heard over the radio intolerable. Yet broadcasts of classical music appealed to her. "Such music can not be rivaled," she wrote in 1925, "and what a miracle that we are *so* entertained as we lie in ease and comfort upon our own divan with absolutely no inconveniences."[31]

The seductive combination of technology and modern culture appeared everywhere by the 1920s in motion pictures. Contemporary estimates placed weekly attendance at between seventy-seven and one hundred million with half the American population attending at least one movie in any year. A movie's ability to entertain depended on its ability to engage the passions of its audience. "Every emotion of which man is capable is played to by this mighty narrator," one study reported, and American cinema succeeded in engaging audiences around the world.[32] In England in the late 1920s Jessamyn West found nothing but American movies in London. In Paris, she met no one who had ever heard of "Indiana, Iowa, and New Hampshire." But they knew about California—"its scenery, climate, fruit, movie stars, earthquakes, gold mines."[33] In the mid-1930s Dorothy Dushkin and her husband David met Igor Stravinsky and David's brother Sam, who had just performed a concert in Chicago. The party went to a movie "of the *thriller* sort—fighting, romance, torture, patriotism, gallantry, etc. They seemed to love it."[34]

Even though American movies claimed a universal appeal to elemental emotions, movies succeeded or failed to the extent that they matched the emotional values and standards of particular groups within American society. Religious movies, like Cecil B. DeMille's *Ten Commandments* attracted enormous audiences with their nonsectarian moralizing. Yet DeMille's *Joan of Arc* failed at the box office because the Roman Catholic bishops opposed its portrayal of the inquisitor.[35] Dorothy Smith, years before escorting Stravinsky to an American movie, took her

Sunday school class to see *Ben Hur.* "The best movie I've ever seen," she wrote in her diary, because of the beautiful portrayal of Christ and because of the cinematic spectacle that included "hair-raising thrills" and colored pictures.[36] Katharine Du Pre Lumpkin, who grew up in the south, recalled a 1915 screening of *Birth of a Nation* on her college campus in Florida. "All around me people sighed and shivered, and now and then shouted or wept, in their intensity."[37]

Although the impact of movies could seem overpowering in the lives of individual women, they served more commonly as guides to modern problems and as clues to emotional behavior. For several weeks after seeing *Mickey,* Gladys Bell, just beginning her teaching duties in western Pennsylvania, took on the persona of the carefree heroine of the Mack Sennett comedy. In the years that followed, Bell often resorted to movies as sources of ideas or insights for the problems she faced. Yet the large number of movies that she saw (she mentioned eleven in her 1922 diary) gave her a comparative sophistication in the use of movies as sources of life ideals. Gladys also read widely in the popular literature of the day, and she tended to find comfort in Victorian romantic ideals, whether these appeared in movies or books.[38]

An even more studied sophistication comes through in the reflections of Ruth Raymond, whose attendance at movies apparently took the place of religious fervor. She studied *Picture Play* and *Photoplay* and wrote of the lives of celebrities along with her accounts of family, friends, and teachers. Ruth's comments about movies often show a critical distance and appraisal. For the first five months of 1935, for instance, she listed thirty-six movies that she had attended, with short comments on each movie. "William Powell and Myrna Loy delicately comic," she wrote of *The Thin Man.* She listed the main cast members of *Marie Valente,* concluding "God bless them all." But of *Gridiron Flash* she commented, "Eddie Quillen with a gal who must have bartered her virtue for the part; the worst football picture to date." She called the plot of *Evergreen* "idiotic" and characterized *The Defense Rests* as "the usual legal melodrama."[39]

As Ruth Raymond's responses to movies suggests, middle-class women did not only passively absorb emotional culture. Rather, they often appropriated cultural materials selectively, sifting them for what they considered valuable at the moment. Although they generally accepted the ideals they saw in movies and read about in the mass-market periodicals, they also struggled to find a fit between their experiences and the culture's messages.

## The Therapeutic Culture

Modern emotional culture depended not only on new technologies in the media but also on a new language. For Victorian women, evangelical or liberal Protestantism provided the most powerful and pervasive language for understanding human life and distress. By late in the nineteenth century, however, the drama of sin and redemption had begun to lose its power. Many Americans assumed that personal problems implied mental distress and searched for treatments that would make a difference. The traditional and widely popular therapies known as mind cure continued their vogue in the 1920s. The best-selling work on mind cure of the 1920s, Emile Coué's *Self-Mastery through Conscious Autosuggestion* offered a program of self-improvement that required the frequent repetition of the individual's goals. Actress Lillian Roth used Coué's method for a problem with one of her hands, and dancer Jane Sherman tried autosuggestion to keep her weight under control. Christian Science, with its classic *Science and Health* by Mary Baker Eddy, often appears in young women's diaries in times of trouble or personal change.[40]

By 1920, however, mind cure would make way for and in some cases assimilate to the new therapeutic viewpoints associated with Freud and psychoanalysis. Marjorie Kinnan's 1918 interview with a psychoanalyst reveals the dawning of the Freudian era in American therapy and the limited inroads that Freudian language had made up to that time. Kinnan believed that she felt mixed up, "as if I were groping in a mist" after the interview because of the "psychic radiation" the psychoanalyst had given off. She believed it would make her morbid to enter the profession and know "the most intimate cores of people's lives and thoughts," which they reveal "under this sort of hypnotic psycho-analysis—under it they deliver up their very souls. It involves sex a great deal, you know—it might be fearfully unhealthy."[41] Even in the late 1920s psychoanalysis seemed new to upper middle-class New Englanders. The author John Marquand "flung himself with a will into deriding the whole bag of tricks," although he and his wife delivered themselves to analysis as their marriage broke up.[42] In New York by the late 1920s, Freudian ideas and the necessity of treatment had gained wide acceptance. The young painter Ione Robinson dreaded parties with her artistic friends because she always felt uncomfortable in conversations "that I don't understand which seem to be mostly about being psychoanalyzed."[43] Martha Lavell studied psychoanalysis for the first time in graduate school and considered it "the most preposterous illogical stuff that anyone could think up. Yet," she continued, "my reaction merely proves them right."[44]

Many of the terms and concepts of psychoanalysis had become popularly accepted in the United States by the mid-1920s. Ruth Raymond, sixteen in 1925, wondered why her "sub-conscious mind seemed determined to dwell on David," a former boyfriend.[45] A few years later a fourteen-year-old Edythe Weiner in Glens Falls gave herself a probing self-examination and concluded that she was "too self-conscious" and had "a foul inferiority complex."[46] Remarks such as these appear almost universally in the private reflections of middle-class women from about 1920 onward. They believed that the subconscious, complexes, and neuroses all lurked within the self, and this added to the sense of the self as a multilayered entity, not entirely rational and not entirely under the command of the will.

In sum, by the 1920s, the profound and secret self that women in the nineteenth century treasured had changed into a far more malleable and public self. Advertising constantly offered to fulfill some presumed desire of the self, whether for social acceptance or a better marriage or romantic love. Desire, and the products to satisfy desire, appeared everywhere in American culture, and many middle-class women derived some emotional satisfaction from shopping for and displaying new commodities. Advertising revenues made possible other guides for emotion, especially the mass-market magazines that proliferated during the decade. Movies also provided instruction on emotional life. Yet the shallowness of this sense of self also often became evident, and women searched for more profound emotional experiences and for a better understanding of the mysteries of their unconscious minds. Taken together, these sources of self-knowledge often showed remarkable continuity. Popularized Freudian themes appeared in movies, advertisers used the latest psychological ideas, and magazines generally promoted emotional styles drawn from a variety of popular sources.

During the 1920s and 1930s, a wide range of ideas presented emotions as far more the product of culture or even personal manipulation than of innate reflexes. Dale Carnegie's popular talks during the 1920s led to his best-selling motivational handbook, *How to Win Friends and*

*Influence People* (1936) in which he offered strategies for shaping the emotions of others.[47] J. H. Denison, as noted above, had already offered his analysis of the cultural support for particular emotional experiences. Sociologists influenced by behaviorism downplayed instinct as a social determinant. George Herbert Mead and others wrote of the development of the self, including emotion, within a social context. "Piecemeal out of his social contacts the child builds up his self," wrote social historian Arthur Calhoun. Margaret Mead, writing home from Samoa in 1925, observed the striking change in the demeanor of the islanders when the curfew-angelus bell rang around sunset. Everyone ran for cover and began reciting the Lord's Prayer, "while flowers are all taken out of their hair and the *siva* song stops in the middle." As soon as the bell rang the second time, however, "solemnity—never of a very reliable depth—is sloughed off."[48]

Just as the self emerges from a social and cultural context, so do emotions. Culture provides the stories, images, and ideals that allow individuals to understand their feelings as this or that kind of emotion. Yet individuals also actively, although perhaps not always consciously, shape emotional experience.[49] Viola White's observations of the revival recognized the emotional weight of images such as the "white-haired mother" and the "glassy eyes of the dying infidel." Writer Caroline Gordon noted the importance of manipulating emotional messages for specific audiences. Editor's at *Scribner's,* she wrote, wanted "stories with real emotion in them," which apparently meant stories about murder or sudden death.[50]

Psychoanalysis, like mind cure, fits into a broader therapeutic viewpoint that held that emotions could be intentionally managed. As we saw above, shopping could offer a means of changing emotions. Probably the most common strategy for overcoming sorrow or depression was to emphasize the good things in life. "Of course I am lucky," wrote Gladys Bell Penrod, in "so many ways that I must pass by my moments of unhappiness."[51] A *Good Housekeeping* article advised women that most worries came from losing a proper sense of proportion. Instead of allowing herself to become wrapped up in these things, a woman should meditate on "those things that are beautiful and of good report, those things that truly make life worth the living. . . . Worry is a sure sign that there is something wrong with one's way of living."[52]

Yet for all their consciousness about the cultural sources of emotion, and in spite of their own attempts to manage them, emotion still seemed to most young women in the 1920s to arise from sources deep within themselves and to appear almost capriciously. "Why should sudden bottomless despair drown me without any known cause?" wondered Dorothy Smith, a young musician just returned from Paris in 1928. Even though she had entered psychoanalysis to deal with her recurring depression, her emotional experience seemed beyond her control and her grasp. "I am well, strong & of normal brain & reactions—I can't be a prey to mental mania or mysterious psychosis." Gladys Bell Penrod, frustrated with her efforts at self-management, wondered why she could not "laugh at the little ungrateful girl who lives inside me, who is always pitying herself."[53]

In the chapters that follow, we examine both emotionology and emotion. For each period of a woman's growth from adolescence to maturity her culture prescribed both relationships and emotional experiences. By studying the self-writing of early twentieth-century women, we discover how middle-class women understood and appropriated this culture. But we can also observe them as they reflect on their experience of emotion, as they compare their experience with their own understanding of cultural expectations. Almost always we find a tension between emotionology and emotional experience. This tension between the desire to fulfill cultural norms and the often ambivalent feelings and passions that made up their lives was at the heart of the emotional experience of modern women.

## 2

# *Flaming Youth*

By age fourteen Beth Twiggar, growing up in Ossining, New York, began writing diary entries that she believed would shock her middle-class parents. For instance, in February 1928 she wrote, "In bed, with cold cream smeared all over my face, nonchalantly smoking a cigarette." Later in the same entry she asked whether her recent excursions into smoking, necking, and drinking showed that she was downgrading or upgrading and then added, "Gosh, I like to think I'm a devil, don't I?" Her question gave her a way of poking fun at the cynical and sophisticated airs she enjoyed describing in her diary. Beth's airs, along with her adolescent experiments with cigarettes and boys, allowed her to explore the emotional and interpersonal styles of her modern contemporaries.

Her dentist father, three times the mayor of their town, and homemaker mother seemed to Beth to be out of touch with the urges that stirred her. She knew that her parents and older sisters loved her, but doubted that they liked her, and conceded that she often acted badly toward them. Beth regretted hurting them, especially her "long-suffering adorable" mother, but couldn't accept the life they led. "I can't help it," she wrote, "I want to do things and be things she [mother] can't understand. I want to be modern and whicked [sic] and sophisticated." Beth didn't end her entry before dryly poking fun at both herself and her family: "So I guess I'm pretty awful. Shall I commit suicide?"[1]

In the decade following World War I many adolescents embraced the identity of "flaming youth." The best-selling novel that popularized that label offered a compendium of youthful assaults on Victorian morality, including open drinking and clandestine sexual experimentation. The novel's author, Warner Fabian, succinctly described "the philosophy of the flapper:" "Duties could wait. Pleasure was something you had to grab before it got away from you." *Flaming Youth* and other works of the 1920s introduced Americans to a youth culture that had largely abandoned the moral imperatives of nineteenth-century middle-class culture.[2] Sensual stimulation and immediate gratification, so important to the mass media and the department stores of the period, provided a backdrop for the sexual independence of middle-class youth.

Most of the young women in this chapter were still high school students, although flaming youth of the 1920s included college students and some working young adults. They had in common their interest in socializing and had yet to turn to the adult concerns of marriage and career. For adolescent girls like Beth Twiggar, peer relations became more important than family or church in providing possibilities for self-discovery, status, and play. Out of these peer relations, young women shaped a distinctive emotional style. Within the heterosexual dating system, young women sought the skills of social performance that would make them attractive to boys and successful among their peers. The possibility of failure, however, always threatened self-esteem. A girl might fail to become popular or be humiliated by trying too hard to win attention. In addition, she would almost inevitably experience conflict between the Victorian moral standards of her parents and the modern demands for peer conformity. Beth self-consciously recognized this conflict. Although her private musings endorsed the values of her peers—little patience with adult values, desire for consumer goods, and above all, striving for popularity with boys and girls—she often found her peer culture and its emotional style limited or uncomfortable. Two days after asking idly if she should commit suicide, Beth had a spell of optimism and happiness: "It is such a pretty, breezy, vital world that it gives me a clutchy feeling in my—well, to be Victorian—in my heart!"[3] Her occasional nostalgia for Victorian feelings showed Beth that she lived in a period of transition.

Whereas the peer culture of the early twentieth century made heterosexual socializing central to adolescence, young women also found passionate friendships with other girls and with older women. These crushes often took on the characteristics of idol worship of teachers or older girls. At times, young women's relations with other women could become mutual and spiritually and physically satisfying. Within these relationships, women explored self-understandings that departed from the peer culture of social performance and personality. Women's experience of intimacy with other women allowed them to shape selves apart from the patterns of the consumer culture and the peer group.

### The Peer Culture

During the nineteenth century, American youth typically reproduced the gender roles of adults. Girls formed powerful bonds with their mothers and with other female relatives and friends that would last throughout their lives. Education was sex segregated, with women studying at female academies, finishing schools, and at the early colleges for women. Boys grew up in the same households as their sisters, but they also entered sex-segregated schools or went to work in their adolescent years. Girls and boys alike worked and played with adults and within contexts created by mothers, fathers, bosses, and other adult authorities. The gendered spheres of American middle-class youth merged only temporarily, and then only as youth prepared for adult responsibilities. When a young man became interested in a young woman, he called on her at home. If she proved receptive and the family approved, the young couple would be given enough privacy to become acquainted and, over time, to build a foundation of passionate desire for the commitment of marriage.[4]

As the nineteenth century drew to a close, a distinctive youth culture began to emerge within the American middle class. It was the high school, the "college of the people," often modeled on American colleges but available to many more American adolescents, that would become the agora of American youth culture. By the early twentieth century, child labor laws forced many teen-aged children out of the workplace, and compulsory education laws forced others into school. Even earlier, high school education had begun to replace low-level work experience as the most important preparation for managerial positions in American businesses. At least some high school attendance became normal for white youth by the late 1920s.[5]

In high school young middle-class women adopted the customs and styles that characterized the youth culture. Adele Siegel, who attended high school on Staten Island in the late 1920s, found the social side of high school far more absorbing than the academic. "I'm terribly lazy when it comes to school work practicing and housework, but I'm awfully energetic when it comes to Woodcraft, playing basketball, going to parties and doing things that are fun." "Things that are fun" included clubs, dances, and sporting events, the "extracurriculum" that taught students both the rituals and values of the peer group.[6] In these social activities adolescents sought status and self-worth through the approval of peers.

The extra curriculum encouraged boys and girls to mix socially. By the 1920s, American adolescents and young adults had accepted and elaborated a set of values around heterosexual sociability that sharply distinguished them from the middle-class youth of a generation earlier. Like the advertisements for the movie of *Flaming Youth* that titillated prospective viewers with promises of red and white kisses, heterosexual excess often appeared in the popular culture of the 1920s as the core of youth culture. High school sponsored activities, amusement parks, and local sporting events allowed teen-agers to define distinctive roles for themselves. As more and more young men and women entered college, an even more ambiguous stage of development became common: adults, still largely dependent on family resources, without full-time employment, prepared for roles in the rapidly expanding economy by studying the liberal arts. High school graduates, whether they went to work or to college, made high school customs and practices normative for adult recreation and courtship in the United States.[7]

The new directions taken by high school and college students during the 1920s could seem strange and even dangerous to the older generation. The generation born after 1900 had noticeably more difficult relations with parents, especially between mothers and daughters. "Each group thinks the other cruel, heartless and unfeeling," wrote Miriam Van Waters, then superintendent of the Los Angeles County juvenile home. Van Waters believed that at home most young women found boredom, indifferent parents, vague talk about morals and "being good." Outside the home, however, everything seemed "smiling, gay, changing, no disapprovals, motion and rhythm in dance-halls and swift cars; unheard of intimacy" and the "vague awareness that though one may be 'bad' the adults who 'live this way' are contented and seemingly rewarded, at least in movies and magazines."[8] Michael V. O'Shea, editor of a series of books on youth, fretted that "the nervous system is frequently so disturbed at adolescence that insanity results."[9] Adolescents seemed constantly on the move in their search for pleasure.

By the 1920s young women took for granted the newness and separateness of youth culture. Young women might echo the experts and moralists worrying over "speed crazed youth" living to "find a thrill," but the sense of newness, of a break with the past, often struck youth in the 1920s as a promise of improvement. "I'm glad I'm living in this age," one college student wrote, "people are beginning to wake up."[10] A high school student in rural North Dakota affirmed her freedom from custom: "Here all women past forty wear black dresses for best. When I get to be forty I'll wear a pink dress if I want to and never mind if the neighbors think I am trying to be young and frivolous."[11] A medical resident in the east reflected on the changes since World War I. "I can think & act; perceive & execute, reason & react in a thousand different ways that my grandmother & even my mother never could." Harriet Louise Hardy wondered about the ambivalent promise of this new freedom, although she felt, "We do not need inhibitions, it is right to heave them away."[12]

Denver juvenile court Judge Ben Lindsey recognized the economic and technological changes that underlay the "revolt of youth" in social and personal matters. "Thirty, forty years ago, youth couldn't have flung such a challenge with the least hope of success. Today, the day of the automobile, the telephone, speed, good wages, and an unheard of degree of economic independence for everybody, it can." Along with new technology, new patterns of consumption arose with the mass market economy of the early twentieth century. The youth of the century's early decades, less assimilated to the Victorian values of thrift and impressed by the advertising of the era that glamorized youthfulness and newness, attained far greater expertise in consumption, and in choosing among marginally different products, than their parents.[13]

Fads and crazes gave middle-class adolescents opportunity to explore the emotional satisfactions of commodities and to refine and display their "wisdom" in commodity selection and also to distinguish themselves from adults by the clothes and possessions they displayed. Pearl Buck, who grew up with her missionary parents in China, returning to the United States to attend Randolph Macon Woman's College, wanted to "belong to my own kind."[14] She quickly learned that to fit in she had to "learn to talk about the things that American girls talked about, boys and dances and sororities and so on." "At DePauw, in 1919," Margaret Mead recalled, "I found students who were, for the most part, the first generation to go to college and whose parents appeared at Class Day poorly dressed while their daughters wore the raccoon or muskrat coats that were appropriate to the sorority they had made."[15] A Broadway actress recalled the disasters she endured when her mother had her dress in *Vogue*-like fashions for teen-age dances: "Young people want to look like peas in a pod, and there is no use trying to make them different."[16] Beliefs and ideas, like material culture, also shifted with each passing fad. In the early 1930s, a graduate student at the University of North Carolina thought her dormitory companions all pretty much interchangeable: "you could unscrew all these heads and screw them on again to other bodies without getting any difference in conversation, outlook or personality."[17]

## Heterosexual Conviviality and the Sexual Revolution

In high schools, coeducational colleges, and the workplace, young men and women had far more contact with one another by the 1920s than had been true in the nineteenth century. This provided the context for the new socializing practices of the era and helped account for the decline in the median age of marriage.[18] Although outlandish clothing and illegal alcohol use added to the racy reputation of flaming youth, it was far more the new social and sexual freedom of young people that set the postwar generation apart. Southern writer Caroline Gordon, who happily reported in her letters when she found a better quality of liquor, had a much different response to "a madcap virgin from Greenwich Village" who stayed with her and her husband Allen Tate in 1926. "I fear I use the word virgin loosely. . . . This child is an unedifying spectacle of what may happen to young people these days! She begins to twitch if the conversation strays from sex a moment, and suddenly began to boast in the midst of dinner last night of her prowess in birth control by muscle contraction—a method she says she learned from some Hindus." Another southerner, Emily Tapscott Clark, only 30, attended "a very young party" where she was surprised to learn how much young people had changed. "The masculine methods are especially startling. They don't stop for amenities of any kind."[19] Dorothy Smith, a Midwesterner with what she referred to as Puritan ancestry, traveled to Paris to study with Nadia Boulanger in 1926. She found herself "with young people who drank a lot & told vulgar stories with relish."[20] On her trip to the Orient with the Denishawn Dancers, and under the watchful eye of Ruth St. Denis, Jane Sherman, a teen-ager from New York, found herself fending off advances from American or English expatriates in virtually every city she visited and discussing sex with her fellow dancers in their humble quarters.[21]

Although discussion of a sexual revolution generally refers to those who took advantage of new courtship or marriage practices, even young women who took no part in dating understood and experienced the changes in heterosexuality by the late 1920s. Ruth Raymond, who was 20 in 1929, kept discovering sex everywhere in her hometown, Lexington, Massachusetts. At a movie she moved once from her seat to avoid "a shabby young man" who kept flirting with her and only rid herself of his attentions by speaking coldly to him. She accepted without question a second-hand report that many of the girls in the local high school had become pregnant. At a local baseball game she overheard girls talking about the local team's players in intimate terms and discussing who various members of the team had sex with.[22]

Like Ruth Raymond, who prided herself on her worldly wisdom, many young women preferred life without Victorian euphemism. Martha Lavell, a college student in the Midwest, proudly reported that her psychology professor congratulated the generation of the 1920s for its willingness "to face the facts." Lavell reflected on just how far she had come herself in her knowledge of sex, from learning of "the man's part in procreation" during her sophomore year in college to studying psychoanalysis in graduate school.[23] Elizabeth Yates, only fourteen, recorded her embarrassment when her mother attempted to explain the physical changes that would accompany menarche. A book on *What Every Young Girl Should Know* did nothing to relieve her ignorance—in fact she hated the "prissy" style that said nothing. She finally had a straight talk with a friend who made her realize that menstruation did not mean she would never be tall enough to play center in basketball. Jane Sherman assured her mother that the talk among the Denishawn Dancers was "NOT DIRTY, just instructive about the things we really ought to know," including birth control and syphilis.[24]

Of course, discussion of sex did not always mean any gain in accurate knowledge. Margaret Mead and her housemates at Barnard College compiled a five-page list of "home remedies" for pregnancy for the benefit of a sixteen-year-old daughter of a friend, who nevertheless became pregnant. Gladys Bell had only a sketchy, and apparently inaccurate, knowledge of birth control when she married in 1925. Ruth Raymond recorded a question from a "sweet young thing" in a class where the professor had just discussed sex hygiene. " 'Just what,' she asked, 'do you mean by "intercourse" and does it *have* to be physical?' "[25]

The combination of curiosity, naiveté, and confidence in exploring heterosexual relations displayed by young women in the 1920s seemed explosive to contemporaries. One prominent sociologist recognized that although the new sexual mores of the machine age could confuse men as thoroughly as women, the "unrest is felt most by those who have heretofore been most excluded from general participation in life,—the mature woman and the young girl."[26] The vamps and gold diggers of the period, along with the knowing girl next door, revealed a less inhibited sexuality than Americans would have found among middle-class youth in an earlier generation. "Girls display their bodies with an abandon that would have made the most hardened woman blush fifty years ago," opined advice columnist Dorothy Dix. "Young women think no more of kissing every Tom, Dick and Harry who comes along and in indulging in petting parties and 'necking,' than their mothers would have thought of shaking hands and holding a casual conversation." Biochemist Louis Berman blamed the excessive pituitary irritations of the post-1914 era for turning what might have been a "nice sedate" girl into an "adventurous never satiated avid pleasure hunter, in whom the craving for stimulation will stop at nothing."[27]

The heterosexual excess of their contemporaries came home to individual women in more direct ways than the sweeping judgments of experts and social critics. Martha Lavell's sister told her that "everyone at school . . . puts on lipstick and rouge and smokes and 'pets' and everything."[28] Jessamyn West, successfully fending off flirtatious men in England and France, worried about her husband attending school that summer in Berkeley, "getting (I hope) his own meals but subject to the wiles of one thousand beautiful and unscrupulous coeds."[29]

The heterosociality of the postwar era grew out of at least two decades of youth culture that encouraged young women and men to socialize with many members of the opposite sex and to explore physical intimacy with their partners. Dating and the "conspicuous heterosexuality" of working-class women had aroused the concerns of progressive social scientists by the turn of the century. By 1920, middle-class youth had adopted much the same style of socializing. Within a decade dating was widespread, even in rural areas, with as many as half of high school freshmen and the large majority of seniors dating.[30]

The dating system that became common by the 1920s began in the high school extracurricular activities of the 1890s, where middle-class adolescents formed social ties with many of their contemporaries and took an interest (or at least felt they should take an interest) in the other sex. Hallie Ferguson, born in 1889, recalled " 'going with' several boys to our group activities." She and the other girls in her high school class discussed boys "endlessly, chiefly on the great problem of whether or not we should allow them to take our arm when they took us home."[31] Clara Savage, a high school sophomore in 1907, spent time with her peers studying, putting on plays, playing basketball, performing music, and going to dances. She had guilty enjoyment from some of her male friends' flirtations, although generally she expressed her most ardent encounters in limited detail: "He showed me he liked me awfully well. I said 'I had a beautiful walk.' 'So did I & thank you for the privilege!' See! See! Well I like it."[32]

By the first decade of the century, middle-class women expected to socialize with many young men; these would include some intimate acquaintances and prospective spouses. Having a wider range of acquaintance would allow a young woman to recognize the worth of the man she hoped to marry, "the one." "Chap books" were available which allowed women to organize the list of men they knew and to record other information, including the place and date of meeting and also opinions of the men. Doris Stevens's chap book included entries as early as 1905, when she was still in high school. Most of the "chaps" appear to have been students at Oberlin College, although she also met many young men at dances or receptions in the homes of friends. The total number of chaps was 109. She gave her opinion on forty-one of the total. She included a variety of judgments about dress, conversation, dancing abilities, looks, and character. She found both outward appearances and finer qualities attractive in different men. Of one she wrote, "Never was there a man with more true manlihood—*very* courteous" (Ross Wiley). Of another, "Fascinating—good dresser—good bearing—swell dancer—*not* a spooner" (Harry C. Biddle). Her mention of spooning suggests that middle-class men had adjusted to the new courtship style with social graces intended to advance intimacy as far as it would go (although not very far) with a variety of young women. Several of Doris Stevens's chaps seemed to take this approach: "Fond of cozy corners—much big *spoon* fond of feminine sex" (Fred Elliott).[33]

As a student at Oberlin, in 1908, Stevens's social life included several young men. She spent most of her recreational time with Russell, probably the same Russell P. Jameson that she mentioned in her chap book. Doris and Russell took walks (sometimes to fire his revolver), played bridge, and attended school events together. Stevens offers no hint of physical intimacy, except a walk of half an hour that she annotated with

" '2 volumes' & ." On occasion the couple quarreled and made up, usually with presents and apologies coming from Russell. Yet the romance seems to have lasted only for the school term. When Stevens went home for the summer, references to Russell disappeared.[34]

Even if socializing with many young men had become common for women by the second decade of the century and physical intimacy had become more casual, prewar middle-class youth still seemed restrained when compared with postwar adolescents. Malcolm Cowley remembered that at his high school in Pittsburgh before the war, "Petting was not yet fashionable: it was called 'loving up' and was permitted only by unattractive girls who had to offer special inducements." One young woman recalled that her future husband was the first "male person who was ever allowed at my home in the evening."[35]

By the war, respectable behavior had changed even for middle-class women. Marjorie Kinnan's mother asked the landlord where women received male callers in the cramped New York apartment house that her daughter was contemplating renting. "Oh, right in their rooms. It's considered perfectly proper. . . . And of course, tho' I try to look out for my girls, I expect them to be able to take care of themselves."[36] By 1919 Michael V. O'Shea hoped that parents and administrators could arrange high school activities so that teens would go home directly afterward: "There should be no loitering, no visiting, no ice-cream parlors, no joy riding, no strolling." But there was, of course, all that and more. Gladys Bell's diary opens in 1919 (she was eighteen) with a report of a midnight picnic on August 8, a date on August 9, a joy ride on August 14, and the first report of staying home on August 16.[37]

The kind of heterosexual recreation that Gladys Bell described so frequently in her diaries had assumed a form by 1919 that would remain consistent throughout the 1920s and 1930s. Boys or young men asked for the company of a girl or young woman to some public amusement— dance, movie, party, or other social event. They went without adult supervision or interference. The male member of the couple paid and frequently in the 1920s provided transportation. After the main event, the couple often went out to eat and frequently would try to find some private place for necking. Whereas physical intimacy became an expected element of dating, the limits on sexual experience depended on the girl and to a large extent on her class. Middle-class women typically placed greater limits on their physical freedom with male peers than working-class women did.[38]

Class also shaped the choice of how the couple spent their time. Dates could be expensive, leading even middle-class young men to complain. Working-class couples still rubbed shoulders with middle-class couples at amusement parks, but none of the diarists in this study mention Coney Island, Kennywood, or other popular parks of the period.[39]

Dancing proved to have greater appeal across class lines. By 1911, open-admission dances in New York sparked a nationwide craze that lasted years. Moralists condemned dancing, recognizing, along with everyone else, the erotic possibilities brought onto the dance floor. Even so, dancing in some form—whether the jazz-driven writhing that Ione Robinson discovered in Paris or the sedate ballroom dances with German partners and well-tutored protocol that upper middle-class girls learned—assumed a central importance in the social lives of most of these middle-class women.[40] At her sister's coming-out party, Elizabeth Yates danced with a boy an inch shorter than she who whispered that he planned to marry her. "I could have slapped him!" she wrote in her diary. Dorothy Smith, back home in Chicago from college, went to a dance at the local high school with a young man and another couple. "It was fun—both were good dancers & I felt like dancing." Staten Island high school student Adele Siegel recorded a party as "the best yet. . . . I danced until I almost dropped." Ann Marie Low, in rural North Dakota in the midst of the Depression, attended dances with various admirers.[41]

Movies would have edged out dances as the most popular excuse for dates except that young women often went to see films alone or with other women. Even so, movie theaters remained popular date destinations, giving the couple a modicum of privacy and relieving them of the duty to make conversation. At least some teen-aged boys took dates to movies to put them in the mood for petting. Moralists deplored, again without effect, the movie habit.[42]

Whereas cars had only minor importance for high-school-aged couples, the importance of the automobile increased with the age of the couple. Jane Sherman, only barely out of high school and traveling in the Far East as a member of the Denishawn Dancers, recorded drives with a young rubber baron in Singapore as their main recreation. She recalled the sounds and smells that surrounded her as she rode out to watch the moon rise and back through the jungle. "All the background for a romantic episode which threatened but did not come off!"[43] Isabelle McNelis, a bank clerk in rural western Pennsylvania, struggled to resolve the question of whether to marry Harry Sickler or not. She sketched one of their dates in her "line-a-day" diary: "Thur—Nice Out—Down to Band Concert at 8:00 Harry & I trying to arrange our future Up the Mountain to talk things over. I can't decide what to do."[44] After a dance with a young man and another couple, Dorothy Smith and her friends went in search of refreshment. "We buzzed over to Natick for a hot dog & nearly rattled the poor Ford to death."[45]

Although cars gave couples opportunities to be alone, the example of Dorothy Smith reminds us that dates took place in a context of more general socializing. If the couple removed themselves from their peers, it was only temporarily. In a larger sense they never left the wider group. Often the line between the couple and the larger peer group blurred. Edythe Weiner went to the movie *Alias Jimmy Valentine* with a group of female friends. "*Everybody* was there," she wrote. After the show she and her friends went to the Commodore for sodas. "You meet everyone you know there. In fact, there are always a bunch of school kids there." Edythe also had small parties of friends to her house. One evening a group of girls gathered there to dance and smoke cigarettes (her parents apparently did not notice) and then used her phone to call boys. Edythe considered her girlfriend group the base from which she would gain attention from boys—"if only I were in with a popular crowd of girls, it would help loads, I know."[46] Dating couples frequently joined other couples for group parties, and parties gave boys and girls opportunities to become acquainted before the more serious social act of dating. Adele Siegel's crowd on Long Island made a party of playing bridge, dancing, eating ice cream and cake, and talking until one. Another evening she used a string of exclamation points and other emphatic markings to show her excitement. "What a hot time we had!!! We sang 'Love Song [*sic*] the Whole World Sings' right through from cover to cover."[47]

Although high school dating might look like—or even turn into—courtship, its more typical role was to establish social status within the peer group and to provide young women with a means of self-understanding. Edythe Weiner repeatedly mentioned her attachment to Jimmie Davison in her high school diary. "Oh, diary, he's so *gorgeous*!! I adore him. . . . If I should ever make him—Whoopee!" Two weeks later, with no loss of adoration for Jimmie, she developed a crush on the star basketball player during an ice-skating outing. She reflected on the quality and source of her feelings after discussing her new infatuation with a group of friends and noting that another girl, an admirer of the same boy, took special notice of Edythe's account. "I seldom get a crush on a boy unless some other girl has a crush on him. Then I first begin to notice him, and find hidden beauty in him." Crushes and other thrilling feelings never meant that Edythe planned to commit herself to these boys for more than the length of a few dates. At fourteen she longed for the acceptance that an attentive boy could give her with other boys and girls. Such acceptance would make her more popular and allow her to feel better about herself. In the calculus of the high school social system, more dates meant more popularity and vice versa. "Oh, I want lots of dates," Edythe pined after returning from a Glee Club concert without an escort. "I want to be popular—I want to be loved. Oh, God! Oh, God! I'm in love with Love, and the feeling isn't mutual, I guess."[48]

The success of a date depended on both personal and peer judgments. The opinions of friends could shape a woman's reaction to her conquests. Ruth Raymond was glad to report that her preparations for a group religious discussion—spending the morning polishing her nails—worked. She met a young man who had asked to call. The next day, though, she discovered from dormmates that he was merely " 'an affectionate puppy' " who had called on several girls already. Raymond had no more time for her prize.[49] Whatever the satisfactions of male companionship for girls and young women, they were generally so thin that they offered no protection from the coolness of one's friends. Sometimes, there was no satisfaction to be disapproved of. Dorothy Smith spent much of a summer day with a young man who took her to tennis and later swam with her. "For an English teacher & Dramatic coach he is a stupid talker. . . . I don't care if I never see him again."[50] Anne Morrow tired of the college men who took her out every weekend: "Nice, good-natured, agreeable, mediocre, platitudinal." She obviously felt some relief in describing one of her escorts: "He is a mass of conventions—his talk, his ideas, his clothes, his car. We went to a conventional movie where a conventionally pretty girl went through the conventions of sex appeal and love. *Hideous.*"[51]

If Anne Morrow, who had many dates, could find the ritual so trying, imagine the dangers for a girl on her first date with a young man she has never met. Marion Taylor was excited at the prospect of her first date which a former teacher had arranged. The string of disasters she described might have provided a silent movie scenario. Her date, apparently trying to meet social protocol learned from an etiquette book, startled Marion when he "sprang" to help her on with her cloak. As they strolled, "he edged around for the outside of the sidewalk, and I forgot that the gentleman is supposed to do that and I nearly knocked him off because I started to walk on the outside too." Crossing the street, he clamped a "vise-like grip" on her arm and seemed to shove her along. Unsurprisingly, they had nothing to talk about. When he took her home, she just wanted to escape although her escort seemed to expect a farewell embrace. "I made various lame remarks and there were several harrowing pauses."[52]

Dating gave young men and women opportunities to become accustomed to members of the opposite sex. Martha Lavell, who vowed in her diary that she would never allow a man to take her out and pay her way, understood the strangeness the genders held for one another. Regretting that she could not wear trousers and shorter hair, she reflected, "If I were a man, it seems to me that women wouldn't seem human to me. They'd seem so unnatural and stilted." Yet it was the artifice of social ritual that allowed men and women to spend time together, to become friends and lovers. Marion Taylor, humiliated but undaunted by her first disastrous date, self-consciously reworked her social skills to attract men. "I am learning to 'jolly' and 'small talk,' to 'flirt' in an embryonic, amateurish sort of way! . . . And I am making more of my appearance than I ever have before."[53]

Taylor, of course, also recognized that having men take her out only served to provide the occasion for "crude, primitive love-making," the necking and petting "universally practiced on a college campus." She could barely suppress her excitement at the prospect of having one of her dates take her "out into the fresh exciting night and put his arm around me again." She knew she harbored little affection for her date; rather, she craved the "sheer physical excitement and the intoxicating knowledge that one is admired and desired."[54] Dating provided a social setting for social recreation that almost inevitably became sexual recreation. The petting parties scandalized and fascinated early twentieth-century middle-class adults and convinced critics that "a social revolution in manners and morals" had taken place. Yet petting parties also showed that even physical caresses could be done among one's peers and were subject to peer judgments. Ernest Burgess, a sociologist, writing in the early 1930s, recognized that the new sexual explorations of American youth did not reveal moral decline but were "phenomena of group determinism," or shifts in the patterns of behavior of an entire generation that typically replaced the strictures of the family with those of "the intimate social group."[55]

Petting allowed American adolescents to domesticate desire, to make commonplace those caresses reserved for the betrothed among the Victorian middle class. Some sophisticated college students would even claim to have made necking a fine art that broke away from the "prevalent conception of eroticism as merely a mechanism of propagation, or as a brute, delightful sin."[56] A pamphlet prepared by the YMCA to help college youth through the confusions of romance received the dubious honor of being referred to by *The Nation* as "A Manual for Petters." *The Sex Life of Youth* took a pragmatically conservative approach toward questions of sex, assuring young men and women that the sex drive was normal and providing seven tests to measure the propriety of petting. Although the authors condemned sex outside of a loving relationship, they also condemned loveless marriage and concluded that some experience of physical intimacy would guide the individual in discovering sexual compatibility.[57]

We can understand the attraction and confusion surrounding the new sexual practices through the experience of Jane Sherman. As a high school student on Long Island, Jane never participated in smoking, drinking, or necking with her peers, and although she was an attractive young woman, she had no boyfriends. Her first date, to a high school prom at age sixteen, included her mother as chaperon. She spent most of her free moments at the Denishawn dance school. Her diary and letters from her trip with the Denishawn Dancers to the Far East from 1925 to 1926 reveal how confusing she found domesticated desire. She quickly discovered that young American and British men in the Orient found the Denishawn Dancers irresistible, and Jane in particular attracted the attentions of young diplomats and businessmen. Her first proposal of marriage came in Manchuria, and others followed in widely separated locations. As men pressed their attentions, presents, and proposals on her, she worried over the meaning of her newly widened experience. "Three men have kissed me in my life, and each one proposed. . . . But should I let every man who proposes kiss me?" As the trip continued, she shared her worries with other members of the troupe and adopted attitudes more in line with the mores of her American peers. A year later she could assure her mother that any kissing she had done was experimental. She was thrilled at first but then disappointed "that there wasn't more kick in them." In a month she would assume an even more blasé attitude about her relations with "V," her most ardent suitor. They dined and drove in the evening, she wrote her mother, but he had her back to the hotel by ten. "No parking, darling! And besides, V. is really all right. He is as harmless as an affectionate puppy, as exuberant and as adoring. Of course I let him kiss me, but that never hurt anyone, did it? Besides, I'm 18 now!"[58]

Both Gladys Bell and Martha Lavell worried about the morals of youth. Martha, on the outside of the dating ritual, could only puzzle over adolescent behavior. Gladys, by contrast, believed she could teach her sister "the difference between a lover's kiss and that of the worldly wise 'petter,' and so save her from the error I made in permitting so much love-making."[59] Edythe Weiner expressed the more common attitude of middle-class girls when she complained about her escort to a dance. "All the kids in the back seat were necking like the devil, and altho he did finally put his arm around me and pull me over to him, he wasn't nearly so hot as the rest, and he didn't kiss me once."[60] Adele Siegel took petting for granted as part of the bridge between boys and girls. On a Woodcrafters hike, "Canio Di Cairano was *very* attentive to me." Afterward, "We stayed out on the porch until real late—after ten. Canio and I got acquainted." Adele, in fact, listed the boys and young men she was involved with at age fifteen, describing their qualities in somewhat the way prescribed by earlier chap books, revealing which excelled or failed at conversation or other social graces. Unlike the chap book, however, Adele's diary entry includes her rating of her beaus when it came to "n," presumably necking. Of one, "A good pal. Can tell him practically anything and he'll answer questions to everything. Don't mind him n." Of another, "Won't go out with him at all. Poor company—tries to please me, however—don't like him very much, and absolutely dislike him n." For Siegel, the thrills of necking were quite separate from emotional excitement. About the young man who excited her the most ("I guess I'm in love with him.") she wrote, "Like him all round except n. at Jane's."[61]

Adele Siegel's list of fifteen suitors shows her success with boys and men (the youngest was sixteen, the oldest twenty-four) and also shows the mix of personal attractions and peer judgments involved in adolescent socializing. After the April hike where she became acquainted with Canio Di Cairano, she became more and more involved with him. In May she looked back over the progress of her affection. The first meeting she retrospectively characterized as "On porch—hardly thrilly." But when a friend "remarks that he said he liked me very much—(slam book) Larger thrill." A week and a half later, "*Like* him tremendously." Siegel carefully stressed that she "liked" Canio to distinguish the feeling from love, a much more serious matter, especially with an older suitor like Canio (who was already attending Wagner College). She seemed well aware that the opinions of friends helped shape her affections. "Remarks of my girl friends, who love to talk about the Everlasting Subject helps [*sic*] to keep him in mind."[62]

Although she shared her friends' fascination with boys, Adele's enthusiasm for romance had its limits. Siegel's diary reflects her impatience with Canio's ardor and with the unwanted affection of other male admirers. One boy, who took her to see a Marx Brothers comedy, "was so far gone, all he could [do] was look at me like—I can't help it—like a dog looks at his master." Another young man who took her to a party "wouldn't behave. I slapped his face hard, and he was very respectful and gentlemanly the rest of the evening." Siegel clearly wanted to balance both companionship and sexual excitement. "This is what I believe about that Everlasting Subject: that I should have as much fun as possible with all the boys I like, flirt just a bit, and 'neck' only with boys I really care for."[63] Popular with boys and with her female peers, Adele Siegel could enjoy dating as recreation, testing the thrills of romance and sexual desires but never allowing either to go too far.

## Having "IT" — Personality and Beauty

The distance between Victorian attitudes toward intimacy and those of jazz age youth points toward a wide-ranging change in the middle-class experience of self. Victorian women and men assumed some deep and private essence as the core of the self. Whereas one's character—the link between self and society—might grow and shift, self remained essentially fixed. In romantic love, Victorian men and women found opportunities to share and reveal this essential self. A decades-long shift in American culture that questioned the depth and immutability of self led Americans to equate the authentic individual with what they saw of the individual. It was during the 1920s that William Sheldon suggested that personality types might correspond to physical proportions, an idea given serious consideration among social scientists and in the popular media. Adolescents and young adults learned to value self-presentation and social acceptance over qualities of intellect or character. "I have spells of thinking, that personality is more important than immortality," Emily Clark wrote to the author Joseph Hergesheimer.[64] Physicality and appearance became the standards for judging personality and even personal worth.

Young women took a keen interest in their bodies and in their physical abilities and the abilities of others. The sexualization of social relations undoubtedly made women more aware of themselves as physical beings. But they did not limit the awareness of their physical lives to their sex lives. Dorothy Thompson, struggling with the problems of learning to ice skate at thirty-eight, believed that her son was "better off than [she] was, because he lives in a world which has discovered that people have bodies."[65] Dancing, as we have seen, gave women one way to enjoy physical activity. Sports provided another. Basketball was the sport of preference for Dorothy Smith and Elizabeth Yates. Adele Siegel, on a date with her future husband, played basketball with him at the St. George Hotel. They also swam and danced before he took her home. Sarah Bradley worked on her basket-shooting skills, but she did better at first base on her school softball team.[66] Many of the women in our group delighted in horseback riding, and although this points to a class distinction in the case of Elizabeth Yates and, perhaps, Miriam Van Waters, the ardent riders also included Ann Marie Low and Gladys Bell, both from humbler families. Summer camp gave further opportunities for healthy living and physical exertion, and this proved the most popular summer vacation for these women. Yates taught horseback riding to younger children at camp, Dorothy Smith taught music, and both Viola White and Winifred Willis went to summer retreats to allow them time to write. Camp would continue as an attractive activity for many of these women beyond their youth. Harriet Louise Hardy went camping to recover her closeness to God, and Miriam Van Waters looked for a renewed sense of purpose on yearly camp vacations.

Watching sports also gave young women an awareness of physical vitality. All of the women who wrote about their high school years either participated in sports or attended sporting events as spectators. Gladys Bell cheered so heartily for her Grove City College football team that she felt her "nerves were on strike."[67] Although major league baseball gained enormously in popularity during the 1920s, none of these women recorded attending a major league game. Many of them, however, went to games of local teams and took a keen interest in the games. "Jack Wylde hit a two bagger," Sarah Bradley wrote of a game between two local teams.[68] Ruth Raymond gave much of her spare time to following high school and town teams in baseball, football, and basketball. In the spring and summer following her senior year in high school she attended seventeen local games. Over roughly the same months in 1930, she went to twenty-nine games. She often wrote in knowing detail about the games she saw. For instance, in August 1930 she went on for five pages describing every major play of a town league baseball game.[69]

Along with sports, cinema and advertising depicted youth and health as central to personal appeal. Middle-class diarists often discussed beauty. Some retained a concept of beauty that referred to spiritual qualities. Gladys Bell wondered if she could hold herself to a high standard: "Morally, spiritually, intellectually and physically beautiful!"[70] Her inclusion of physical beauty, however, underscores the place that appearance assumed in her life and also the assumption that physical beauty might bend to the will. In a wide-ranging discussion, mainly about sports, Ruth Raymond considered with her father "the fact that lack of beauty often mars a girl's character."[71] Novelist Elinor Glyn wrote that "plain women are always at a disadvantage" in the Darwinian struggle for mating. A common assumption of the early twentieth century was that proper diet and exercise could make all women beautiful. Martha Lavell took it for granted that she could achieve a perfect body, which required that she gain both weight and strength.[72] Middle-class women believed that they could become beautiful if they exercised conscious control and used the products that the economy made available; they learned to worry if they failed.

After the turn of the century the weight that once would have given evidence of robust good health seemed excessive and unappealing. American women came to see unwanted weight as a personal failing. One physician wondered why "girls with a tendency to get fat and gross" did not consult experts or books "on the science of reducing comfortably, and then see to it that they stay slender?"[73] As athletes young women experienced themselves as fit and energetic. Yet even the most active young women could find themselves fighting off a few pounds. Jane Sherman, giving nightly dance recitals during her tour of the Orient, went from 110 to 120 without realizing it, and her weight continued to climb in spite of debilitating diets. The weight gain, unpardonable for a Denishawn dancer, threw her into despair. Dorothy Smith and Caroline Gordon approached 120 from the other direction, giving them cause to rejoice.[74] Dieting could sweep through a college campus, as it did at Bates College in 1923. Gladys Hasty wrote home that everyone in her house was trying to reduce "and it is a continuous series of, 'Gee, I'm so hungry' . . . 'Hey, what did you eat this noon.' . . . 'Look can you see I'm a little thinner.' "[75]

Young women also worried about their hair. The adolescent girl, according to psychoanalyst Phyllis Blanchard, talks incessantly "of the 'Castle clip' or 'Mary Pickford curls'; . . . her one concern is to see that her newly put-up locks are arranged according to the latest vogue."[76] Journalist Clara Savage Littledale in one of her *Good Housekeeping* articles discussed the concern that a woman's hair might evoke. "Even the most sensible among us bemoan gray hairs, begin to look for them at twenty-five, worry about them." Shaping hair to cultural demands, and providing a host of other services all summarized under a single term, fueled the growth in the number of beauty parlors, from five thousand in 1920 to forty thousand ten years later.[77]

The right appearance meant new standards for skin as well as hair. The heroine of a romantic novel of the period referred to her beautiful white skin as "one of my assets—part of my capital."[78] The cosmetics industry was a $180-million business by 1930. Psychologist and advertising executive John Watson managed to convince Americans to buy an underarm deodorant that required the wearer to keep the arms raised for ten minutes while it dried so that it wouldn't harm clothing. The advertisers who touted the wonders of soap, facial creams, and deodorants cocreated the cultural presumption that beauty could bend to the will. They also knowingly exploited and aggravated women's anxiety that they failed to measure up to the standards that their culture held out for them. Margaret Sanger's advice in a book to young women seeking marriage and happiness reflected the importance of personal appearance and the assumption that beauty could be achieved through effort and expenditure. "The care of the body," she wrote, stressing the value of proper habits, "both outwardly and inwardly, the bathing and thorough cleanliness of all of its orifices, give the girl an assurance of sweet-smelling cleanliness which gives her an invaluable assurance and confidence in her own power of attractiveness."[79]

Although some young women did find assurance about their appearance—Edythe Weiner believed she was more attractive than most girls, even though in her own judgment she remained unpopular—it was far more common for high school girls to lament their looks. Marion Taylor found just about everything about her face unsatisfactory—thin, lifeless hair, pug nose, forehead too high. Elizabeth Yates found fault with her hair (frizzy) and also with her figure.[80] Beth Twiggar admitted that she was pretty, but only at times, and "awkwardly loathesome [*sic*] at others." She lamented again and again in her diary that she was too tall. "I can't get used to being so big—I *won't* say large."[81] One southern woman remembered that when her picture was first taken, at age twelve, she expected to see that she looked "like Mary Pickford or Norma Tallmadge." What she saw ruined her illusions of beauty: "I saw myself for the first time as completely and hopelessly ugly."[82]

Beth Twiggar wanted to look like her petite sister, who in addition to being "slim, short, slender" had "it."[83] By the late 1920s, Americans had changed "an impersonal neuter pronoun" into "the symbol of personality." Elinor Glyn, novelist and screenwriter, promoted "it" as an internal essence that inevitably attracted the opposite sex. In the 1927 movie *"It,"* the comic figure of Monty goes searching for "it" in a department store. He walks along a lingerie counter where women clerks are lined up for inspection, as though in a beauty pageant. When he spots Clara Bow, he knows he has found "it." That an unselfconscious essence should make itself known through physical appearance suggests how cinema equated good looks and goodness. It also points to the sexualization of selfhood, since "it" could mean either an interesting personality or sex appeal. "When a mere schoolgirl boasts of having 'it,' " a contemporary psychologist groused, "she means simply that she is the possessor of a personality that would attract men."[84]

Personality did not mean merely good looks. A physician offering advice for girls on how to win men without becoming too free with their bodies said that men will be attracted to women who are "friendly or affectionate or a jolly partner for an outing."[85] Edythe Weiner spent a study period in the school library reading a story "that contained some awfully true things." According to her source, for a girl to become popular, she "must have *four* things: A. good looks. B. good clothes. C. nerve. D. practice."[86] Personal qualities other than beauty still counted, although how much they weighed in the balance depended on the circumstances of various women. Stage actress Lillian Roth believed that she moved from singing to starring roles in the musicals when a showgirl friend convinced her to slim down from 135 to 116. She attracted the attention of an important producer who had formerly only acknowledged her in passing. "Perhaps it wasn't the talent you had, or the personality," Roth concluded, "it was the form divine." Ruth Raymond, on the other hand, who saw herself as attractive, nevertheless spent dance after dance watching others dance. "Tell me," she asked a friend at one dance after two men had asked her about other women, "haven't I any sex appeal?"[87]

To have "it" a girl or young woman had to be pretty and she had to find ways of attracting the attention of boys or young men. Yet "it" did not presume intelligence, and most young women learned that obvious ability was a liability. A seventeen-year-old admitted that the movies gave her lessons in love-making and showed her "that bad and pretty girls are usually more attractive to men than intelligent and studious girls."[88] In "*It*," Clara Bow's character twice finds herself confronting a class barrier—her ignorance of French. She manages both times to dodge the problem, showing that native wit and nerve are more important than education. A popular advice columnist wrote that men don't like "superior women."[89] Ruth Raymond's father learned from a conversation on a bus that Ruth's achievements in school had probably worked against her: "all of them were always ashamed because you knew everything and they didn't know anything." He presumed that was why no one danced with her, and he told her so.[90] Marion Taylor could not understand how one of her friends could assume such "silly baby ways" around boys or why the boys seemed to like it. Her father told Marion that when the right man came along " 'he' will care more about the cute little curl behind my ear than for my opinions on the whyness of the unknowable."[91] Edythe Weiner recognized that her cleverness at school probably hurt her with the boys. "That's why, lately, in school, I've tried not to appear too smart."[92] The peer culture of the high school gave status for excellence in sports or other areas of the extracurriculum and for popularity with peers but not for good grades.

In her self-analysis and secret shame over being unpopular, Edythe Weiner wished that she could see herself as others saw her. "Then I'd know my faults and be able to correct them."[93] In the American culture that emerged by the 1920s, the judgments of one's peers became fundamental marks of personal worth. For adolescents, they were definitive. And high school girls, who depended on boys for invitations to dance or to go out, found themselves at the mercy of male judgments. Jessie Lloyd cried at night over being ignored at high school dances and convinced herself that she was ugly. Reflecting on her lack of success at various dances Ruth Raymond decided that what she needed "wasn't a chance at a man—it was an Act of God."[94] Ilka Chase, later a successful actress, wrote that "nothing makes me happier than to realize I cannot possibly relive my youth." As a debutante she was invited to all of the important balls for the year after high school, yet she spent most of her time waiting along the wall pretending to enjoy herself until her "face ached from smiling brightly, and then the laughing little excuse that you really had to powder your nose, and the escape into the ladies' room."[95] To avoid such humiliation, girls sought popularity. Edythe Weiner's reading brought home another "truth" about the peer culture: "If it gets around that a girl is unpopular, she might just as well move to another state or enter an old ladies' home!"[96]

As young people relied more on their peers, they often found themselves at a greater distance from their families. Rather than wear an unattractive woolen shirt to school, Edythe Weiner put up with her father's anger, abuse, and punishment. She hated going to the movies with her family, "because if any of the kids see you, they think you were so hard up you didn't have anyone else to go with."[97]

Submitting personal qualities to the judgments of their peers prepared adolescents for an economic system that demanded social skills for success. The peer culture gave American middle-class adolescents guidelines for understanding themselves and for evaluating self-worth. It became the context in which high school students learned how to act with one another including how to achieve acceptance, gain interpersonal intimacy, and enhance self-esteem. The value of one's personality depended on one's success with others. For the peer culture, the personality consisted of physical fitness and attractiveness and skills at socializing. Girls flirted with boys; with other girls they discussed the "Everlasting Subject," that is, their relations with boys. With both genders they demonstrated interest and awareness of activities valued by the group, such as sports and other elements of the extracurriculum, and indifference to academic subjects.[98]

## Emotion and Social Performance

Success or failure at social performance largely shaped the emotional lives of young women. Beth Twiggar, whose diaries cover most of her high school and college years, allows us to follow a social performance with great variability and a wide range of emotional experience. Beth lived in a comfortably middle-class family, the youngest of three girls. Her diaries are chatty and self-reflective by turns, with entries often dashed off in the heat of anger or humiliation, or reflecting calmly on some triumphant moment in her young life. As with other girls, Beth's life as an adolescent often conflicted with her family's ideas for her. "God Damn my family anyway. Bickering and pettyness [*sic*] and picking continually," she complains in one passage. She runs through a litany of the nagging complaints thrown at her and ends by reporting a fit that she threw back. "I was heaving and swearing and growling and shriekily protesting and now here am I in my room alone, a little worn out, but satisfied."[99]

Family played only a minor role in Beth's diaries. Most frequently Beth wrote about peer relationships, particularly about boys and dates, and she reflected on her personality and the popular acceptance that dating represented. "I'm sadly boy-sick," she admitted in one passage. Like Edythe Weiner, praying for lots of dates, Beth Twiggar summarized her goals succinctly: "I wanted to be popular, to go out, to dance, to know boys and boys and boys." Beth believed that her peer culture offered her possibilities that her mother could never understand. She self-consciously placed herself among the flaming youth of her day: "I love dates and boys and whoopee, road houses, smoke and jazz. I'm not quite so far gone as to say I've developed a craze for necking and drinking, but the two are symbols of my summers [*sic*] debauch."[100]

Beth's desire to attract boys led to self-consciousness about her appearance. She worried about her height—at least as tall as her father, enough to "blight the life of almost any girl"—and her weight, "Oh, I'm reducing. No kidding." After the inspiration of the film *Gentlemen Prefer Blondes*, she decided she wanted to become a gold digger. But when she looked in the mirror, she felt that the only gold digging she could do would be in overalls "with an ox!" Her desire for beauty shaped Beth's consumer consciousness. She could quickly list numerous cold cream and facial preparations—Ponds, Dagger et Ramsell, Woodbury, Ecloyer, Coty, Venician, Penaud, Elizabeth Arden, Rubenstein—and delighted in the results of an Elizabeth Arden bath product: "Verily Elizabeth is a witch!" Feminine undergarments enhanced her sense of beauty. "Step ins positively inspire me!" she wrote as an introduction to the varieties of colors and trimmings of the garments she sewed for herself.[101]

Beauty existed for Beth Twiggar as social performance. Desire for sophistication led her to read *Harper's Bazaar,* to practice smoking cigarettes in front of her mirror, and to experiment with cosmetics. Feeling beautiful and sophisticated might enhance her self-esteem, but for confir-

2.1  Beth Twiggar at age sixteen. Courtesy of Beth Twiggar Goff.

mation of self-worth Beth looked for evidence that she had achieved popularity with both boys and girls. Such a measure of self-worth was maddeningly public and quantifiable in the number of boys she attracted. Unfortunately for Beth, even this measure was subject to personal and peer judgments.

Beth enjoyed listing her success with boys: "Steven, Billy, Newton.

And others not so nameable," she wrote at the end of one summer vacation. "Methinks Beth has been flirting! Well, we girls do want our fun!" The following winter she compiled a longer list, including Steve, Billy, and Newton, along with earlier and more recent conquests. Lists like these gave Beth Twiggar a chance for self-examination, to see if she was approaching her goal, "to have boys on waiting lists." She hoped to match the success of a girlfriend who was "some *hot* mama!" The number of dates, however, could never stand alone as a criterion of success. When a boy "made certain advances" at a movie in Tarrytown and later promised to write to her, she felt excited until she learned from a friend that he was "great at picking up. So I'm a little ashamed of myself for being so easy." On the other hand Steve, already listed twice, gained in Beth's estimation when a friend told her she thought he had "sex appeal and *it* and a few other things. So now guided as I always am by the opinion of others he has doubled in attraction for me."[102]

For Beth, boys, dates, necking, and popularity all came as a package. "I want a boy friend," she complained during a lull in her social life. "I want to be cuddled (Me the Mammoth) petted, necked and improperly delt [sic] with. . . . I want to be sought after caught often and generally popular." Her diaries show that she grew more comfortable with physical intimacy and more competent at it. Of her "first love," Herbert, she wrote, "I wiggle when he tries to neck me. . . ." Even if it was uncomfortable, she could still revel in the description. ". . . I lie in chairs with a boy beside me . . . his hand getting fresh and his face getting close." A year and a half later, a more experienced Beth would spend time with an older man. " 'God Girl,' " he told her, " 'you certainly can love!' " A knowing Beth commented, "But he was wrong. I can't love, I can merely neck." Necking carried its own satisfaction, although it was not clearly a product of sexual excitement. Beth Twiggar, at the end of a disappointingly quiet weekend, complained, "I wanta be necked! I do! It gives me a sensation I love."[103]

Yet the pleasures of sexual excitement and social success had to be balanced against the dangers of peer disapproval. Adolescent females still found themselves at the mercy of a double standard that could punish them with personal humiliation and even public shaming. Girls "owned" sex, to the extent that boys, short of assault, required their dates' permission or at least tacit acceptance of their advances. Yet, as Beth painfully recognized in her self-reflection, a desire to remain popular with boys meant that girls had to be generous with their wealth, risking the scorn of the same boys they hoped to attract. Teen-aged Pat, in *Flaming Youth,* for example, became the topic of a male discussion at one of the many parties described in the book. "Too easy," commented one young man. "She's got a teasin' way with her," said another.[104]

The downside of popularity came painfully home to Beth. She learned that one boy had remarked of her to his friends "that there was gold in them thar hills." This was followed "by a mean chuckle." From her sense of herself as growing in popularity, she suddenly confronted a reputation of being too eager and of attracting boys as a mere "convenience, an appendage" of a more popular friend. "Who the hell wants to take out Beth Twiggar?" was the record of one boy's comment that she put at the head of a long diary entry in which she reflected on her feeling of loss. Humiliation made itself apparent to Beth as physical pain. "I am feeling unutterably badly," she wrote. "I am hurt, battered, wholly crushed," as though she had begun to feel the "mauling and hauling" we saw her describe earlier. The boys' comments "are making me squirm and suffer." Without the "joyous illusion" of popularity, she returned to a sense of herself as unattractive, unlovable, and fundamentally flawed. "Hate me!" she wrote to herself at the end of her narrative.[105]

Sexual modernization allowed adolescents to more readily accept physical desire as a normal part of life. Yet the benefit of this widening recognition accrued mainly to boys and men. Girls and young women, who found they had wider latitude for physical enjoyment, also faced the lingering condemnations of Victorian morality. For all her impatience with her family and with her mother's incomprehension of what it meant to be modern and sophisticated, Beth Twiggar could still occasionally experience renewed "self-respect" when she refused to allow easy familiarity. "I want other people to like me and people my own age to respect me!" That Beth Twiggar and other middle-class young women of the jazz age should find themselves drawn to the new sexual freedoms but still at risk from the old sexual morality reveals the incompleteness of the new attitudes toward women's sexuality. No wonder that one of the wishes the fourteen-year-old Beth Twiggar had for her fairy godmother was to have no conscience.[106]

Middle-class adolescent women in the 1920s discovered a world of thrilling heterosexual possibilities. New forms of physical intimacy became common as boys and girls dated as couples. The thrills of closeness were combined with those of becoming the center of attraction for many young men and a recognized success in their peer group. Yet the emotional satisfactions of these triumphs came at the risk of losing social acceptability, of a sense of loss of self-worth, and of humiliation. For boys, who also had the possibility of greater physical intimacy, humiliation was rarely a threat. In fact, the humiliation of young women could become a means of protection for young men who could use a former date's behavior as a topic of scornful derision.

The emotional experiences of heterosexual sociability for middle-class high school girls depended largely on peer approval. Dating and popularity did not simply follow from the possession of "it;" these social customs enacted "it." Social success meant sex appeal, which meant a good personality, which meant social success. Rather than bringing passion or idealized love, sex appeal meant acceptance by boys but also by girls. A young woman attending University of California Los Angeles showed the complicated mix of social ambitions and personal attractions when she characterized her desire for a man as a longing "for companionship, for the thrill of it, for admiration, for self confidence, for show purposes, for an escort to take me places, for the satisfaction of curiosity, and for surcease of Spring Fever."[107] The peer culture, blending into the mass culture of movies and advertising, shaped heterosexual relations and adolescent personality.

### Homosociality and Emotion

Young women were capable of far less public and far more fervent feelings than those generally associated with dating. As these girls became young women they often found that some individual man became more and more important in their lives and they began to attempt to understand love. Although we explore romantic love in the next chapter, the experience of a deeply felt passionate commitment to another girl or woman was common among adolescent women in the early decades of the twentieth century. These relationships offered both profound satisfactions and deeply felt pain. Homosocial or homosexual relations gave adolescents emotional experiences far less structured by peer groups than heterosexual relations and with fewer cultural expectations to conform to.

The 1920s now appears as the decade when the romantic friendships so common for middle-class women in the nineteenth century began to disappear or to become identified with pathological behavior. One study of college sexuality in the 1930s suggested that passionate attachments between women had become less common. Claiming a "heterosexual counterrevolution" may go too far, but it is clear that during the early decades of the century a strong emphasis emerged in the youth culture on winning dates; among young women in college and at work, finding and landing husbands became a pressing concern.[108]

Our work strongly suggests, however, that it was not until at least the 1930s that heterosexual relations began to completely replace passionate female friendships among middle-class adolescents. Among the thirty-nine women whose diaries or other personal papers we studied, eighteen, nearly half, wrote of affectionate or passionate relations with other women during adolescence or later. The nature of these relationships varied so greatly it is difficult to offer any single term that characterizes all of them. They all included friendship, but they achieved levels of warmth, idealization, or devotion that friendship does not adequately describe. This closely matches the findings of Katherine Bement Davis in a 1929 study of one thousand college women. Of these women, 505 had experienced "intense emotional relations" with other women. Davis attempted to separate these relations into three categories—those with some physical expression, such as hugging or kissing, but not recognized as sexual (293); those without physical expression but considered sexual (78); and those that were fully sexual with genital contact (234). Women entered these relationships primarily as adolescents or young adults, with 43.5 percent of the relations beginning before college and 35.5 percent beginning during college. These relationships continued after the high school years, and even after college, for the majority of women. The relation could last for a few months up to a few years. One college woman told a sociological investigator, "we all tasted homosexuality in some degree."[109]

Psychology and psychoanalytic theory became vital for understanding and marginalizing intense friendships among women. According to one psychoanalyst, "One of the commonest perversions of the libido among adolescent girls is the fixation of the affections on members of the same sex, and absolute indifference or even aversion to male companionship." Margaret Mead remembered studying Freud at Barnard in 1920 and worrying about past affections for women.[110] Martha Lavell's diary shows a growing psychological sophistication. "I'm beginning to believe I'm rather abnormal in regards to liking boys," she wrote while an undergraduate. Two years later, with further study in psychology and familiarity with Freud, Lavell stated her situation differently. "Evidently

my emotional development has never reached the heterosexual stage."
She believed that because she had no father, transfer to a male love
object never took place for her. Even so, she recognized that she felt
especially "susceptible to an attraction for women. . . . It *isn't* normal, I
know; but what is one to do about it? . . . And no matter how much I
fight against it, dismiss it from my mind immediately, that feeling returns
again & again."[111] Psychoanalytic psychotherapy enabled Dorothy
Smith to recognize the homoerotic content of her longing for female
friends, from early adolescence into adulthood. Therapy helped Smith to
overcome homoerotic impulses and to affirm her attraction to David
Dushkin, leading to their marriage after her analysis ended. Yet in spite
of narrowing cultural acceptance, women's love for other women often
continued. Even after her marriage to David Dushkin, Dorothy Smith
Dushkin still yearned for a special companionship with another
woman.[112]

As these examples suggest, young women learned to understand homosocial relationships as dysfunctional only after they reached college. Yet
even for young adult women, relationships with other women frequently
remained the most important emotional connections outside their families. High school girls in the 1920s felt little of the change in cultural
norms, and college women often ignored the norms they discovered in
the classroom. When they wrote of affection for other girls or women,
they did so with no trace of guilt or anxiety. "I do love Effey," Azalia
Peet wrote in 1913, "but I don't [want?] to confine my love to her. I love
Faith but this ought not to interfere with my loving some other girl just
as much."[113] The same matter-of-fact style appears almost twenty years
later, in Adele Siegel's diary: "Jean L. and Jane P. certainly are affectionate. Well, I'm glad they love me."[114] Women took for granted that they
would love other women, and also that they would express their affection physically and publicly. A boy in a Massachusetts high school in
1928 complained about the frequency of female attachments at his high
school: "They walk down the corridors all twined together like a figure
eight."[115]

An exceptional concern by Beth Twiggar stands as testimony to the
unexceptional nature of affectionate friendships among high school girls.
Beth had a special relationship with her friend Peggy for several years. It
was different from her usual friendships with girls and different from
anything she described experiencing with boys. Beth experienced this
and other crushes as an enduring, unambiguous desire to be near and

receive attention and affirmation from the girls she admired and perceived as superior to herself. The experience of the crush was overpowering, coloring all of her perceptions. "I love that girl," she wrote of
Peggy. "I admire and respect her. Nothing makes me happier than when
I have her approval. Nothing is so delightful as to be alone in her presence."

The crush might place the private self in as much jeopardy as dating
could place the public self. "I am being submerged in her personality,"
Beth wrote of her affection for Peggy. "I'm hurt by her indifference, I'm
sensitive to her moods. . . . I am not my own. I am her slave." In her
reflection on her problem, Beth considered it "an astonishing thing for
one girl to like another that way. It is a harmful, degrading thing." Yet
Beth was not complaining of intense friendships with women, only the
lack of mutuality and dependence she found in her relation with Peggy.
"Loyal friendship is a commendable and admirable thing, but the blind
adoration which I have for Peggy is actually ignoble." The problem, she
concluded, originated with her. Her dependence on Peggy showed "the
weakness, the futility and the lack of determination which are me."[116]
For Beth, the experience of vulnerability associated with her crush became intolerable when the object of her affections failed to reciprocate
her admiration.

By the 1920s, girls loved other girls as an expected phase in adolescence. It was not unmentionable, only unexceptional. The girls themselves most frequently referred to their passion as crushes. Katherine
Davis wrote of women who had intense emotional relations with physical affection as the "regulation 'college crush' type." Girls, their parents,
and experts could all view the relations as normal as long as they carried
only the "legitimate amount of emotion that belongs to friendship."[117]
Girl's relationships with other girls did not preclude enthusiastic interest
in boys. When Beth broke a date with Peggy to go on a date with a boy,
Peggy became furious. "I don't blame her," Beth wrote. "But I can't see
her, somehow, acting otherwise if our positions were reversed."[118] One
work warned that "individuals may let relationships among their own
sex, which are sound enough to begin with, hinder the development of
relations that open the possibility of marriage."[119] Homosociality could
only exist safely if it made no impact on the development of heterosexual
relationships. Yet passionate friendships were far from trivial. Young
diarists might spend pages on their success or failures with boys, but
they often described far stronger affection for young women than for

young men. Boys and dating allowed girls to assimilate to a culture of consumption and social performance. Crushes on other girls brought private experiences of intimacy and passion that they rarely found with boys.

Marion Taylor left a particularly good account of her high school crushes. Born in 1902, Taylor grew up near Los Angeles. Her divorced mother, who worked hard to provide for her two girls, was not emotionally demonstrative. Beginning at thirteen, and continuing through high school, Marion would have crushes on a series of her teachers and other girls. "Ah! Only a girl knows the sensation of being crushy!" she wrote in an early entry about Miss White, her first crush. Marion experienced her attraction to these teachers as the most intense and important part of her life in those years. She ordered her days around contacts with Miss White and practiced small rituals to express her devotion. Marion shared hot chocolate from her thermos every day at lunch with Miss White, and she pinned a test with Miss White's handwriting on it to her underwaist.[120] She thought about the woman constantly.

For Marion, the infatuation felt far from trivial. When some of her girlfriends told the teacher about the crush, Miss White told Marion that it would soon pass. "Well—there's where she's mistaken," Marion wrote defiantly. In fact, her affection for Miss White persisted through junior high school. Three years later Marion wrote in a letter she never sent that "my love for you is no little thing—it's not just a crush—a school-girl's affection; it is all of me; it is the biggest thing in my life."[121] Her regard for Miss White eventually changed into a feeling of friendship and respect, but the experience of love for Miss White continued as an important emotional backdrop to Marion's later crushes on teachers.

As long as she continued to direct her affection toward teachers, Marion created love objects that were distant and easily idolized. Beth Twiggar also wanted her crushes on a pedestal. Even when they were classmates she had to feel that the girls were much older than she and superior. Marion knew that her teacher idols could never be a "chum" or an equal. Even while she enumerated each teacher's outstanding qualities, she acknowledged that her crushes originated with her own need to adore someone rather than with the compelling attractions of the particular woman. This fits with the psychological literature of the day which found that an idealized love for an older person "is almost invariably a part of every girl's development."[122]

Even idealized love could make a girl vulnerable to pain. If one of her crushes failed, even unthinkingly or unknowingly, to give Marion attention or regard, she might fly into rage or sink into despair. Early in her affection for Miss White she wrote, "Nothing could hurt me more than if she had a bad opinion of me." Years later, after not seeing Miss White for two months, Marion ran into her on her walk home. Instead of walking with her, Miss White went on by herself. "I just hate Miss White! I'm mad at her forever," Marion wrote. Marion also feared that her affection for teachers made her disloyal to her mother. Like Beth Twiggar, she described herself as scared that her strong feelings might sweep her away or threaten to override her self-direction.[123]

In spite of the dangers of idealization, adoration fulfilled a number of emotional needs for Marion. Her feelings for Miss White and others allowed Marion to see women in a positive light. They provided models of femininity that were distinct from that provided by her mother. She studied their style and hoped to emulate it as she grew older. She probably decided to go to college because of her intense devotion to these women and in spite of her father's resistance. Clearly she desired the youthful vigor and feminine attractiveness that these women showed her. Her relationships, although one-sided, allowed Marion to see herself as a valuable individual. When Miss White or later crushes returned her affection, she felt thrillingly good about herself. The affection she received gave her the nurturing that her mother did not provide. Crushes also allowed Marion to come to terms with her own life. As she admired Miss White's nose or another woman's petite stature she dealt with disappointment over her own appearance.[124]

Marion shaped her sense of herself as an individual and a woman through her experiences of affection for these teachers. By studying various women's ways of being womanly and successful, she could imagine herself as someone in their positions. Like her heros, Marion eventually became a teacher. Her crushes also gave Marion a rich and varied emotional life, one that did not remain entirely secret. Miss White knew of Marion's affection, and other teachers must have seen Marion's ardor for them as a school-girl phase. In their understanding responses and affectionate interest, they gave Marion some validation for her emotions and allowed her to understand her emotions more fully. Through her crushes Marion learned what it meant to feel passionately about others. Still, crushes on teachers precluded mutuality and so limited the satisfactions that Marion could expect from these relationships.

As we saw with Beth Twiggar, love for a girl or woman did not preclude attraction to boys. As a senior in high school Marion Taylor reluctantly admitted that she had "fallen hard" for a boy in one of her classes. Later, in college, she yearned for the physical closeness of men and "primitive love-making." Yet she still found women who excited and attracted her, and she clearly distinguished her affection for women from her desire for men. "I don't see how love for a man could be half so thrilling," she wrote of her attraction to a woman professor at college. "A man could never be so far off, and mysterious, and tantalizing and fascinating and intellectual and *spiritual*."[125] As with her earlier crushes, the college professor could easily be idolized. For Marion, loving women generally meant loving them at a distance.

Marion did find one young woman, however, whom she could both love and be close to. As a college student Marion became friends with Henrietta. Some gaps in Marion Taylor's diaries make their friendship impossible to fully analyze. Yet Marion recognized that this relationship differed from others. It allowed her to live out her affection in a way that her crushes could never allow. "I feel a volcano within me which bursts every once in a while," she wrote. "Just restlessness and longing for I don't know what. But I am happy too with Henerey." Marion had always been reserved with people, and even though she sometimes wrote of longing for affectionate caresses, she typically took satisfaction in loving at a distance. One of the ways her dates with boys and college men differed from her crushes was that she wanted to pet with the men but had little attraction for their other qualities until she met her future husband.[126]

With Henrietta, however, affection included both love and desire. "I get more excitement out of showing affection! I never have until that other night, and some way, something—reserve I guess—gave way then, and I've wanted to express my affection for her ever since!" In fact, she felt compelled to show her affection. "I have a crazy desire to kiss her about every minute, and I hug her all the time and feel so thrilled and excited." For Marion, the breakthrough came at a definite moment. Suddenly she discovered a relationship that could combine the distinctive pleasures of love and physical closeness with someone whom she considered a friend. "I just love her to distraction, as thrillingly as I used to love my lady-loves, but more satisfyingly." The only advantage that a romance with a man might have over her affection for Henrietta is that it "would tickle one's vanity, and excite with the novelty of it," but by contrast it would "not be half as satisfying, not so congenial, not any more thrilling." And, finally, love-making with a man could have a different conclusion than with a woman—"I can love Henerey all I want, and you'd have to be so careful with a man."[127]

For Marion, the combination of love and desire would return in her romance with the man she married. In him she found a congenial companion and lover and someone whose exotic past and personal accomplishments allowed for some of the same adoration that she had lavished as a high school girl on her teachers. Although equating her adolescent crushes with her mature love may seem too facile, there clearly exist some connections. As a teen-ager she had written that the man she wanted to marry (if she married) should be older than herself, someone who could offer her intellectual companionship.[128] Her husband was just such a man.

## Conclusion

Teen-agers and young adults of the century's first decades elaborated a peer culture that allowed them to shape their own social and sexual practices. The peer culture shaped personalities that would allow men and women to deal effectively with the demands of a mass-market economy and of a society in which the individual dealt with strangers every day. Modern society required middle-class women to adjust to rapidly changing social situations and remake themselves according to the interests and demands of peers. We have seen Edythe Weiner earnestly reading magazines for the "truths" that would allow her to achieve popularity, and Beth Twiggar applying the cold creams that promised beauty.

When personality succeeded—proving that one, in fact, had personality—popularity followed. Suddenly a girl found herself out of the stag line at dances and dancing with several partners in one dance. Yet popularity might prove ephemeral. Boys might talk; a girl might gain a reputation as being easy. The evidence of popularity might, in fact, turn into shame as it did for Beth Twiggar. Or, like Ruth Raymond, a girl might remain in the stag line and despair of her sex appeal and her personality. Humiliation and self-doubt were the emotional compliments to the excitement of popularity.

The emotional lives of girls and young women also grew through their relationships with other girls and young women. Crushes might offer a girl the chance to deepen a friendship. Often it meant adoring a distant girl or woman. Through crushes, however, girls felt deeper affections than they typically did for boys. Only in later life would most women discover passions for men to match those they had harbored for teachers or older girls. American culture in the early twentieth century taught women that romantic love and companionate marriage would give them the intense affection and companionship that they sometimes found with women friends, and that these adult relationships would open a full life for them.

# 3

## *The Single Woman*

In 1919 eighteen-year-old Gladys Bell began keeping the diaries and journals that would record her emotional life for the next sixty years. She grew up on a farm in southwestern Pennsylvania and by age eighteen had earned a teaching certificate. The first few pages of Bell's first diary show the transition from adolescence to life as an independent woman with almost dizzying speed. Beginning in August, the diary's brief entries report on her social life and on her first teaching experience. Within a month she had broken up with one boyfriend and quickly found another. Her dates sound like those of high school girls. "To Indiana [Pennsylvania] and the Grand to see 'Mickey.' Fine! Then to the 'cafe' for sundaes. They looked sort of astonished to see Glad in Indiana." A few days later Bell went to a dance and noted that she had "a jolly time with my many pals," going on to list the men who had danced with her (including the man she would eventually marry). By November the diary assumes a more serious tone as Gladys worked out a misunderstanding with one of her beaus, leading to their agreement to marry. Her father gave his blessing. The next day, however, she wrote, "Changed my mind." This did not sit well with the prospective fiancé, and Gladys felt both pressure to accept this proposal as well as a longing to enjoy her freedom. "Must I *soon choose* or can I do as others at eighteen and a half, walk onward alone and happy?"[1] Gladys would never be alone, exactly, but she would put off marriage for almost six years.

Women like Gladys Bell who postponed marriage until many years after completing high school often experienced a period of life without clear boundaries or goals. For many women marriage constituted the primary, and sometimes elusive, goal. Single women's social activities, including their romantic and sexual practices, attracted the interest of researchers. In 1934 Robert Latou Dickinson and his assistant Lura Ella Beam explored singlehood in a volume based on case histories from Dickinson's decades-long gynecological practice. *The Single Woman*, along with the predecessor volume, *A Thousand Marriages*, proposed to answer the question that Dickinson had posed in his 1920 address as president of the American Gynecological Society: "What, indeed, is normal sex life?" Dickinson and Beam found the women in their study to be generally healthy and well-adjusted. Comparing a sample of women born around 1900 with another group born a generation earlier, Dickinson and Beam noted that all the contemporary single women "beyond childhood had had heterosexual experience either emotional or physical or both," yet none had venereal diseases. As compared with the earlier group, the single women of the 1920s were far more likely to be engaged and somewhat more likely to have lost their virginity. Although women still sought love, they had also come to believe "that love is not constant" and in disappointment over lost love they learned to separate sexual desire from "emotions and beliefs."[2]

*The Single Woman* presented a picture of healthy and triumphant heterosexuality for American women. The spinsters of an earlier generation seemed to be "disappearing before the flapper or the younger generation, who can have free contact right through life, with knowledge of birth control . . . " as one of the women had written to Dickinson. The minority who became sexually active outside marriage could control their fertility and so enjoy sex without fear of pregnancy. Singlehood, in fact, seemed a period of preparation for full selfhood in marriage and for the full realization of sexuality. Homosexual women also came within the case histories studied by Dickinson and Beam, and although these women had health and success in life to match heterosexual women, they seemed more of a throwback to an earlier period when a larger proportion of professional women remained unmarried and often found intimate companionship among other women. For women who remained single through their lives, as well as for women who married, the early years of independence in college and work became an important time of maturing from youth into full womanhood.[3]

As suggested by the example of Gladys Bell, Dickinson and Beam's celebration of female heterosexuality overlooked complex emotional developments in the lives of young women. The transition from youth to adulthood, represented in choices about love and career, frequently created personal conflict. The passage became even more complicated and confusing for modern youth whose marginal status might extend for years and whose culture offered skills for gaining social acceptance but not for self-affirmation. The emotional experience of middle-class women often contrasted sharply with widely accepted emotional ideals. Cinema and popular fiction offered women narratives of romance, enhanced by desire, fulfilling and transforming their lives. Although women generally accepted these ideals, they also experienced feelings of ambivalence about love, men, marriage, and desire. When love did arrive, it often resolved these feelings of ambivalence—at least temporarily—but it rarely appeared as an overpowering and unambiguous experience. Instead, love seemed like another confusing experience in the lives of single women, even if they believed it was the experience that would transform all others.

## Singlehood

Just as adolescence in the 1920s could extend from junior high school into the college years, singlehood included women both studying beyond high school and working. After they left high school, women faced important decisions about their lifecourse. College and work attracted a growing majority of middle-class women by the early decades of the twentieth century.[4] All of the women whose personal papers we have examined went to college or worked before marriage, if they married at all. These years became an intermediate and indeterminant stage beyond adolescence when middle-class women achieved greater independence from their families and moved toward self-definitions for their adult lives.

The flapper was the most common image of single women in the 1920s. According to Zelda Fitzgerald, once a young woman discovered that " 'boys *do* dance most with the girls they kiss most,' " she "bobbed her hair, put on her choicest pair of earrings and a great deal of audacity and rouge, and went into the battle."[5] The battle here referred to the public recreations and heterosexual conviviality that young women took up with delight. The flapper seemed so taken with her new sexual equality with men, and so wrapped up in her life of pleasure, that she could hardly pause over problems of identity. The flapper image, however, can obscure the emotional turmoil that young women faced during their years of singlehood.[6]

For single women out of high school and subject to the competing attractions of career, marriage, friendship, and independence, decisions about the future often proved difficult. A fundamental issue for self-definition was the question of marriage—whether or not to marry and, if so, to whom. Popular images presented romantic love and desire as forces shaping women into fully integrated—and married—persons. Yet the feelings of competence and independence that women gained from college and work could leave them with a sense of the limits of married life. Even desire, which seemed to promise an untouched path to love, offered only ambiguous guidance to women coming of age in the early decades of the century.

Within the middle class, distinctions of wealth and position made striking differences in the meanings and forms of singlehood. For Sarah Bradley in Boston and Ilka Chase in New York, the year following high school meant a round of social events as debutantes. Their families viewed work, and even college, as goals for women of lower social standing. After their mandatory year, however, Sarah Bradley and Ilka Chase left the social round with some relief—Bradley to do volunteer war work and then to go to Radcliffe College, Chase to become an actress. Another wealthy middle-class diarist, Elizabeth Yates, recorded her parents' expectation that her older sister would come out as a debutante during the year following college rather than accept a position as an instructor at Smith College. Elizabeth watched in dismay as her sister complied with parental pressures to meet social responsibilities rather than take work that she wanted but did not need. Elizabeth, on the other hand, would ultimately hold out against her parents' plans. She never became a debutante, and rather than follow her sister to Smith, she spent a year at a boarding school after high school and followed her dream of becoming a writer.[7]

By the 1920s college was becoming a far more common goal for young women, whether from the upper middle class or further down the social scale. Those with college educations had grown from 4 percent of the population in 1900 to 12 percent by 1930. By 1938, 1 percent of the entire population of the country was currently enrolled in college. The numbers of women enrolled in college had grown much faster than the college population as a whole, with women making up 21 percent of the college population in 1870 but 47.3 percent in 1920. Many of the women entering college in the 1920s came from families in which college had already become a tradition. Anne Morrow, from a wealthy family, attended Smith, as her mother and older sister had done. Other women attended college in spite of limited family support. Gladys Bell took a year off from teaching in rural Pennsylvania to attend Grove City College from 1922 to 1923. Ann Marie Low, whose family struggled to maintain their farm in the North Dakota dust bowl, worked at her school library and during the summers so she could attend college in the midst of the Depression.[8]

The college years extended and deepened young women's involvement in the peer culture. With college, many young women lived away from home. This, combined with the intellectual demands of study, encouraged young women to move toward independence from their families. In her journal, Gladys Hasty reflected in 1922 how her months at college had begun to affect her life. "We work and play together all day, and at night we do not go home to talk over with older people what has happened; we go back to our dormitories where we are associated with no one who is older than we are, and wrestle with our problems together or alone."[9] Martha Lavell, who read avidly as a teenager, only considered herself to have begun reading in earnest in college. New ideas and possibilities for thought swept her away, and she soon found herself rejecting organized religion and arguing about God with her grandmother: "Evolution is the basis of my belief: therefore no Adam and Eve for me."[10]

The college years may inspire young women with new possibilities in thought, as they did for Martha Lavell, or with new opportunities. Gladys Hasty found her freshman year at Bates College "almost unbearably exciting." She hoped that Bates women would become more active in politics "and in civic improvements of all kinds." For most college women, the attraction of college accompanied training for some vocation. By the late nineteenth century, college attendance for women had grown along with the numbers of women entering professions. College education still resulted in jobs as teachers for many women, but growing numbers of women entered such traditional male bastions as law and medicine in the early twentieth century and they dominated the new field of social work. During the 1920s, women earned about one-third of all graduate degrees awarded.[11]

Clara Savage's work as a reporter for the *New York Evening Post* gives a sense of the variety of women's work in the years before World War I. "Spent the morning with one Miss Finney visiting Irish scrub women on the West Side," Savage wrote in 1914. "It may be the way to do charity but I have great doubts. I felt so embarrassed to-day because she asked so many personal questions of the poor Poor." During that same year she interviewed Frances Perkins, who was then investigating workplace safety, and attended a lecture by feminist leader Charlotte Perkins Gilman who made Savage *"furious."* She also met labor leader Mother Jones and interviewed peace activist Lillian Wald, social scientists and administrators Katherine Bement Davis and S. Josephine Baker, and Anna Howard Shaw, head of the National American Woman's Suffrage Association (NAWSA). Savage, who in 1915 took over as the head of the press section for NAWSA, felt herself part of a wider women's struggle for a more just society and more opportunity for women.[12]

Even Clara Savage, with her busy schedule, sometimes felt lonely. After a long Saturday of work in early 1914, she lay on the couch in her Manhattan apartment feeling tired "and *lonesome* for—oh! Well, merely for a house, husband and baby! Want them awfully!"[13] By the 1920s, marriage would color all of young women's choices during their years of singlehood. From the 1870s until about 1920, 40 to 60 percent of college women never married. At elite women's colleges like Smith, Wellesley, and Vassar near the turn of the century, only about one-fourth of the graduates married. By the 1920s, however, neither college nor work for women represented a choice against marriage. As early as the 1919–1923 period, 80 to 90 percent of the graduates of the top women's colleges married. Many colleges joined popular periodicals in praising marriage and encouraging it. Advertisers presented marriage as a career, and colleges offered new curricula to prepare women for the wifely duties as hostess, dietician, purchasing agent, and nurse. Vassar established its Institute of Euthenics to bring together social and natural sciences to solve the problems of family and child care, to incorporate "into the consciousness of every college woman" the values of scientific parenthood. A study of college sex written in the 1930s noted that "competition for dates is keen and the socially timid suffer accordingly." Sororities helped by stressing the social skills needed to capture and keep a husband. In reflecting on her years at college in the 1920s, Pearl Buck recalled that "No girl thought it possible that she might not marry."[14]

*3.1* An office of the *New York Evening Post* when Clara Savage worked there. Schlesinger Library, Radcliffe College.

Among the women whose papers we have studied, the best demographic predictor of marriage or lifetime singlehood is date of birth. Only a minority of these women chose life without marriage, although a higher percentage made this choice than for the American population as a whole. But of women born before 1900, one quarter remained single, while for those born in 1900 or later, only one in seven never married. The quality of the decision for singlehood may have also differed for the two groups. Devotion to a career, especially one embedded in reform, offered an attractive choice for women in the late nineteenth and early twentieth centuries. They could expect to work and live with other women, committed reformers like themselves. Lives of service seemed more compelling alternatives than the private satisfactions of home and family. By the 1910s, however, service and career seemed to Clara Savage only about equal to marriage in its appeal.

*Romance*

By the 1920s, popular culture presented single women as committed to a life-transforming struggle to find and capture the right man to marry. Elinor Glyn offered chapters in *The Philosophy of Love* on the best means for women to attract and ensnare the man of their choice. Anne Hirst, a columnist for the *New York Post* and the Philadelphia *Record*, wrote an entire book, *Get Your Man — and Hold Him*. She encouraged young women to make the most of their personal attributes, "be they face, figure or mental equipment." "You must be distinctively something in order to bring that handsome young man you covet across the room to your side."[15] Like Glyn, Hirst imagined a fierce competition among women to capture the most desirable men. Although both writers urged women to examine the faults of their potential mates, they took for granted that most women's ambition focused on snaring a man.

For women at the opening of the modern era, finding the right man to marry meant finding love. Eugenics advocate Paul Popenoe warned in his marriage advice manual against the "Romantic Platform." In this scheme, love appears at a sudden "psychological moment," "looks you in the eye, and then *it is on*." When love appears, everything else becomes secondary at best. And if this mysterious experience passes as suddenly as it appeared, another will take its place as the supreme experience of life. Popenoe dismissed this concept of love as "infantile philanderings."[16] By the 1920s, however, the romantic platform had become a staple of the popular media. Whereas some narratives of love might depart from the love at first sight followed by complications followed by marriage scenario, both movies and popular literature almost always presented love as the most important experience of an individual's life and the source of personal transformation.

One large-scale study of the messages offered by movies in the 1920s and 1930s found that sex and love were the main themes of 57 percent of movies in 1920 and about half of movies in 1925. In more than a third of films analyzed, love meant an experience of attraction when the couples first meet, and in another quarter of the films love follows on the second or third meeting. What the investigators termed "Love as a growth" appeared in only 5 percent of movies. The movies, concluded the study, portray love within "a Cinderella conception of acquaintanceship."[17]

The plot of the movie "*It*" revolves around the concept that a woman and a man will know at first meeting that they are meant for one another. During the first scenes of the movie, Clara Bow's character, Betty Lou, has to maneuver her way into the path of department store heir Cyrus Waltham just so the two can meet. Once they do, their romance begins and in what remains of the movie's seventy-two minutes the couple only has misunderstandings about sex and morality and overcoming class differences. Elinor Glyn, the movie's writer and the creator of the concept "it," believed that love "is caused by some attracting vibrations emanating from the two participants." Love depends "not on the will of the individual, but upon what attracting power is in the other person." She described "it" as a "nameless charm, with a strong magnetism," in other words a surplus of the "attracting vibrations."[18] For people who possessed "it," love at first sight would make perfect sense.

Although movies had a limited number of reels in which to conclude stories of romance, novels of the period could develop stories of love at greater length and with more subtlety. Most of the popular novels of the 1920s relied on proven formulas for romance. Advertisers, who took the popularity of romance in fiction, magazines, and movies as a sure insight into the mentality of the "matinee crowd," wrote scare copy to match this perception of life, with romance lost to falling socks, bad breath, or blemished skin.[19] Although the psychological moment of romantic love might be beyond their control, using the right product could guarantee that women didn't miss those opportunities that appeared.

Young women took the romantic ideals of the culture seriously. Azalia Peet grew up in a world still Victorian. She was twenty-six in 1914 when she wrote, "And still the Prince lingers." "I wish he would come," she wrote two years later and added, "I feel as if I had been a wee bit robbed because this experience has been denied me."[20] Four years later Elizabeth Yates would read the description that her sister had written of her tall and tender "well-beloved:" "When we meet, our eyes will say more than our lips, and we will know that we were meant for each other." When Yates discussed her own ideas about love, she drew on the same cultural store her sister had used. Each person, alone, is only half of a whole personality, she wrote, "and the whole reason for living is to find the other half and make a whole."[21] Martha Lavell, a student at the University of Minnesota in 1928, quoted from song lyrics to express her feelings about love and her hope for a man who would find her. "*Is it so terrible for me to dream such things?*" she wondered.[22]

When they looked forward to love, women believed that it could not be "merely physical," as Jane Sherman wrote. Of course, she believed, "there must be bodily attraction, the little silliness and all which is just the opening of a door to a real and lasting love which is deeper than the first stage." A few months later she repeated that love "musn't be flippant, and oh! It *must* be companionship idealized to love."[23] In discussing love with two friends at college, Ruth Raymond found them disagreeing over the relative importance of the spiritual and physical in love. "I said I didn't know much about physical or spiritual, that I thought you just looked at a boy and knew he was right for you, and *stuck*." She concluded that love "was a sort of fate. It got you *stuck*."[24] She might have been writing advertising copy for the movie *"It."*

Even though the lives of women often admitted to more drama than Hollywood's scriptwriters could dream up, they generally experienced love as less dramatic and less sudden than called for in scripts. In her months of acquaintance with author John Marquand, Helen Howe, an actress in her late twenties, felt a growing sympathy and attraction for the older, married man based on common interests and mutual admiration. "In those days John simply filled a place on my horizon of newfound older brother—only kinder and more encouraging to me about my work than either of my brothers would ever have thought of being."[25]

In between writing to her mother about her work with muralist Diego Rivera, Ione Robinson included the information that she had met an American working in Mexico as bureau chief for Tass, the Soviet news agency. Later, a little guiltily, she admits, "I have a feeling that I'm falling in love with Joe." Their romance had all the makings of a Hollywood comedy or perhaps a spy movie. "I like best the days when he spends the whole lunch hour composing poems to me on the back of the menu," Robinson wrote home. But Joe rejected such bourgeois products as poetry and pretty dresses and chided Ione when she wore ribbons or silk. Since Ione knew Max Eastman, Joe—or his superiors—assumed that she knew something about Trotsky's whereabouts. At least he kept asking about Trotsky. One evening when she visited Joe and his friends, everyone stopped talking when she stepped into the room. "It is really very difficult being in love with a Communist," she admitted.[26]

In less exotic surroundings seventeen-year-old Gladys Hasty discovered her psychological moment with a distant cousin who took her and her aunt to a Maine beach-side resort for dinner and dancing. She danced the tango with Paul and that night at Aunt Mollie's she couldn't sleep. "It must be love, I thought, because I had never felt like this before." She felt guilty about her passion for a married man and managed to avoid Paul for the rest of the summer. But she worried that if she really loved him she might never have such feelings again. She left for college in the fall still hoping *"more than anything* to feel about a man who isn't married the way I felt about Paul, last summer." Perhaps her cousin's unattainable status had given him the added attraction in Gladys Hasty's imagination to make her psychological moment possible. It fulfilled an adolescent girl's image of love at first meeting, yet in her own mind her cousin was out of reach.

When she met a young man at college who attracted her, Gladys found her feelings far less distinctive and far more difficult to understand. When she talked with her boyfriend, Herbert Carroll, he "always understands what I mean that I don't say" and she realized that she knew what he meant even when he didn't say it. "Then I just felt—oh, I can't explain *that* either." As she grew closer to Herbert in the months that followed she wanted to understand better what exactly she felt for him. She listened to other girls and searched for clues in Russian novels and French plays. "Man or woman," these sources seemed to agree, "if you were in love, you knew it. But how did you?"[27] For Hasty, the assurance only came after months of questioning, and it came only slowly as she watched the warmth that her parents felt for one another after many decades of marriage, as she saw the easy sympathy that Herbert and her father formed with one another when he visited her home, and as he continued to express his steadfast regard for her. At least part of the romantic platform failed for Gladys Hasty. Love didn't appear at first sight, as she believed it had for Paul, and she didn't recognize it instantly when it did appear.

Even when experience failed to match the script, the narrative of romantic love might shape the way that women thought about their relationships. Dorothy Thompson, Berlin correspondent for the *New York Herald Tribune*, met novelist Sinclair Lewis in 1927 shortly after her divorce. Almost immediately he asked her to marry him and he persisted in courting Thompson in the months that followed. Sinclair Lewis "occupies my mind," Thompson wrote two months later; "he and he alone intervenes in my dreams at night and is the sole object of my daydreams." Like her teen-aged contemporary Jane Sherman, Thompson believed that she could have a complete life only with one other person— "what I want is to find that person and build a life with him which shall have breadth, depth, creative quality, dignity, beauty and inner loyalty."[28]

In spite of the power of the cultural ideal of romance, unmarried middle-class women often saw through the romantic platform. " 'Falling in love'—what does that mean[?]" wondered musician Dorothy Smith. "Not just a sleek young man courting a fluffy young lady & both of a proper age." The woman remains a "cucumber" until "plop, one falls in love." That hardly matched Smith's experience of "dizzy aggressions & retrogressions." When an older and unattractive man asked if she liked to fall in love, Emily Tapscott Clark told him that she "hated it, because it upset me horribly." Helen Howe, who had followed her passion for John Marquand into an affair that her family found sordid, waited through his divorce from his wife and then faced his drifting away from her. She felt devastated when she heard of his engagement to someone else at a dinner party. The prospect of finding a young man to complete her life attracted Ruth Raymond on some days, although on other days she believed men were "a snare and a delusion" and planned to carry insecticide to slaughter any of the "anxious earthworms" she met. Ann Marie Low dated an older man for years before recognizing how impossible life with him would become. When she looked at his John Barrymore profile and wavy hair, she didn't see her prince but "a tombstone on which is written the epitaph of dead dreams."[29]

Just as Gladys Hasty struggled over the question of whether she really loved Herbert Carroll or not, many other women found themselves unable to choose among suitors. Winifred Willis felt drawn to both Bill and Bub before finally marrying Tommy.[30] Jane Sherman, as we saw in the last chapter, collected marriage proposals in virtually every stop on the Denishawn tour of the Far East. The dating system that made acquaintance with many young men possible also made knowing any of those men well relatively difficult. Women might find themselves in the role of consumers, choosing among several men on the basis of seemingly marginal differences.

Young women struggled with their own feelings and their culture's messages when they experienced desire that could not fit the cultural script. "I believe that more than half the misery in the world comes from mistaken assumptions about love," Viola White wrote in her diary. She found herself repeatedly in love with women and men whom she could not approach, such as a married professor at her graduate school, or, such as Beatrice, who "regards me with gratitude when I let her alone."

Yet White never questioned the value of her love for Beatrice. "It liberates one's spirit from the mollusk shell of identity, and it gives intense meaning to the most trivial incident. You may thereafter be tormented or ashamed, but you are never bored." As Zelda Fitzgerald wrote to her husband after years of struggle, "love is bitter and all there is."[31]

Clara Savage, whose desire for marriage predisposed her to accept the cultural image of romance, found instead that her relations with men were a confusing mixture of affection, regard, and desire. At the end of one relationship her beau told her that he didn't love her and that she didn't love him " 'enough.' " She accepted his pronouncement but couldn't sleep that night: "there was something like the blade of a razor in my chest and the upper edge of it kept moving & cutting a little as it moved. Having tears inside of you makes it. And I thot of how a good many men have found me attractive physically, and how no man has ever really loved me." In the same diary, she wrote that "So much of the happiness in being in love comes from looking forward to something. It seems as though that were the biggest element in it. Once you take this away, the bottom drops out of everything."[32]

In a culture that promised happiness and meaning through the experience of love, the greatest threat of emotional distress came from being jilted. Anne Hirst included a chapter for women whose boyfriends or fiancés had abandoned them, providing a variety of tactics to help women survive and recover from their mistreatment. Five years after her own crisis of lost love Clara Savage Littledale would offer her counsel to those with broken hearts in *Good Housekeeping*. Face the situation, she advised, try to understand it, realize that this does not mean you are unlovable, change your surroundings if possible. She wrote out of her own experience of feeling the piercing pain from unshed tears. But after advising young women to take control of their emotional lives, she concluded her advice with a plank from the romantic platform—fall in love again.[33]

The confusion that young women experienced over romance and marriage seems on the surface to contradict the trend toward heterosexual conviviality in adolescence. That dating could become courtship appears clear from the trend toward the convergence of the date of graduation from high school and the marriage age for women. Girls in high school met many boys in the dating system and more and more frequently one of those boys was "the one," that is, the one they married. An advice manual for college students recommended that if young people have "several friends of the opposite sex" simple mathematics would keep them from making hasty and wrongheaded decisions about marriage. Popular author Floyd Dell believed that dating served biology. Men had evolved to compete, women to choose.[34]

Yet even when women accepted the rituals of the dating systems and the assumptions of the romantic platform, they still experienced anxiety and confusion as they made decisions about marriage and career. Middle-class women coming of age in the 1910s and 1920s could only lay claim to a tentative self. They frequently lacked confidence in their ability to live independent and productive lives and had little reliance on their ability to make decisions about marriage. Azalia Peet, who would ultimately commit her life to service as a missionary, still wondered in her late twenties what "all embracing ideal" should shape her life. "Is a life devoted to *mere* helpfulness to others, disregarding self, the real goal? . . . Is the well rounded development of the artistic nature not a bigger, broader more comprehensive ideal?"[35] Peet's concern over the development of the self reflected widespread doubts in early twentieth-century culture over the core meaning of self. Unambivalent values seemed to disappear along with the local economies and "island communities" that gave way to the mass market and consumerism in late nineteenth-century America. At the same time religion assumed less time and passion and the symbols of religion held less compelling meanings for middle-class Americans.[36] The cultural ideals that took the place of religion and communal values in shaping the self—consumerism, romance, even social reform—held out the hope that they could make individuals feel whole. "Nothing but a great love or a great cause will ever concentrate all the atoms and make me a weapon of efficient service," wrote Viola White in 1926.[37] For some women, love and marriage did mean a movement toward wholeness. For others, the self became less tentative as they practiced their professions or gained other experiences of competence and independence. Their growing sense of self, however, might make the decision for marriage seem more like a loss than a gain.

Because young women typically remained dependent on their families until after college, they could rarely see themselves as fully competent. Some women seemed unable even to take the most elementary steps toward confident self-assurance. Anne Morrow, who followed her mother and sister to Smith College, struggled with her slowness on tests and her inability to believe in herself. She apologized to her mother for telling her about a success in one of her classes, and when she won a school literary award she went from feeling "dazed" with happiness to a conviction that she didn't really deserve the prize. We have seen that Elizabeth Yates's sister turned down an offer of employment from Smith on her parents' insistence. Later, when she fell in love with a poorer man, her parents again intervened and squelched the match.[38]

Whereas the wealth and class expectations of their families handicapped both Yates and Morrow in claiming independent lives and confident selves, women from sharply different backgrounds also felt that as single women they could claim only tentative or provisional identities. Ann Marie Low, who grew up on a farm during the late 1920s, worked with her father and never seemed to lack confidence in her dealings with boys and men. Yet after giving the valedictory speech at high school on "making a life," she wondered, "What in billy-blue-blazes do I know about making a life?" Ione Robinson, who left her mother to move to New York to pursue her desire to become a painter, found a growing sense of meaning in her work. Later, however, when Rockwell Kent made the seemingly capricious demand that she burn all of her early paintings, she complied "out of pure spite, just to show him that I could and would make new ones."[39] Robinson's decision to burn her pictures shows an ambivalent self-assertion based on self-doubts but also on her growing confidence in her artistic ability.

As young women lived through their years of singlehood, they frequently recognized the tentativeness of their identities and also their movement toward greater self-confidence. Simply growing older seemed to bring about change. As a senior in college, Martha Lavell noted the changes in her personal life since her freshman year. "It is no longer hard to make friends. No more of that crushing feeling of inferiority that handicapped me in the presence of any girl." Distinctive experiences, such as travel, could make the change even clearer. Dorothy Smith expected study in Paris to allow her to "live more fully & express myself in every way." Jessamyn West, also traveling in Europe, began "to feel more myself, or at least more of the self I like to be" as she grew close to the companions she lived with in Paris. She also gained markedly in confidence. On the ship to Europe at the beginning of her summer of study, she would never have confronted the purser and demanded better accommodations as she did at the end of the trip.[40]

For most middle-class women, independence and self-confidence grew with competence in career or profession. Viola White recognized her need to gain control of her life and to live independently. At age thirty-eight she decided to take "account of my gifts and limitations and set forth systematically to develop the former." Elizabeth Yates, benefitting from her sister's experience, defied her family's discouragement and held firm to her desire to write. As she gained acceptance as a feature writer, Lella Secor discovered the "bounding, pulsing, thrilling joy of life within me; that old feeling of confidence in my powers—as yet not fully tried or tested—and the sublime sort of certainty that I shall be able to fight my way, however difficult the obstacles."[41] Lella Secor would continue to feel sublime certainty when she joined the peace movement trying to forestall American entry into World War I. Working full time on peace activities, she met a sympathetic young graduate student in economics who would eventually become her husband. But when Philip Florenz first proposed, in March 1917, Lella Secor told him she was too busy to be engaged.

In the 1920s, as in the 1910s, career and marriage often seemed incompatible. Only about 12 percent of professional women were married in 1920, and even though a growing portion of married women worked during the following decade, the great majority of these were domestic workers. During the Depression, the constraints on married women pursuing careers became even greater, because many employers refused to give married women work. Ann Marie Low's cooperating teacher wanted to marry but knew that she would have to give up her job and that she and her fiancé could not live together and support his mother on his salary alone. Low, planning for a career in journalism, knew that a "married woman loses all independence and any chance at a career of her own."[42]

The conflict between marriage and career played an important role in the larger conflict that women felt between marriage and self-definition. Marriage remained the goal and destiny of most American women. When they worked, most women expected to marry later. "It's the best and biggest thing," wrote Clara Savage of marriage, "but there are other experiences I want first." But choosing a career, as Dickinson and Beam pointed out, "is a choice against marriage insofar as it removes uniqueness and places marriage among alternatives." Women who found a sense of purpose and growing competence in their work—Lella Secor's sublime certainty—might well look askance at the dubious promises of married life. When Clara Savage Littledale later asked, rhetorically, in a *Good Housekeeping* article, "can a girl afford to marry?" she reflected the concerns of many women over the loss of independence that came with marriage.[43]

Among the problems discussed by Littledale in her article was the difficulty that many women felt in finding and choosing the right man. Littledale, along with Judge Ben Lindsey, recognized the important role of career in allowing women to feel something like equality with men. "The result," according to Lindsey, "is that many a youth finds himself subject to rather contemptuous inspection by the young woman of his choice." With no compelling need to marry, and with more self-confidence based on their competence as professionals, women might find the failings of young men more apparent and their own independence more dear. From striving as adolescents to be "wanted or chosen or considered desirable, by a member of the opposite sex," young women moved toward valuing themselves for their own achievements.[44]

### The Ambiguity of Desire

Personality—self as social performance—may have been the most widely accepted concept of self by the 1920s, but a concurrent trend within both academic circles and popular culture assumed an underlying, biological meaning for self. Chemist Louis Berman in 1922 proposed the view, accepted by many physicians, that every manifestation of behavior had an explanation in the operation of the endocrine glands. Many social scientists, led by Harvard professor William McDougall, presented human behavior as the product of multiple instincts. The important works on the psychology of advertising written in the 1920s encouraged advertisers to appeal to "wants" grounded in such basic drives as the need to acquire, possess, escape pain, and find emotional excitement.[45] Psychologist Joseph Jastrow also treated human nature as fixed and further offered specific male traits: "The one selected trait of the male from the club of the cave-man to the masculine protest of Adler is mastery." Elinor Glyn's *Philosophy of Love* included chapters on "The Nature of Woman" and "The Nature of Man." Both chapters began with sections describing and explaining "fundamental instincts." "Man is a hunter," wrote Glyn, "a hunter always." But even modern women are still willing to be ruled.[46]

As a "biological fact," sexual desire should have given young women in the 1920s a clear connection to their underlying nature. Warner Fabian's flappers and Ben Lindsey's jazz babies titillated or shocked Americans with their eagerness for sexual pleasure. Social research showed that heterosexual intimacy had become common among unmarried youth. Information gathered by psychologist Lewis Terman in the 1930s showed that of women born before 1890, 13.5 percent had sexual intercourse before marriage. For those born in the decade after 1900, the figure rose to 50 percent, with an even higher percentage for women born in the following decade. Dickinson and Beam found the growing heterosexual experimentation of the period a healthy precursor to good married sex. A later study of college sex identified a wide range of healthy sex experiences for young women, from the ordinary caresses of "love-making" to experiments that included intercourse.[47]

But even researchers who supported sexual expressiveness found that young women often harbored ambivalent feelings about sexual pleasure. Psychologist Elton Mayo believed that ignorance about sex was a widespread problem among adolescent women. Dickinson and Beam found that many young women (and a small number of young men) remained ignorant of the sex act until after marriage. And although some young women separated sex and emotion, the researchers found that most women still tended to look for sex within the context of love relationships. This accorded with the widespread assumption that for women sex had more to do with emotion and the desire for children than it did for men. "The sexual impulse of woman is not the simple momentary desire of the male," wrote one psychoanalyst, "but a highly ambivalent emotion in which fear is intimately mingled with desire."[48]

In popular literature and in the cinema of the 1910s and 1920s, the heterosexual pleasures available to women led to marriage or ended in disaster. The eroticization of images in advertising and cinema coexisted with a continuing condemnation of unchastity for women. Clara Bow's character in *"It,"* for instance, pursues Cyrus Waltham with scrappy and flirtatious abandon. But when he kisses her after their first date, she slaps him, telling him she's not that kind of girl. In *Hot Stuff* a college woman "pretends to drink and smoke and neck because she thinks fellows prefer whoopee—girls," but the leading man "calls her bluff," turning her toward romance and away from the excesses of the flesh. Jessamyn West tried to explain to her husband that a woman might delight in the attentions of a man but remain incapable of returning "that desire in kind"—"frank delight" might show "satiety." "The woman must appear to repulse and scorn."[49]

As we saw in the last chapter, the joys of necking included excitement over social success, attention from attractive boys, and sexual desire. The accounts that girls gave of "primitive love-making" never dwell exclusively on physical satisfaction. Jane Sherman could not understand her own reactions to the attentions of her beau: "sometimes his kisses thrill me but usually they don't." Young women often experienced the desire of others as confusing or frightening. Viola White felt drawn to speak to a soldier during a rainy night's walk, but she feared approaching him might stir up the boy's "sensuality." Jessamyn West received repeated propositions, from men and women alike, during her summer of study and travel in Europe. Before she became accustomed to these she considered the encounters as a reflection of personal failing.[50]

The passion of men could come as a threat to women who had never come to terms with their own desire. By age twenty-one, Winifred Willis could recognize the "muffled, inarticulate passion" she inspired in men. "It is the sort of thing men always feel at first," she reflected, "before they decide they'd rather die than marry me, & *will* die if I don't yield to their immoral demands." Later, involved with two men, she separated her desire for the two of them. She had no longing for Bub's body but felt she could marry him for his companionship. She would never marry Bill but longed for his body. "So you see Journal," she concluded, "I have only one tragedy left—the only one I have ever had—Virginity."[51] Willis experienced her own passion as "muffled, inarticulate," and found embracing it difficult until later life.

Dorothy Smith was more attracted to girls than boys during her adolescence and managed to remain "self-sufficient & coolly independent" toward men until her early twenties. During a music summer school at age nineteen, however, she met an older, married man who penetrated her reserve, although "not without considerable embarrassment & resentment on my part. I couldn't get used to such an intense & masculine sort of person all at once." Whereas she believed that her first male interest taught her many essentials about "the other sex," she nevertheless felt relieved that he was married. Smith found her first approach to heterosexual desire disturbing, and she remained aloof from men until her months of study under Nadia Boulanger in Paris when she began to feel the "enormous undercurrent of sex appeal." Even so, she had not surrendered to the current and felt that "it is all slightly repulsive." Smith would struggle later in analysis with the ambivalence of her desire for her fiancé. "Must I respond to him as a trembling red hot wire," she wondered, "or may I push him into the airy sunshine along with the trees and love him as I do them[?]"[52]

Clara Savage charted the ambiguity of desire in her own life. "When I was growing up," she wrote in 1916, "love was one thing and the sexual act another entirely separate thing. The latter was bad and indecent except between the married and then it was for the purpose of having children." She only realized that sexual passion played a leading role in love during her college years, and then only as an intellectual insight. After college, perhaps as a result of her own passionate relationships, she "began to wonder if they couldn't be separated—if desire wasn't a good thing in itself without insisting on having it dressed up as love."[53]

Savage's thinking clearly reflected both the needs she felt in her own life and the growing awareness within American culture of sex as a natural and desirable element of human life. A single woman and a professional in New York City during the prewar years, Savage dated several men and also had passionate relations with several women. She undoubtedly knew radical thinkers from Greenwich village. In 1915, during her confusion over sex and love, she read Edward Carpenter's *Love's Coming-of-Age*, a widely influential work that proclaimed "Lust and Love" as "subtly interchangeable" or perhaps one and the same. Savage thought the book "pretty good and true." Perhaps reading Carpenter helped Savage to a better understanding of her own desire. Carpenter's insistence on the primary value of lifelong marriage for love, however, may also have helped Savage reaffirm love as the only sanction for sex. "For me," she wrote, "there could never be any joy, any sense of fulfillment, anything but a ghastly emptiness and horror in a sex relationship without love."[54]

Because young women experienced great ambivalence about desire, when they finally discovered unambiguous sexual passion, it often came to them as a revelation, an erotic moment to match the psychological moment of romantic love. Dickinson and Beam included a first-person account of a woman's sexual awakening, from her love for another woman in college to her friendships with men in Europe during the war. After returning to the states she met a man who captured her heart. "My whole being," she wrote, "was swept as if by fire. The physical effect was so severe that one night the lips of the vagina parted and I formed the first realization of the aperture." Dorothy Smith, as her engagement to David Dushkin continued, had "day dreams of passionate sensual possession of others—forcing my will & pleasure upon them." After months of a growing friendship, the twenty-eight-year-old Helen Howe suddenly one evening found herself in the arms of John Marquand. "There was nothing I could have wanted to hold back," she recalled. "It was for this utter, complete self-giving that I must have been keeping myself."[55]

Even when the erotic moment came more than once, it always surprised women. Winifred Willis found it with several men. Her ambivalence toward desire began in adolescence and included images at once frightening and fascinating. She dreamed of "bodies crushing down on me—of terrible satisfaction—of unholy cravings." She would wake up exhausted but "ready to go out on the street after some sort of love." Her romance with Bill, whose body she desired, ended with their parting, but not before she found Bill's body in bed with her. "I found at that night & since that my pygmy will always set me on fire with desire," although she knew she would never love him. After leaving Bill, she began to date Tommy with whom she felt no passion until they came home from a night of dancing and dining. He stayed at her apartment that night, and they slept together, as they would on many future nights, although without having sex. She wrote later, "When I lie back in his arms & give him my lips I forget everything else except the sweet, gentle, greedy feel of him."[56]

The intense desire of the erotic moment surprised women and liberated them to surrender themselves to their passion, although not necessarily to the "immoral demands" of the men who inspired this passion. Diarists Howe, Smith, and Lockhart, like Dickinson's unnamed patient, enjoyed their lovers' caresses yet remained virgins until marriage. Dickinson and Beam described this as "an intermediate stage of all-but-coitus in which union has not been consummated but only vaginal chastity is preserved." Those women who "went the limit" generally made love first with men they loved and, in most cases, expected to marry. Beth Twiggar kept her virginity as her claim upon self-respect in the face of her reputation for being easy. Her first intercourse was with her fiancé. Although that marriage never happened, Twiggar kept her most intimate physical caresses for men she loved. Marjorie Kinnan experienced repeated frustrations in trying to find time and opportunity for a tryst with her fiancé. "We lost our chance Thanksgiving," she wrote to Charles Rawlings, "when I had the apartment absolutely to myself—all day and until 9:30." Kinnan nevertheless dreamed of her lover and looked forward to " 'an orgy of lust' " on their honeymoon.[57]

Desire and love would become important elements of the emotional lives of most young women coming of age in the 1920s. Yet most middle-class single women had not abandoned themselves to desire and many found it difficult to abandon themselves to love. Romance, so important in the cultural prescription for the young, female self, made up only part of a complicated mixture in the lives of single women. Career and independence also made powerful appeals to young women, and personal histories of family life could yield views of marriage at odds with the cultural ideal. For women with a strong and clear sense of the purpose and direction of their lives, love and sexual awakening could come as expansive and promising. For women lacking such self-assurance, desire and romance seemed both threatening and confusing.

## Ambivalence and Acceptance

As we saw at the beginning of the chapter, in only a few months as a single woman, Gladys Bell experienced both the struggles of establishing herself in her career and the ambivalent appeal of romance and marriage. Later notes show that in 1921 she fell ill with "nerves" and had to close her one-room school in Seitz early in the spring. To help recover her health, she traveled to Washington, D.C. The reason for Bell's indisposition remains unclear—perhaps pressures from work had overwhelmed her. Yet she took up teaching in the fall at Whitesburgh, so she obviously found continuing attractions in her career. Her 1922 diary begins on her birthday, March 3. "Twenty-one and happy, contented for once, and occupied," she wrote. A few days later she reported on her improved health and on sleeping "sweetly" for the first time since 1920.[58]

Among other concerns, social pressures around marriage had contributed to Gladys's ill health. She wrote about a date to a musicale, where "the crowd was tolerable, but I simply cannot feel 'their way.' I'm out of place, bored or weary-disgusted with some things, especially *husbands* and *domestication*." Marriage remained a persistent concern for Gladys Bell during the next several years. In the spring of 1922 she dated two young men, Marlin Penrod, whom she referred to as Red, and James Nelson, Jr., whom she always called Junior. Red Penrod, a big handsome man who drove a truck for Sterling Oil, could appall Bell with his wild

3.2 Gladys Bell in 1925. Courtesy of Mr. and Mrs. DeLane Penrod.

ways, but he also had a knack for delighting her with his sweetness and
devotion.[59] Although better educated than Penrod, Nelson lacked steady
work seems to have struggled in the early 1920s to launch himself
in business. Both wanted to marry Gladys. Finally, on May 18, she became engaged to Red Penrod. Still unable to reconcile her confusing
mixture of feelings for the two men, Gladys found herself overcome by
longing, wonder, and happiness when she met with Junior a few weeks
later. Her solution was to accept Junior's proposal of marriage and to
make clear to both men that she needed time to decide between them.

Dickinson and Beam celebrated engagement as a "midsummer mad-
ness" that gave "unimpeded expression" to both romance and "personality" and allowed greater continuity between the single life and marriage. For many women like Gladys Bell, however, engagement had
become a transitional stage in courtship that allowed further assessment
of the prospective partner.[60] In the months after she gave her tentative
promise to Red and Junior, Bell looked to her culture for a clear guide
to the meaning of love in her life. She could identify with characters in
movies, taking their situations or personality as representations of her
own, as she did in 1919 with the character of Mickey from the Mack
Sennett comedy by that title. During her confusion over her choice between Red and Junior, she found guidance in the movie *Island Wives*,
which depicted "labor, sacrifice poverty—and *love*, against riches, ease
luxury and indifference." In mid-1922, Gladys felt that Red Penrod offered the greater material security, but she felt drawn to Junior Nelson
more powerfully. The movie, Gladys believed, "twas meant to help me
decide my destiny."[61]

Bell had no hesitation in accepting the romantic platform. Love would
transform her life, she believed. One of the novels she read claimed that,
"In Life's great choral symphony, the keynote of the dominant melody
is Love."[62] Gladys reproduced the novel's praise in her own reflections
on love. "A mighty, unconquerable, force born of Heaven," she wrote,
"which peoples the world, makes happiness, creates harmony, instills
higher motives, and—what doesn't love do?" In fact, Gladys added,
"what is *life* but a fulfillment of love's demand[?]" Love shaped the
whole life and it came not as action of the will but as a demand, as
something beyond the self and overpowering the will. She compared her
feelings for one of her beaus with "a great whirlpool drawing me gradually to the center of its passion." Yet, if Gladys could sometimes feel
the tug of affection, she never felt confident enough that the passion of

the moment was genuine love. "I'm longing for someone to crush me to his breast . . . ," she wrote just before Penrod proposed. "Can it be possible that I'm in love? No—I don't think I am."[63]

Her ambivalence about romance proved too great for Gladys to resolve in 1922. After a trip to Michigan in the late summer, she returned to Pennsylvania and broke off both of her engagements. She attended Grove City College during 1922 and 1923 and returned to teaching the following school year. By 1924 Gladys Bell would again face decisions over marriage. Throughout this period she tried again and again to match what she learned about love from her culture with her own experience.

Gladys experienced her ambivalence about romance as confusion over the direction of her life. Hoping for an overpowering experience that would transform her life, Gladys found herself unable to make the decisions and commitments that would set the direction of her life. "Women may seek for peace and joy and happiness," she wrote in 1924, "but after all the most blissfully peaceful and restful moments of a woman's life are those in the arms of him who loves her," and later that year she hoped that her love would "draw [her] personality to its height and beauty." But she could never be certain that any of the men who attracted her most and who wooed her most ardently qualified as the one man who could give her the peace and the self-development she wanted. Unable to find her ideal man in real life, she began a correspondence in March 1923 with a dream lover, an imaginary beau who may have been based on someone she knew but who nevertheless represented her ideal, the one who could inspire the kind of transforming passion that Bell had learned to expect. "I wonder if I'll meet you soon," she wrote in one of her early letters, "or if you are only a 'phantom of Dreams.' "[64]

In November 1924 Bell tried to resolve, or at least end, her confusion by accepting a second proposal from Red Penrod. "Well, I mean it this time," she wrote the next day, and the two would marry the following April. Yet the new engagement only aggravated her ambivalence about the place of love in her life. "For Goodness Sake!" she wrote just four days after the engagement, "I'm in an awful stew—I don't want to be married, yet," keeping in mind her recurring (although generally mild) illnesses, "I don't know whether it is good for me to be single under the circumstances." As the date for the wedding approached, Gladys kept trying to reconceptualize her resolve to marry as a "modern arrangement" of convenience or as a practical step based on economic necessity.

Bell admired Penrod and felt affection for him, yet she refused to believe that her regard for Penrod was the passion she had waited for. "Love to me is something as yet undefined and unexperienced," she wrote in December of 1924, and in April of the next year, just weeks before the wedding, "Funniest thing of my life is that I never 'fell in love.' "[65] Even as she prepared to marry, it seemed that only a dream lover could satisfy Gladys Bell.

Bell's doubts about love mirrored her doubts about the self. Several months before her second engagement to Penrod, Gladys Bell wrote that her success as a teacher and her year at Grove City College had given her greater confidence both professionally and socially. "My mentality has been wonderfully expanded and in many directions." She prided herself on her success as a teacher and knew that she could live without a husband's support. At times, her expansive sense of her accomplishments and ideals made it difficult to imagine that any man could meet her requirements for a husband.[66] Yet Gladys experienced herself as incomplete and, as we saw above, expected the love of a man to give her life fullness and integrity. For Gladys, love represented the most important of the strategies she followed for self-fulfillment.

The freewheeling and slightly racy morality of *Flaming Youth* and of the movie *The Perfect Flapper* attracted Gladys, as did the independence of a career. Yet she lived in a rural society where parents and friends expected her to marry. These conflicting goals help account for both her nervous troubles of 1921 and her self-doubts. The highly mutable personality of modern American culture seemed always paper thin, for Fitzgerald's Amory Blaine as well as for Gladys Bell. Both the fictional character and the schoolteacher searched for some fundamental core of self beyond the demands of social performance. Gladys believed that she could achieve a full, rich sense of self and an abundant life through discovering her own inner potential. For a young woman from a more comfortable background in an urban area, this might have led to psychoanalysis, as it did for Dorothy Smith, or to philosophical speculations, as it did for Winifred Willis.[67] Gladys Bell searched for a fuller self within the quasimystical advice literature of the period.

Marie Corelli's *Life Everlasting* would serve Gladys Bell as Mary Baker Eddy's *Science and Health* and Emile Coué's *Self Mastery through Conscious Auto-Suggestion* would serve other young women of the 1920s. The work gave Gladys both a cosmic context for self and a system for managing her life. According to Corelli, the individual soul could partake in the Divine if only the individual would remember her eternal reality, that is, her genuine self. Once discovered, the genuine self would guide the individual through all the confusions of life and give her the power of directing her own destiny. Those who embraced sickness became ill.[68] Those who embraced health and happiness would have them for the taking.

Inspired by Corelli's novel, Bell felt confident that she would enjoy "strength and brightness in spite of dark clouds" through the exercise of will power. "I shall try my power over others and forget to be sad and moody." Her quest for psychic health centered on her efforts to control her emotions. Bell attempted to gain direction of her emotions by looking on the bright side, by cultivating healthy habits, and by simply persisting in good cheer. "My life is seemingly full of beautiful and soul-satisfying service, light pleasure and usefulness," she wrote in a typical effort at emphasizing everything good about her life. She believed that "Happiness is a Habit to be cultivated or discouraged at will," and she hoped to sustain happiness through such strategies as "Smile at least 20 times a day," and "Abstain from fretting or worry, regardless of circumstances." During a later time of trouble she hoped to take herself in hand with a Corelli-like pep talk: "Self-pity is deathly and self-analysis is as good as medicine so let us have more of the latter my little woman, and see if we can't feel better, have a better time, look prettier and give the world a smile and lots of dimples full of sunshine."[69]

While Bell's mental discipline and efforts to form good habits gave her some calmness in the face of emotional struggles, they rarely gave her the control she desired. "I'm losing my grip on myself," she lamented in 1924. "I can control my mental state if I assert all my will to that point but still I lose my temper." If her weakness of will proved frustrating in the face of bad children at school or relations with her parents, it proved devastating in her search for true love. Instead of finding the kind of transformative love promised by Corelli, the "immortal union of two Souls in one," Gladys found her sense of self in turmoil as marriage approached. "I wish I could slip away into no-where and forget it," she wrote of her impending marriage. A few weeks later she could find no anchor for self anywhere: "Can't find joy in my work any more. Can't see any use in being married, don't believe in love or marriage for myself and I don't want to be away from home." As her wedding day came closer, Bell wrote again and again of her melancholy and lack of direction. Just a few days from the date, she felt herself "near hysteria."[70]

The ambivalence that Gladys experienced toward desire compounded her confusion over marriage and her reluctance to accept her feelings as love. Gladys thought of herself like the perfect flapper in the movie of that title as "joyous but not immoral . . . virtuous but not old fashioned." She believed she could help her sister understand the difference between a lover's kiss "and that of the worldly wise 'petter.' " Yet Gladys viewed the prospect of physical love with considerable anxiety. Like most adolescents and young adult women of the decade, Gladys Bell enjoyed the casual caresses of dating. How little this taught her of intense desire became clear when she made her trip to Michigan in the summer of 1922. While staying with her cousin, she enjoyed her youthful attractiveness and wrote home that she "vamped two men inside of an hour with my wonderful eyes." She went too far, though, when she playfully flirted with her cousin's husband. When her cousin left for a few moments one day, the husband "seized his opportunity." Although Gladys admitted that she "shouldn't have permitted him to kiss me or hold me in his arms," she refused to accept any responsibility for the brief embrace: "too sudden was the movement to enable me to prevent the mischief." But in addition to placing her in a compromising situation, the incident also brought Bell literally face to face with sexual passion. "I wonder what mental anguish, or mental desire makes a man turn pale, his lips tremble and his voice to waver." She made plans to leave two days later, but on the night before her departure her cousin retired early and the husband again took Bell in his arms. This time the embrace did not last a moment but two hours. "Surely God saved me again tonight," recorded Gladys, "for never before has any man been so absolutely slave to his passion as that man was, in my presence."[71] Rather than recognize her own desire and willing involvement, Gladys set her experience down as a warning from God about the uncontrollable passions of men.

The prospect of marriage made Bell's ambivalence about physical love ever more apparent. She hoped for a mate "sufficiently strong to conquer the animal passions of his nature." Her experience in Michigan, though, made her doubt that such a man existed as she recalled that "man roused the first bitter sarcasm of disgust and disdain—man impregnated my soul with suspicion and man deadened . . . the power to love."[72] Happily for Gladys Bell, Red Penrod proved to have both the love for her and the will to give up intercourse on their wedding night. Only several weeks later, after anxiety and trepidation on Bell's part, did they fully consummate their marriage. Like many women, Gladys Bell eventually found satisfaction in married sex and it became part of the satisfaction she found in marriage.

Gladys Bell experienced both romance and desire as ambivalent passions. She had appropriated the cultural images of love as the fulfillment of self and as an overpowering transformation that absorbed the self. Drawn to both of these ideals, Bell also found that her own growing sense of competence and independence contradicted the cultural ideals to some extent. Nevertheless, she felt that she had to marry, in spite of her reasoned and emotional aversion to marriage. The prospect of physical love also failed to settle her mind about marriage. Rather, her ambivalence about her own desire and her distrust of the desire of her lover made her grieve all the more her loss of innocence and independence. Marriage for Bell, as for most middle-class women, would settle these feelings of confusion. In a sense, the issue of what the self would become was surrendered to the ideal of the self as a married woman. Although this gave some relief, it also left other possibilities for self unanswered, preempted by the demands of married life.

A minority of women decided against marriage. For these women, singlehood was not a transition with a well-defined conclusion in marriage. Dickinson and Beam found that work gave some women a wide enough variety of satisfactions to take the place of sex and companionship. Another minority of women found both sex and companionship outside of marriage. The professional women among their case studies seemed to have had relationships that often lasted many years. Dickinson and Beam also showed that a significant portion of single women were homosexual. Some of these women had full sexual lives with other women, whereas others followed "relationships of companionship" or "chief interest" over a period of many years.[73]

Dickinson and Beam tended to support the common sense of medical and advice literature in assuming that the psychic or physiological propensities of women determined their attitude toward both men and marriage. One physician blamed the attitudes of "old-maidish, cold, and reserved" girls on their "psychopathic, reserved, over-religious, or sexually anaesthetic" mothers. Only disaster could follow if such girls married. Novelist Elinor Glyn recommended to women who were "cold by nature" to "make up your mind to join that increasing body of females whose real interest is not in man or children, but in things and careers." Similarly, homosexuality appeared as a fixed condition—if not exactly a pathology, it was not exactly a compliment either. After Katherine Bement Davis's study of college women, both scholarly and popular literature recognized the prevalence of passionate relations among women. Those women who persisted in such relations, however, came to be seen as a particular type of sexual being. The category of homosexual, which had replaced the medical term "invert" by the 1920s, assumed a fixed sexual orientation.[74]

Our work supports neither the view of single women as "sexually anaesthetic" nor the belief that women who love women lived out unvarying psychological or biological imperatives. Personal papers almost inevitably reveal the passionate longings of young women. Even those women who seemed, outwardly, the most reserved nevertheless yearned for affection and even physical caresses in their writings. We also found little evidence of exclusively homosexual orientations. Just as girls like Beth Twiggar could delight in their crushes while pursuing dates and necking with boys, young women frequently had profound, loving relations with women and men at the same time. Even among women who had long-lived intimate friendships with women, interest in men seems to have comfortably coexisted with love for women.

Although the image of life without marriage in the 1920s included loneliness and emptiness, young women often found full lives in work and service. Harriet Louise Hardy was one such woman. Firmly committed to her profession, Hardy rarely wrote of loneliness or of confusion over the direction of her life. Born in 1906, Hardy grew up in New Jersey. She graduated from Wellesley College in 1928 and then attended Cornell Medical School. Later in life Hardy would reflect that she had never married because she was "wedded to medicine," but as she completed her medical studies and embarked on her life's work, Hardy experienced the attractions of companionship and love and pondered the place of passion in her life. Her steady sense of self and purpose allowed her to recast each experience as another facet of a full, rewarding life.[75]

Hardy's ideals of self resembled those of an earlier generation of professional women. A commitment to service and a strong spirituality characterized her reflections on her own life. "I know I was born to be a doctor," she wrote during the early months of her practice. "I love people in distress; I feel for them endlessly and can work myself ragged for them." She knew that her middle-class family had given her a privileged upbringing that allowed her to gain skill and experience "to make the world a finer place to live in." Even her frustration over mistakes she made and her fatigue were "annulled by the love my patients give me and their gratitude. . . . I am so tired I ache but I am ready to go back to the ward—I will find something to do, important, human, satisfying."[76]

Although Hardy had such a clear sense of herself as a physician that she would refer to medicine as "the Goddess I worship," both medicine and service to others existed for Hardy within a context of spirituality that pervaded her life and work. An Episcopalian, she wrote repeatedly of her faith that "God is reaching for us" and working through us. She referred to her work as a "tremendous responsibility" chosen by her but also an expression of the will of God. "The Self in me is God-given; belongs to God; will be shaped & molded by God till the self of the small s is no more and only life-with-God is practicable." This surrender to the will of God did not diminish Hardy's ability to experience her strength and independence as an individual; rather, it allowed her to see her commitment and profession as having transcendent value. When a Catholic priest told her that south Philadelphia was full of people who prayed for her out of gratitude, she wrote in her diary, "God make me worthy of it!"[77]

A sense of self defined by service, career, and faith made Hardy almost Victorian. She felt at times "essentially independent, alone, apart, sufficient perhaps too much so—still there it is!" Yet her self-sufficiency never precluded strong emotional ties to both men and women. One young man who took her to a play during her residency in New York made her feel "young & warm & exuberant"—"we are alive, flesh & blood and glad of it." A year later she enjoyed dining with the same man and realized "that I am very fond of S & enjoy being near him."[78]

Hardy recognized "a very feminine streak" in her personality but also believed that, on balance, she was mentally and physically more male than female. During Hardy's residencies in New York and Philadelphia, female friends inspired her greatest passion. Her first reference to E (Hardy referred to her lovers, male and female, by initials), a fellow female resident in New York, described "a most unique night" of work together on the same ward. "But the whole thing was pleasantly permeated with the quick flashes of friendship, the warm grasp of a wanted hand and the myriad of little things that make human relations so satisfying, so sane." As their relationship grew, Hardy experienced her love for E as enormously and powerfully satisfying: "its strength is incredible; its influence endless." Six months later, on a visit to E, Hardy quickly rediscovered the "sense of belonging that I feel when we are together."[79]

This relationship had little in common with schoolgirl crushes. Both women were adults, both professionals. Unlike an earlier relationship that had seemed too demanding for Hardy, she experienced her love for E as mutual and reciprocal. She characterized her feelings as responses to "certain essentials—the need of souls for each other; the infinite satisfaction in close companionship; the deep pleasure in intimacy of personalities." In its mutuality and in the power it carried for both women, Hardy's relation with E resembled the ideal of romantic love. Yet, in spite of the intensity of her emotions, Hardy felt confident in her love for E. E's love for her "almost makes me afraid," Hardy wrote, but she still felt certain that all would work out. "Sometimes it seems fraught with danger by its very intensity," she wrote, "again its peace seems an essential benediction to my busy life. I have a confidence that it will turn out well—there is a purity of purpose in both of our attitudes that will keep us—God grant it so!"[80]

Hardy's reflection on her feelings for E shows the confidence she felt in her own sense of herself and her reliance on divine help. It may also point to Hardy's fear that the love she bore E might turn into a sexual relationship. If so, she believed that she and E could control their desire. She continued to have faith in her inner resources to deal with passion and disappointment. During a week that she described as "shot thru with emotional content of a fierce and painful type" Hardy relied on "a certain private life that is full and rich."[81]

Several years later Hardy called on those same inner resources to carry her through a far more disappointing relationship, this one with a man. In her first position as a physician, at Northfield Seminary for girls in Northfield, Massachusetts, Harriet Hardy came to know R, who worked at the same institution. Her attraction to R shaped her emotional life for more than a year. "I have come to love and cherish R," she wrote early in their acquaintance. Almost a year later, his "slightest attention," she wrote in one entry, gives "meaning and color to my life." If Hardy's love for E implied romantic love, her desire for R made it evident. "I have read so often in Miss Millay's verse and elsewhere of a lover's longing and it has seemed touching but remote from my experience. It is no longer so."[82]

Unlike her earlier loves, however, Hardy's love for R went unrequited. "Alas," she wrote early in her relationship, "perhaps he never thinks of me." Six months later the realization had become more and more clear that they would not become lovers. "I have spent hours steeling myself to the idea that I shall never have R and can do without him and then he calls me and it all goes." Later, when she had resigned herself to giving up her hopes for R, she felt a "futility and loss and uselessness and uncertainty" that she had never experienced before. Hardy learned to accommodate even these negative emotions and to find herself calmer and less desperately lonely in the months that followed. In failing to gain R's love, singlehood again became Hardy's future. She looked ahead to study and medicine, work with students, and winter sports. "My old optimistic self bobs up its head to say I will learn much from this experience."[83]

In a memoir of her life written in 1983, Hardy remembered the period after 1936 as a "turning point" in her personal life. The memoir says nothing about R and her disappointments. Rather, she recalled having "a happy social life" while at the same time "finding reasons for refusing offers of marriage, just as I had done in medical school." At least in retrospect she understood the later 1930s as the time that she decided in favor of career and gave up on the possibility of marriage and family. "I believe that I am truly wedded to medicine," she wrote. "So while I had and have friends of both sexes, my primary allegiance is to medicine. For me at least, this has been utterly satisfying."[84]

Although decisions about the course of her life entailed far greater ambiguity than her retrospective summary suggests, her statement reveals a core truth about Hardy's inner strength. Hardy's optimism and commitment to a life of service are evident from her life's work. In 1939 she became college physician at Radcliffe College and in 1945 began the studies on the effects of beryllium poisoning that would make her a national authority on industrial toxicology. She established the National Beryllium Registry and the Occupational Medicine Clinic at Massachusetts General Hospital in 1947. Later she would become a professor at Harvard Medical School.[85] As we have seen, Hardy felt powerfully the attractions of romance in her life, yet she could overcome the shortcomings of her relationships with R through her strong commitment to her life's work.

The different experiences of Bell and Hardy in facing emotional crises undoubtedly point to a range of personality differences between the two women. The two examples suggest that the emotional experiences of women in the 1920s were shaped by the resources available to the self. Women who felt confident of their competence and purpose could face emotional crises with greater resilience and so manage their emotions more successfully. They could also open themselves to the intensity and conflict of romantic passion and, perhaps, of desire, more easily than women who lacked a firm sense of self-identity. Gladys Bell, who felt fully the tentativeness of singlehood, found steady conflict in the question of marriage. The question of whom she should marry became so important that only an unrealistically ideal mate could make the decision an easy one. Hardy, who escaped the tentativeness of singlehood by embracing work and career, faced no such demands on her sense of purpose. Hardy also carried with her a sense of transcendence that allowed her to place her actions and decisions within a cosmic scheme. Bell wanted such transcendence, yet her attempts to gain it through mysticized positive thinking failed. Hardy, who experienced herself as competent, could more readily experience the self as transcendent.

The examples of Bell and Hardy also show the power of culture to shape experience. The romantic platform of the 1920s and 1930s that presented love as the unique and transformative experience of life convinced most women. Although women may have realized that the romantic platform promised not only the fulfillment but also the loss of self, the ideal of love set the standards that women used to evaluate their own experiences. Those women who embraced the alternative of a life committed to career might escape the cultural calculus and find love and fulfillment on different terms. Yet the example of Harriet Hardy makes it clear that women required great self-assurance and competence to find satisfaction outside the culture's sanctioned pathway to fulfillment and happiness.

# 4

## *The Flapper Wife*

Shortly after she married Lorin Thompson in 1924, writer Winifred Willis came to believe that she was fundamentally unsuited to marriage. Although she loved her husband passionately, she found that the harmony and intimacy of their courtship and first weeks of marriage quickly gave way to periods of emotional estrangement. She attributed virtually all of their problems to her own personality and vowed to remake herself. "Already I am struggling to conquer myself," she wrote several months after her wedding; "my nerves, my habits, my selfishness, my irritable instincts of the recluse, just for his sake. . . . Many times a day I whisper '*For him*,' and so succeed in conquering some meanness in myself."[1]

Two years later the tone of her diary hadn't changed. Winifred still loved her husband passionately, yearned to be his perfect mate, and struggled to overcome her shortcomings as a wife. The characteristics that made her happy as a single woman (independent and solitude-loving) and that contributed to her success as a writer and poet (introspective, sensitive) hindered her in her efforts to emulate the models of modern married happiness that she believed would satisfy her husband. "He wants a home, children, friends, social activities, popularity, success . . . I have been a drag on him, pulling him down, discouraging him, communicating to him the slow poison of my own inevitable philosophy, which gnaws forever, destructively, at the healthy tissues of my being." Willis felt it necessary to take radical steps toward saving her marriage, which she deemed more valuable than selfhood. "If I am to change all this, to be glad and happy, to bear children, there is only one course for me—*I must deny my very self*. I must not only learn rigid surface control; I must suffer a complete inner negation."[2]

Following World War I, one of the most widespread images of the new roles for women was that of the flapper wife. Although Willis did not consider herself a flapper, the crisis she experienced as a new wife mirrored the difficulties that popular experts predicted would challenge a generation of young women. Gloria Gregory, the heroine of Beatrice Burton's 1925 novel, *The Flapper Wife*, also suffered in a marriage she considered a mismatch. Gloria believed that a woman in marriage had the choice of becoming either a slave or a doll. Unlike her mother and grandmother, she was determined not to become a slave. On her honeymoon with Dick, she spent heroic sums on clothes and perfume, and when they returned to their new home, she insisted on having a housekeeper. "She would never be a household drudge, her hands shriveled with washing dishes. Her nails broken. Her dresses smudged with pastry flour." When Dick insisted that he didn't make enough money to hire servants, Gloria became hysterical, and in the end she got her way.

This marriage, begun with such contrasting expectations, deteriorated rapidly. Dick wanted children; Gloria found the idea repulsive. She preferred to spend her days shopping and her nights dancing or going to parties, ignoring Dick's complaints of having too little money and too little energy. While Dick was hard at work, Gloria rekindled a romance with a handsome actor who supported himself by cadging off of women. And when Dick was forced to take a trip to recuperate from an illness brought on by too much work and too little wifely care, Gloria seized the opportunity to pursue Stan, the actor, to New York City where she hoped to find work on the Great White Way.

In the end Gloria and Dick reunited, but only after Gloria's humiliation and rehabilitation. Her actor boyfriend had already married when Gloria arrived in New York, and the Broadway producers were unimpressed with her beauty—except one who offered her a role on a casting couch. Crushed, Gloria returned to her hometown, took a job, and learned the skills of housekeeping. In the final pages of *The Flapper Wife* Dick and Gloria embrace. "Ah, it was good to be here," Gloria reflects, "to surrender herself!" She asks her husband, " 'Did you ever stop to think how nice it is for two people to care for just each other . . . and to have little children because of their caring so?' " Dick agrees: "I've been trying to tell you that all along, Flapper. But you never would believe it before, would you?"[3]

The image of the flapper wife gave expression to anxieties felt by many in the roaring twenties that marriage might not be included among the "new interests, new attractions, new ideals" of the new woman. A sand painting in Asbury Park, New Jersey, showed "the agonies of a man married to a flapper as he holds a small baby on his knee at the hour of two." A *Literary Digest* article warned of the "jazz-baby" who would soon tire of the "monotonies of matrimony." Part of Hollywood's stock in trade during the decade was the story of a married couple making a difficult adjustment from fun-loving singlehood to married life.[4]

Although the flapper wife represented the concern that modern life made young women unfit for marriage, marriage itself was the target of an opposing strain of criticism. Journalist Samuel Schmalhausen, who invented the idea of a sexual revolution and of the new morality, claimed that when a woman discovered the satisfactions of sexual love she "positively prefers to be sweetheart and mistress rather than wife and mother." Psychiatrist G. V. Hamilton, who carried out one of the earliest scientific studies of marriage, pointed out that most people can adjust to almost any situation, yet they "fail to make of marriage anything like a tolerable situation for themselves." Even many "who go on living together find in marriage a hateful bondage, a dreary, long-drawn-out harassment and a stultifying relationship." "There's no place like home," wrote Samuel Schmalhausen, "except a lunatic asylum."[5]

Gladys Penrod, whose quandaries as a single woman we discussed in the previous chapter, read Burton's novel shortly after she married. She wrote that "it was a stroke of luck that I ran across 'The Flapper Wife.' That is surely an honest portrayal of our present day marriage and its meaning." Although Gladys accepted the book's warnings about the dangers of modern women and modern attitudes, she also took comfort in the story's resolution. "After all *love* is all that is worth living for. . . ."[6] Gladys placed her hope in a revised, modernized version of marriage explained and described by social scientists and journalists alike. The young wife in Sidney Howard's *The Silver Cord* described what modern marriage had to offer her husband: "A hard time. A chance to work on his own. A chance to *be* on his own. Very little money on which to share with me the burden of raising his child. The pleasure of my society. The solace of my love. The enjoyment of my body."[7] The wife, although young and modern, exhibited none of the flightiness of the flapper. Rather, as a biologist, she penetrated to what she believed was the core meaning of marriage. It fulfilled the sexual desires and parental instincts of the wife and husband, it offered companionship with affection, and it gave women and men an opportunity to achieve full adulthood through independence from childhood ties and through work.

Women appropriated the new ideal of marriage and worked to make it a reality in their lives. Yet the new roles and satisfactions of modern marriage proved formidably difficult to achieve. Old values often collided with new expectations; biological drives, seemingly the engine for the success of modern marriage, more frequently disappointed cultural expectations than fulfilled them. And women found themselves caught between cultural ideals of modern women and modern wives.

### Companionate Marriage

Although companionate marriage usually refers to the ideal of marriage that crystallized in the United States in the first decades of the twentieth century, the model of marriage as loving companionship between husband and wife had been generally accepted by the middle class in the Northeastern states by the middle of the nineteenth century. From about 1830 until late in the century the style of courtship in the middle class fostered romantic love—passionate and transcendent desire for another unique individual. Marriage advice literature in the nineteenth century dealt with disharmony in marriage by urging couples to find ways to foster greater commitment to the marriage and affection for one another. As William Alcott, a widely read writer on the marriage issue, put it, "Mutual love is the only guide to connubial happiness."[8]

Yet the distance between men and women, bridged during courtship, generally returned in marriage. The middle class that formed in the towns and cities of the young republic created homes in which the father was frequently absent, at work in the countinghouse, the office, or the retail stores. Men created their own spheres of homosociality in fraternal organizations and recreational activities. Women, alone with other women and children, shaped a home life that was distinctively feminine. Women assumed the most important role in child rearing, and the bonds between mother and child grew very strong. This helps explain the continued importance of bonds among women friends and relations, warm and even passionate feelings that could last over decades. This also meant that the husband might return to his home as a stranger, someone whose authority still prevailed but whose values had been abandoned.

The separate spheres of men and women helped define the gendered roles and possibilities of each sex and also shaped the marriage, giving husband and wife specific satisfactions and responsibilities within marriage. Unfortunately, the separation could seem like distance and indifference.[9]

Important shifts in American society would alter the American family structure by the turn of the century. A continuing decline in the birthrate, led by middle-class women, meant that wives at the turn of the century would have the care of far fewer children than their grandmothers had. Women had more time for activities outside the home and, potentially at least, more time to spend with spouses. The separation of genders also declined, as women moved into the workplace in clerical positions and in growing numbers of professional positions. The youth culture of the high school and the new courtship styles that emerged around the turn of the century also undermined the separate spheres. The proportion of women who married rose and the age of marriage declined for women and men from 1890 until the 1920s.[10]

Reformers and intellectuals, from anarchist Emma Goldman to sex researcher Havelock Ellis and feminist Charlotte Perkins Gilman, attacked the Victorian family for its stultifying effects on women, sexuality, or society as a whole. Many turn-of-the-century intellectuals questioned the transcendent value of the middle-class ideal of a closed, private marriage for life with complete sexual and emotional exclusiveness. By the early 1900s popular authors such as Edward Carpenter and Ellen Key had offered ideals of men and women freed from the nineteenth-century monogamous marriage for life. Addressing a different agenda, purity crusaders introduced sexual issues into political debates during the Progressive era through their concern over the proper education of youth, the reformation of fallen women, and the containment of venereal disease. Efforts of reformers from a variety of perspectives had the effect of destroying the double sexual standard and opening sexual matters to wider discussion.[11]

By the 1920s a new ideal of companionate marriage had become so widely accepted that it seemed like a settled matter. The birth control reformer Mary Ware Dennett wrote that "one of the very prettiest sights which present life affords is the way in which a relatively small but rapidly increasing minority of young people are living their mated lives and producing their wanted babies." Author Floyd Dell, in 1930, believed that human instincts, once free of repression, would reestablish human relations on the basis of free, individual choice. This would mean courtship in which men pursued and women chose marriages based on romance and created permanent unions in which men and women fulfilled their parental drives.[12]

John Watson, the behaviorist, writing about the same time as Dell, maintained his position as one of the harshest critics of marriage and family life. "The home remains, I suppose, a place to change one's clothes in, to have cocktails in before going out for dinner, and a place for spending a few hours in sleep (even in this respect the rule is not unbroken)." Yet later in the same essay, as Watson took a speculative look into the past, he imagined a world startlingly like the one Dell envisioned, where freely promiscuous young people formed exclusive unions based on compatibility. "The ideal happy family situation (and the only one I know) is thus a man and woman living together with plenty to do, with or without children, in a secluded cave, hut or blind, with little contact with other human beings, with no scars from early training and no yoke from religion and mores." Watson's primitive society, as it happens, provided a model for modern companionate marriage, including dual careers ("plenty to do") and life in the suburbs ("in a secluded cave . . . with little contact with other human beings").[13]

Whether they took a pugnacious attitude toward marriage in general or only the flawed marriage of narrow-minded ancestors, advocates of modern marriage understood it as a sharp break with the past. And, as modern marriage assumed an ever more pervasive role in American culture, women took the leading role in demanding, forming, and benefitting from it. With their new independence in heterosexual courtship, young women often appeared "oversexed," yet this new independence, combined with the use of contraceptive devices, meant that married love could be "enriched and greatly reinforced by completely fulfilled sexual communion." By the 1920s becoming a wife meant becoming companion and partner, roles that included more sharing as well as equality in family matters, and perhaps even financial independence. The experience of young women in the business world, in fact, not only led them to demand greater equality in marriage but also changed their attitude toward housework. The flapper does not believe housework is hard, wrote a contemporary psychologist. "She has seen too many meals come out of tin cans and delicatessen stores. . . . Her problem is much more one of finding a man who can afford to keep her at home."[14] The pleasures of consumption joined those of the flesh as advertisers made the fruits of mass production into prerequisites for the good life and the good marriage.

### Fulfillment in Marriage

Taking to heart the ideology of companionate marriage, women in the 1920s and 1930s actively sought marriages of companionship and love, good sex, and consumer delights. They also accepted, in some form, the "measure of success," as described by sociologist Ernest Groves, as "the extent to which the relationship encourages the development of the character and personality of both husband and wife."[15] Modern marriage held out the promise of allowing women to form fully independent, adult selves. That the meaning of independent adulthood for women remained confusing appears in the journal of Anne Morrow. The fiancée and later wife of the aviator Charles Lindbergh, Morrow searched for examples of the "humdrum divinity" of married life in her travels before and after her own marriage. She wanted to see how women could be happily married and still "self-contained," how couples could work in equal partnership and maintain loving regard for one another. She also considered possessions—the flowers that women cultivated, how they furnished their homes—as important expressions of the inner life of the couple. "Their house was a strange combination of the newest and best in radio, plumbing, appliances, etc.—and lights inside a red and green glass parrot," she wrote of one couple that she and Lindbergh stayed with.[16] She concluded that the right kind of relationship could harmonize even such discordant taste in furnishing.

The right kind of marriage could only proceed from the romantic passion that some single women believed would transform their lives. This passion seemed to provide marriage with a halo for weeks or months. Most middle-class women believed they had found the happiness and fulfillment that marriage promised. Within days of her marriage, Isabelle McNelis Sickler, in rural Tyrone, Pennsylvania, wrote, "I love my husband more every day." Lella Secor, unconstrained by the line-a-day format that Sickler used, gave her enthusiastic appraisal of her husband as "the most charming, tender, thoughtful and delightful person in the world." Rather than a sharp change in their lives, marriage for Lella Secor and Philip Florenz was "just a delightful continuation of a rare and beautiful comradeship. . . . I have never known any union so sweet and beautiful, so spiritual and soul-satisfying as ours. I dwell in the sunshine of Philip's great soul, and my heart sings with happiness." Ione Robinson, who returned with her husband to their New York apartment just after their wedding, felt "as if I'm sitting in heaven and just starting my real life."[17]

Robinson's sense that her life had only just begun is a striking testimony to the power of the ideal of marriage. She had pursued her devotion to art across the United States, to France and then Mexico, and had worked with artists as successful and as different as Rockwell Kent and Diego Rivera. Marriage, although not consciously or conspicuously the goal of young professional women, almost always seemed like the end of a search for them. It could give them a sense of having found a full and complete self. After her marriage, Elda Furry, from Altoona, Pennsylvania, found that her husband, comedian de Wolfe Hopper, could not always recall her name because it sounded so similar to the names of his exwives. She consulted a numerologist who suggested Hedda, a name her husband managed to remember. "At last," recalled Hedda Hopper, "I had an identity of my own, and was on my way."[18]

Dorothy Thompson, already a successful foreign correspondent, believed that her marriage would make sense of her life. "Not that I belong to you or you to me," she wrote to Sinclair Lewis, "but that we two together belong to something bigger than either of us, and thus, being together, serve it."[19] Love and marriage held the power to give her something that her international renown as a journalist had so far failed to provide her.

### The Failures of Marriage

Although women sought, and generally found, love, affection, companionship, sexual pleasure, and even material comfort in marriage, disappointment in some element of marriage appears frequently in the private writings of middle-class women. After the passions of courtship, both men and women might find marriage more humdrum than divine. Financial difficulties or unsatisfactory sex could undermine the pleasure of either partner. For women, however, the shortcomings of marriage proved far more difficult than for men. In abandoning the separate spheres of Victorian marriage, modern marriage eroded the social networks and customs that had provided support for women analogous to the supports the world of work provided for their husbands. Modern marriage was presented as a total institution, where partners would fully satisfy their emotional and sexual needs and realize true selves. Men, however, continued to have the challenges and consuming interest of work. By 1930 only 12 percent of white married women worked, and limitations upon married women working became even greater during the Depression.[20] Married women had the home and children, as they had in the nineteenth century, but they lacked the cultural support and the network of contacts that formed the separate sphere of nineteenth-century women. When marriage didn't work, it generally didn't work most for women.

A large body of popular and scientific literature from the 1920s onward found that marriages often failed to meet the companionate ideal. In Muncie, Indiana, Robert and Helen Lynd found "little spontaneous community of interest" in marriage and a lack of honesty between husbands and wives. G. V. Hamilton's study of marriage placed most of the marriages he examined in categories ranging from "doubtful success" to separation and divorce. Dorothy Dix, one of the most widely read advice columnists in the early decades of the century, warned that the differences due to sex, heredity, and upbringing could threaten the companionship in companionate marriage. Like other guides to marriage, Dix wrote that couples marry an image of one another as much as they marry the real person, but once they begin to live together "they find out that they have married ordinary human beings instead of angels and motion-picture heroes. Comes the clash of personalities."[21]

One of the most common fears represented by the image of the flapper wife related to her lack of restraint within the consumer culture. Both social science and popular literature of the period recognized the importance of "an adequate economic arrangement" as part of the complex set of relations, goals, and projects of modern marriage. By the early 1930s two-thirds of a family's income went to the purchase of retail goods. A prominent sociologist characterized the economic arrangement of most families as "making money and *buying* a 'living.' " Advertisers recognized women as the main consumers in the household and pitched their products to appeal to women's desire for a well-run and well-fed household. Legitimation for women's role as consumers appeared in ads and magazine articles touting women as household managers.[22]

Popular advice literature and advertisements stressed the emotional value of properly managed households. A well-run home would eliminate at least some of the sources of tension between husband and wife.

As the wife became ever more competent as a housekeeper, she would gain greater self-esteem while her husband would accept her as a replacement for his mother. New products and new approaches would allow women to operate their homes more efficiently and give them more leisure, to gain a fuller life, and to raise their children better.[23]

Yet the pleasures of a well-run home and new products could easily collide with a family's budget and with older values of thrift and saving. Sociologist Robert Lynd recognized that emotional issues could flare up between husbands and wives over differences in the extent to which one of the partners had assimilated the new values around consumption. Differences in values appeared in popular culture as moral issues. An advice book for college youth about dating and courtship warned against mates who would be extravagant in spite of the limited means available to newlyweds. An *Atlantic Monthly* story offered the pathetic figure of a hard-working small-town dentist whose bank account "remained always in an embryonic state, for Mrs. French drew out as fast as her husband could put in." One of *Good Housekeeping*'s "little lessons in married life," suggested that a "psychological expert" lecture prospective husbands and (especially) wives on the coming changes in their lives. "Realize, Mary," the expert tells the bride, "that you are still pretty much a strong-willed, egotistical, and selfish child." You think you will give up anything for John, but marriage will mean giving up one small thing after another for years to come. Live within your husband's income, a popular marriage guide commanded. "Every man has the right to expect that his wife will. . . . Women can be wonderful managers if they are loyal and honest, and if you aren't naturally a good manager you can learn to be."[24]

Hamilton's study of marriage linked the couple's ability to manage finances to the success of their marriage. Couples in the study with the highest level of income were more satisfied than couples with lower levels, and couples that had saved money since marriage were more satisfied than those that had saved none. Most married couples, of course, lacked the income to both consume freely and save, thereby almost insuring that they would find themselves at odds with one strong cultural value. Divorce proceedings during the 1920s reveal that the pressures of trying to provide material abundance could lead to marital problems. Women, as "the purchasing agent[s] of home and of society" found themselves vulnerable to the charge of mismanagement. William Ferris, for instance, told his mother that his wife, Margy, was "silly and extravagant."[25] Mrs. Ferris accepted this as an adequate explanation for their divorce.

Gladys Penrod considered herself a conscientious consumer, yet she wavered between doubts over her family's finances and her attraction to commodities. Although Red Penrod worked throughout the Depression, Gladys and Red faced shortfalls in their income as they struggled to pay their debts. Faced with the limitations brought on by the Depression, Gladys felt the need to reflect on the varied roles that purchases filled in her imagination. "I guess the debts worry me more than my lack of clothing," she wrote, apparently resigned. Yet the very next paragraph opened, "I really must have some new dresses if only for the sake of keeping my husband's eye on me." Gladys believed that consumption should contribute not only to the family's bottom line but also to the stability and quality of the marriage relationship and to the emotional well-being of the woman. Her longings agreed with advertising of the period that presented a wide range of goods as necessary to sustain love in marriage. "It never pays," she wrote, "to sacrifice too much because of debts. . . . A woman craves pretty clothes and I guess has to have them to fill correctly her role as wife, mother, best girl and companion." Clothing could fulfill both personal and interpersonal needs. Gladys suggested both functions later in the year when she returned from collecting signatures for a local political cause. She had gone to the "mansion" of one of the wealthiest men in town and met both the owner and his wife. Gladys wondered, later, what they thought of her in her simple ensemble and without any makeup. "Could they tell whether I was nervous[?] I guess I wasn't very. But it was because my clothes did not embarrass me."[26]

Later the same year, Gladys considered purchasing an electric range. Just a few weeks before she had lived through a "financial panic" over the need to raise money for taxes. Yet she thought that the family budget could manage the $10 down payment and $5 monthly payment. She considered both the practical and emotional advantages that a new stove would provide. "I could exist with the old oil burner," she conceded, "but it doesn't bake, and the fumes and smoke drive me to distraction." A new stove served a purpose in social interaction. "Nearly every house has a good stove if nothing else." The direct personal benefit, however, held hope for benefits for her family. "My life seems sort of without aim now. Perhaps I could create a new hobby—good meals."[27]

## Married Sex and the Threat of Frigidity

One of the leading experts of the period on women's household management claimed for a fact that the strongest instinct of women, and the major one that advertisers should appeal to, was the drive for "sex love."[28] This close alliance of sex and consumerism also went to the heart of modern marriage, where the emotional satisfactions of new goods would join with a vital and newly liberated sex life. Samuel Schmalhausen presented his heterosexual declaration of independence as the self-evident truth "that the sex relation is not to be dedicated primarily to procreation but quite naturally to recreation." Behaviorist John Watson noted the pervasive presence of sexual themes in the culture of the day—movies, novels, newspapers, and magazines. As a consequence, " 'Virtue,' 'purity' in the old sense, rarely exist and are not even considered desirable. But new values are coming into vogue: individuality—clear-sightedness—lack of illusion with life— . . . independence in thought and action."[29]

Studies during the 1920s and 1930s by physicians, psychiatrists, and sociologists supported the changing values of the new morality and stressed the importance of sexual pleasure within marriage. The truth of science became the precepts of marriage guides. One guide, written by physicians, warned that "a successful marriage can hardly be expected where sexual attraction does not exist, or where the marital sex life is unsatisfactory and inadequate."[30] Yet, as a popular columnist wrote in her guide, if you make the effort to learn how to please your husband sexually, "you'll get a magnificent cooperation and appreciation by a husband who is inordinately grateful that you can meet him in his own bed and be a grand companion."[31]

The growing availability of artificial contraception, and the growing phalanx of physicians and social scientists who supported the practice of contraception, seemed to make sexual pleasure even more available to the married couple. A study of marriage by Robert Latou Dickinson and Lura Ella Beam noted that women typically reacted with shock to the first use of contraception but that the practice "gradually falls into routine like brushing the teeth."[32] Studies of different middle-class populations from the late 1920s found large majorities of married couples using some form of contraception on a regular basis. With contraception making unwanted pregnancy less likely, it is no wonder that Marjorie Kinnan could take delight in quoting to her fiancé that the " 'most correct honeymoon is an orgy of lust.' "[33]

In spite of the broad agreement in American culture over the desirability of good married sex, middle-class women experienced desire as a complicated and often ambiguous combination of motives and urges. Necking and petting before marriage seemed to turn into playful reality the culture's images of sexual desire. Yet, as we have seen, physical pleasure had ambiguous attractions for most young women. One advice columnist explained petting as "a combination of curiosity, natural instinct and an overwhelming yearning in the very young to establish once and for all time the truth that They Have Sex Appeal."[34]

Chastity until marriage—or at least until engagement—remained a strongly held moral imperative for most middle-class women. Even though more women had what one study called "illicit sex" before marriage, most women had intercourse first with the man they married. Some respected voices warned of the dangers of sexual repression. John Watson derided the "sex superstition" that told girls "the hymen is the symbol of virtue, that it must be jealously guarded."[35] Judge Ben Lindsey pointed out that society convinces young women that sexual intercourse outside of marriage is somehow worse than the caresses that might lead to intercourse. Psychoanalyst Phyllis Blanchard believed that inhibitions against sex impulses could create a "sex tension" for women that would find no relief, even in marriage. "There is still an appalling mass of young people," warned birth control reformer Mary Ware Dennett, "who are enmeshed in the wretched clutter of a stale and nasty undercurrent of sex thought and feeling, and who vibrate between ignorant fear and turgid allure."[36]

Both Dennett and Blanchard hoped that as modern marriages embraced equality in sexual affection the expressive independence of the sexual revolution would become the standard for "mated lives." Nevertheless, prerevolution sexual morality played an important and often a leading role in married sex. In Hamilton's 1929 study, only fourteen out of one hundred women recalled that "pleasure predominated" in their first experience of sex. Thirty-two felt disappointed, twenty-two experienced little or no pleasure, and eleven remembered it as painful. As we saw in the last chapter, Gladys Penrod dreaded the prospect of giving up "her girlhood to become the possession of a man, his by every right, to cherish or to defile."[37]

Young wives who failed to satisfy their husband's or their own sexual needs found strong cultural messages telling them that they lacked full mental or physical health. One advice work on *Love and Happiness* lamented that cold women were victims of an outdated morality imposed on them by "psychopathic and man-hating mothers." Gladys Bell Penrod wondered if sexual failure meant a physical deformity requiring surgery. Women might also come to believe that they had become the source of sexual maladjustment. Frigidity became the summary term for any problem in the psychological or medical lives of women that robbed them or their husbands of sexual pleasure. Wilhelm Stekel, whose two volumes on the topic appeared in 1926, asserted that "the most frequent of the sex-diseases of women is frigidity." He gave as a scientific conclusion that forty to fifty percent of women suffered from it.[38] Hamilton's study of marriage placed frigidity within a broader range of sexual problems for women characterized by inadequate orgasm. Almost half of the women in the study fell into the category. He concluded that, "Unless the sex act ends in a fully releasing, fully terminate climax in at least 20 percent of copulations there is likely to be trouble ahead." The marriage, of course, may suffer. The women themselves will likely experience restlessness and tension; of the forty-six women considered inadequate in orgasm, twenty had been diagnosed at some time as "seriously psychoneurotic."[39]

### Companionship and Role Confusion

Consumption and sexual pleasure were to support an affectionate companionship between husband and wife, "a partnership deal between individuals of equal personality," as one woman in the 1910s termed it. The increasing proportion of women who married between 1890 and 1920 accompanied the widespread acceptance of a "democratic" model of marriage in which husband and wife shared equally in the cares of the household. Just as more women found professional possibilities outside the home by the turn of the century, some suburban men became attracted to an ideal of "domestic masculinity" that valued time spent at home with wife and children rather than among male friends and colleagues. Periodical literature by the 1920s encouraged greater intimacy and expressiveness of feelings between the married partners along with appropriate emotional management. Married love would rise on a foundation of mutuality and companionship.[40] Eugenicist and marriage adviser Paul Popenoe stressed both comradeship and equality—marriages run on a "fifty-fifty basis" were happy in 87 percent of cases he surveyed. For men and women alike, the ideal of modern marriage offered friendship as well as affection, emotional expressiveness as well as physical pleasure.[41]

As with financial crisis and sexual failure, women often appeared in the popular media of the 1920s and 1930s as the principle reason that companionship failed. "I like to go to dances and parties," a young flapper wife wrote to Margaret Sanger, "and have innocent flirtations. I like pretty clothes and admiration. My husband cannot understand why at my age I am so frivolous." Novelist Elinor Glyn mourned "young men under thirty tied and bound to impossible young women" because they could not muster the will to "resist the passion in its first stages." A *Good Housekeeping* article pointed out that marriage gave women everything they want in life—a home and children. Men, on the other hand, lose their freedom in marriage and at home don't even have a closet, sometimes not even a chair, to call their own. No wonder they take so little interest in the home and the children.[42]

Advice literature frequently gave women the responsibility for making the ideal work or making it fit the reality of married life. Margaret Sanger believed that women had to "keep romance alive in spite of the influence of the prosaic demands of everyday life." Another advisor offered detailed instructions on just that matter, plus tips on sexual attractiveness and household finances. Columnist Anne Hirst believed that the man you marry may not be the man you thought you were marrying. If so, then "adapt yourself to this new being and make for him the kind of home he wants. If you do, he'll stay in it." Dorothy Dix went even further in suggesting alterations in the companionate ideal. She provided many cautions for married couples, suggesting that intimacy could become a problem. Men want to be "treated as good fellows" but they also "enjoy being bamboozled by women who turn out a nice artistic job." Spouses should be good to one another but they also have to observe limits. Otherwise they will encourage weakness and selfishness in the other. Dix considered jealousy a form of insanity, rooted in the delusion that "any man or woman . . . can supply another individual's whole need of human companionship."[43]

Most middle-class women began marriage, at least, with more faith in the companionate ideal than Dix had. Yet, whether they believed in bamboozling their husbands, or in bolstering their self-esteem, or in providing the perfect domestic situation for them, women found themselves responsible for the success of companionate marriages and yet dependent upon husbands who often lacked a clear recognition of and commitment to their own roles.[44] Women in widely disparate social settings found themselves distressed at behavior of their husbands' that they could not understand and seemingly could not control. Two weeks after her wedding Ione Robinson wrote that she had begun to feel "that I am nothing." Her husband, Joe, an ardent Communist, discussed politics with guests at dinner. "I find myself setting the table, cooking the dinner, and washing the dishes as though I were not present, as far as the others are concerned." Within a few weeks of marriage Isabelle McNelis Sickler spent her first night alone. Other such nights followed, and Isabelle's patience with her husband's absences shortened, especially after she became pregnant. Dorothy Thompson, still yearning for a romantic partnership, despaired of the vagaries of Sinclair Lewis's behavior. "I want to write you a love letter," she wrote, "but I can't. . . . It would be like writing to someone imaginary. Do you exist, and are you you, and what *is* you? I have known so many yous."[45]

### Fixing Modern Marriage

For women, modern marriage proved almost impossibly complicated. Although popular authors assumed that marriage provided women with their most cherished desires, early research into marriage found husbands more satisfied with marriage than wives. Experts advised some form of emotional management. "If your husband seems to be unreasonable," wrote one columnist, "put yourself in his place before you sass him back, and perhaps you'll find he has a perfect right to ask what he does." Or, perhaps couples needed to reduce their reliance on the volatility of romance. Psychologist Elton Mayo, like other "rational" critics of marriage, rejected romance: love was "an ailment of adolescence" and warned that the it "must be got over" before the real marriage can begin. "Persons become attached to dogs, cats, furniture and what not," wrote one physician. Marriage had less to do with love than with "admiration, respect, association, mutual interests, reciprocal assistance, attachment and becoming accustomed to each other."[46]

Both the defenders and the critics of marriage urged structural changes. Judge Ben Lindsey coined the term "companionate marriage" to refer to his ideal of a trial marriage that childless couples could easily end. This would help young people deal with the complexity of courtship and make marriage more likely to succeed. Lindsey's idea of trial marriage inspired attacks from conservatives but also attracted interest and often support from writers concerned about marriage. Behaviorist John Watson offered a similar idea in "progressive marriage."[47]

Although examples of actual trial marriages are difficult to find, the concept appealed to many women. Actress Ilka Chase approved of those couples who "believe in a tryout before the New York opening. They . . . consider a pig in a poke an unnecessary risk under any circumstances." Chase believed that couples who lived together before formal marriage acted out of "common sense," and the ideal of trial marriage appealed strongly to reason and to an objective view of marriage. Martha Lavell, who believed that psychology and eugenics held "the future of the world in their hands," believed that marriage should only exist for having children and only be available "to the physically and mentally fit. . . . Any other relation should be sanctioned *outside* of marriage."[48]

Lavell, however, wrote in the privacy of her diary and apparently never followed her own permissive formula. The new morality for middle-class women included trial marriage for only the most radical, and sometimes not even for them. Jessie Lloyd, a journalist and supporter of labor, liked the idea of allowing couples to try life together before marriage. "Give them a quiet year, I thought, to see if they'd make it, and then, if they did, celebrate with a big housewarming." A radical herself, and the daughter of radical (and divorced) parents, she had grown up hearing free love ideas discussed with approval. Yet she knew that neither of her parents would stand for a free love union for her. When she and radical journalist Harvey O'Conner began their life together, they lived together only until he could gain a divorce, then sailed to Baltimore where they could be married more quickly than in New York.[49]

Even though trial marriage still "flouted social standards" in the 1920s and 1930s, middle-class marriage continued to change in the direction urged by Lindsey and Watson. When she saw the movie *Companionate Marriage* in Glens Falls, New York, in 1929, fourteen-year-old Edythe Weiner wrote that it might "be all right for some people, but even if I am old-fashioned, I prefer the old kind and a quick divorce if you're unhappy." During the 1920s the growing divorce rate often appeared as proof of what V. F. Calverton called "the bankruptcy of marriage." In 1887, Calverton wrote, one marriage in 17.3 ended in divorce. In 1924 it was one in 6.9. As Calverton recognized, divorce did in practice what Lindsey proposed that trial marriage would do.[50]

No sweeping legislative changes made divorce readily available by 1920. Throughout the decade the state of New York granted divorce only in cases of witnessed adultery—the "delicto must be graphically flagrant," as Ilka Chase recalled. Men and women who no longer wished to be married had to find friends to commit perjury and then submit themselves to "public humiliation." Yet if the courtroom meant public humiliation, divorce itself carried less stigma for most members of the middle class by the 1920s. The change seems to have take place in a single generation. Pearl Buck's brother, eleven years older than she, separated from his wife but waited for years, until after his parents died, to divorce her. The sharpest jump in the divorce rate took place between 1910 and 1920, from 4.5 per 1,000 to 7.7 per 1,000.[51]

As suggested by the teen-aged comments of Edythe Weiner, the rising divorce rate represented changing expectations about the goals of marriage and also reflected the widespread acceptance of divorce as a solution for failed marriages. Divorce made modern marriage possible, giving women a sense that they could still find happiness and fulfilling lives if marriage did not give them the love and companionship they expected. Prior to her own marriage, Gladys Penrod considered Lindsey's ideal of trial marriage and both before and after her wedding contemplated the possibility of divorce.[52] Many of the women whose papers have revealed so much about the inner lives of middle-class women found divorce the only solution to difficult marriages. Several divorced more than once. Ione Robinson, as we have seen, married and divorced twice by age twenty-four. Dorothy Thompson married three times, Beth Twiggar and Marjorie Kinnan Rawlings each divorced once. Caroline Gordon divorced Allen Tate in 1946, then later remarried him and, years later, divorced him again.

Yet marriage remained a strong cultural value for women. It held the promise of full selfhood. Even if cultural attitudes treated divorce much more lightly, women who experienced it felt it as a personal failure and profound loss. Marjorie Kinnan Rawlings looked back on her marriage as "fourteen years of Hell." In the end, she had to break free "from the feeling of a vicious hand always at my throat, or of going down in complete physical and mental collapse." "Some hours I wish I were dead," Ione Robinson wrote as her second marriage collapsed. It had failed in spite of her efforts to make it work on any basis, "to adapt myself to him, to build my life around his."[53]

Even though social science idealizations and personal hopes rarely included divorce as part of the modern marriage, the high value placed on married sex, consumerism, and companionship almost guaranteed that many marriages would fall short. Women's psychological development may have played a role as well. Current theories on women's development, whether they rely on intrapsychic processes or cultural forces, view American women as flourishing within a dense network of relationships. By the 1920s, the marriage ideal had become thoroughly modern, eschewing women's networks in favor of a hierarchical model in which one friendship—between husband and wife—became paramount.[54] Without the supportive relationships of an earlier generation, modern women relied upon a companionate ideal for fulfillment of their most cherished desires. In practice, this meant relying on husbands who might not provide the income to meet their housekeeping needs or the partnership and companionship to meet their emotional needs. Some women would try in vain to make difficult marriages work. Others would succeed in spite of their problems, although generally by moving away from widely held cultural ideals. Two women offer contrasting insights into modern marriage.

### Living Marriage: Two Contrasting Experiences

Winifred Willis was born in 1902 in Brooklyn. Health problems interrupted her schooling, and after grade five she received little formal education. Instead, she read voraciously and committed herself to writing. She kept journals for years, but her surviving journals begin in 1923, the year she published her first short story. Along with literary success the year held emotional turmoil with the end of a longstanding romance with Bill Rawlins and the beginning of her courtship with Lorin "Tommy" Thompson. Within months Winifred Willis realized she was in love with Tommy.[55]

"We are soon to be married," she wrote a few weeks later. "I did not know love could be so perfect, and yet so quietly certain." For Winifred Willis, passionate attraction to Tommy and marriage carried the possibility of renewing and remaking her life. The prospect of such a powerful passion, and of the changes that it implied, frightened her as well as drew her toward it. "How terrible that he is all, *all*!" she wrote shortly

4.1 Winifred Willis in Maine in 1923. The picture was taken about the time her diary opens (earlier entries were lost or destroyed). Schlesinger Library, Radcliffe College.

before her marriage. "His warm love enfolds me, envelops me, stands between me & the cold loneliness of life." When they married on May 24, 1924, Willis recorded the event in words strikingly similar to Ione Robinson's: "This is the attainment of happiness and the beginning of life."[56]

The first months of her marriage stood for Winifred Willis as the fulfillment of love and life. "Married life is a headlong rush, interspersed with oases of rich, unbelievable peace." At times they had days on end of closeness and happiness that Winifred relished. At other times, however, she felt a distance or tension between them that she took as a sign of some shortcoming on her part. Two months after the wedding she wrote of her struggles "to conquer myself, my nerves, my habits, my selfishness, my irritable instincts of the recluse." She wanted, in fact, to develop an entirely new temperament, one better suited to the worldly success that Tommy looked for. As she wrote two days later, she lived to "fulfill Lorin's ideal of all he has ever wanted me to be."[57]

In the area of household management, the adjustments that Winifred Willis adopted proved remarkably similar to those made by Gloria Gregory, the fictional flapper wife. In spite of Tommy's well-to-do family and his job as a bond salesman, the young couple found themselves faced with financial stringency. When they sat down to go over finances after a few months of marriage, Winifred was shocked to realize that they spent twice what Tommy earned. Tommy, she recorded, knew this all along but wanted to make her realize it without simply insisting on his way. Like the flapper wife, Winifred began as a spendthrift but then quickly recognized the error of her spending habits and reformed. By seeking a frugal life that balanced the couple's desire for leisure and status with their financial means, Willis hoped to create the kind of cozy home that should have allowed affectionate companionship to thrive. In the months that followed they restrained their spending and changed their entertainment habits. She recorded with satisfaction: "Now we go to plays, dine out occasionally, have laundry & house-cleaning done regularly (not by me!!)&, without being unduly extravagant, do pretty much as we please." She believed that this allowed her to become "a gay & happy companion with nothing on my mind—& very little in it."[58] Winifred Willis understood the fable of the flapper wife and benefitted from its moral.

Financial concerns that seemed so readily resolved would return later, aggravating bigger problems for Winifred and Tommy. Winifred expected a loving partnership, and in moments of passionate affection for Tommy she readily accepted the need for personal change to make that possible. Her feelings varied widely, however, as their relationship swung between loving closeness and clashes over emotional hunger. "A regrettable incident out in Westchester, when I kicked his shins black & blue & flung my hat over a cliff, brought me awake to certain childish tendencies in myself which if not seen & conquered, would eventually end any marriage—even ours." Although she readily blamed herself, she also found herself frustrated by Tommy's reserve, "his neglect, his long silences, his curt brevity."[59]

For Winifred the companionate ideal meant a union of mutual and unwavering love. "Each bond that comes to strengthen my hold on Lorin and his on me, makes me happier. The perfect peace of love, the sense of belonging, the absolute willingness to belong forever—that is happiness." Yet, time and again, they seemed to lose their chance for happiness. She searched for explanations in gender differences—"men are more stolid." They cannot be lovers as well as husbands, and as husbands they "ask physical love & pleasant companionship." Between Tommy's approach to marriage and her womanly approach lies "a state of desire unlimited." The gap between their understandings came home to her as a wounding criticism from Tommy that she spent her whole day waiting for him to come home. "What he doesn't understand is that if I had every hour of every day packed with interests, I would still wait all day for the hour of his coming home. Does he want me to be independent of him? I can't be! He is all I have in the whole big lonely hellish world."[60] Her longing for passionate togetherness would continue to plague her, and the inability of her marriage to give it to her meant that she remained unsatisfied.

The love that Winifred felt for Tommy, the thrill that his presence could give her, seems to have remained without physical expression. During their passionate romance Tommy and Winifred spent many nights sleeping together, yet Winifred kept her virginity until marriage. When she finally surrendered to her husband, the result was "cold, sick, disappointment, the sense of failure, and of having failed him whom I loved." Although couples generally worked out sexual issues in the early months of marriage, the problems that Winifred experienced in her first, unsatisfactory intercourse continued to plague her and led to further problems in her relationship with Tommy. He could not give her the emotional warmth that she craved, and she seemed unable to give him the sexual satisfaction that he hoped for. Winifred placed the blame on the sexual morality that denied girls and young women "casual, sexual experiences" like those she believed men enjoyed. Another young woman described a friend whose problems sounded remarkably similar to Winifred's: "Said she was a virgin when she married and now wished she hadn't been."[61]

The sexual and emotional problems faced by Winifred and Tommy grew more destructive as their living situation became more difficult. The remaining years of their marriage showed that it was not a flapper mentality but images of a world of economic possibilities that created the major financial problems for Winifred and Tommy. The couple yearned to share more fully in the decade's prosperity. Tommy believed he deserved better than his $60 a week salary, and the couple invested a sizable gift from Tommy's father in oil and radio stocks. They dreamed of a home away from New York and a life of industrious comfort like the one Tommy's father and mother lived. The vagaries of the economy, however, would rob them of even the frugal pleasures they had earned. Their investment of the gift from Tommy's father turned into a bad speculation, and soon the couple had to move out of their own apartment and live with Winifred's mother. In the following year Tommy lost his job when his firm broke up. Even though Tommy found a new job, he became engrossed in his work and Winifred felt a distance growing between them. In any event, the job proved short-lived, and the couple moved from one difficult living situation to another, with Tommy's fortunes apparently heading steadily downward. In November of 1927 Willis wrote that they had returned to New York, "dead broke, no job as yet. My hands are full with child-care and housework."[62]

Financial hardships took a heavy toll on the couple. Unemployed much of the time, Tommy spent his days looking for work. Tommy became resentful of life with her mother and then sister and accused Winifred of being too dependent on him. Although Winifred felt the sting of poverty, her reaction to their situation turned far more on the changes in their relationship. "Only for him do I want money," she wrote, "so that I may always seem beautiful and well-dressed and attractive to him—so that he may never tire of me!" Like Gladys Penrod, she believed she could keep romance alive with the appropriate personal care and clothing. Yet as Winifred found herself torn between care for her child and for other members of her family, she also suffered from a growing distance between herself and Tommy. Her marriage ended in 1928, followed only a few months later by her own nervous collapse.[63]

For Winifred Willis, the promises of modern marriage proved false in almost every possible way. Although she could surrender herself to an all-consuming passion for her husband, the sexual satisfaction and companionate partnership at the heart of modern marriage failed to flourish. She found her own sexual response lacking, and she could find no way to resolve the distance between her emotional needs and her husband's emotional reserve. The financial difficulties they faced aggravated their other problems and made the marriage unworkable. Only years later, in another marriage, would Winifred Willis find the companionship and passionate affection she thought her first marriage would provide.

Dorothy Smith, born in Chicago in 1906, was not as well integrated into the youth culture of the day as some of the other women we have looked at. She recorded a dance during her teen years as highly unsatisfactory. The interesting boys, the ones who attracted her, did not seem to find her attractive. Instead, she yearned for companionship with other girls and looked forward to going to a boarding school in New England as an opportunity to find the kind of friendship she longed for. Even with female companions, however, Smith seemed to have experienced trepidation. On the one hand, she felt her desire was so strong that it would overwhelm her friend, and on the other she built up walls of reserve that friends found difficult to penetrate.[64]

Smith accustomed herself to men only slowly. An acquaintance with a married man during summer school gave her opportunity to discover new insights about men, but she remained largely aloof from men. After college, however, she went to Paris to study composition with Nadia Boulanger. She looked forward to the trip as a way of breaking free from the more repressive aspects of her Puritan upbringing. It seems to have worked. In Paris she met and became friendly with many men. In particular, she became acquainted with David Dushkin, a Russian Jew whose family had moved to America. The two began a friendship that would continue after they returned to the United States.[65]

As she and Dushkin grew closer, Dorothy Smith found herself unable to understand her own feelings. She experienced unspecified problems that led her to psychoanalysis. As her analysis progressed, she came more and more to see Dushkin as an object of love. As she worked though conflicting feelings toward her parents, Dorothy experienced a new free-

4.2 Dorothy Smith Dushkin, with daughter Lelah. Sophia Smith Collection, Smith College.

dom in her emotional life. "David suddenly appeared more desirable and I seemed to want to marry him." Like other young women we have seen, Dorothy experienced romance as ambivalent and yet, in the end, convincing: "This very warm tenderness I feel for him must resemble love pretty closely. Marriage with him seems desirable and too good to miss."[66]

As her marriage approached, Dorothy hoped for greater freedom of artistic expression, in part because she would no longer be teaching in a traditional school and in part because David was a musician who kept company with other artists: "I hope next year being with David & seeing more artist types I shall be freer & more eager to create. I belong to the creators not to schools." This speaks to her expectation that in marriage she would fulfill her identity. However, in contrast to other women for whom marriage itself seemed the fulfillment of a woman's identity, for Dorothy it was the particular lifestyle that she believed she and David would establish together that would allow her to be more fully herself. Dorothy feared the confinement of tradition and convention. "I have a horror of growing like moss on its walls as those about me." She believed that David's openness to new experiences would prevent her from becoming stagnant in marriage.[67]

As a newlywed Dorothy felt pleasure and satisfaction in David's affection and in her sense of liberation from both conventional attitudes and artistic inhibitions: "Being Dorothy Dushkin is a glorious pleasure and a satisfying one. It's strange that I feel more natural with that name than I did with my old one."[68] Like other newly married women, Dorothy Dushkin experienced the halo effect of marriage. Yet it persisted for her as she and David became working as well as loving partners.

Dorothy's marriage, begun with such tentativeness, would depart from the companionate ideal in many important ways. She loved her husband, but she never longed to lose herself in his personality, as Willis had, and in fact she maintained her emotional autonomy. In contrast to Willis, Dorothy worked with her husband in the school that they established. She could see herself as competent and productive, something other women could easily lose within modern marriage. However, Dorothy also longed for and nurtured relationships with other women, intense and even romantic relationships that provided her emotional satisfactions that she did not gain or even expect from David.

In her marriage, Dorothy retained a sense of individuality and personal space. When she struggled over her goal to become less narcissistic, she decided that she should submerge herself into something apart from herself. But she had trouble deciding what that would be: "Now in choosing the thing into which I should be submerged, I am not a missionary of any sort—I have no flaming cause. Also I have no love of persons sufficient to occupy me entirely—nor no religious ritual to absorb me—no one thing will do. I must I think resolve myself to being absorbed in whatever turns up."[69]

What turned up was her children, a music school, friends, and a warm but never all-consuming love for her husband. Dorothy drew confidence and satisfaction from a harmonious relationship with David, with whom she continued to share many interests, and an invigorating and smoothly functioning business. In the first years of their marriage, she and David started their own music school, giving lessons and concerts in their home. Dorothy took a relatively small role in the school in its early years as they struggled to launch it. "I keep on the sidelines and have several private piano pupils as well as teaching in the Montessori School twice a week singing & rhythm."[70]

As the school grew, and as the Dushkins continued their own musical creation, they worked closely together as musicians, teachers, and business owners. David initiated discussions with Dorothy over his school-related concerns. Dorothy took this companionship and teamwork as a given. After they built and moved into a new house (where they held their school) Dorothy more explicitly acknowledged the importance of her contributions as her husband's counsel and support. "My days are broken up with a great variety of tasks. I keep the books, send bills & pay them, oversee a lot of music arranging, order & examine new music, discuss everything with David, answer the phone, teach 7 pupils, play in orchestra & oversee the house management & the babies . . . remind David of a hundred things he must do & buy his clothing & see that it's kept clean, practice piano & singing."[71]

As the above passage suggests, child care remained Dorothy's responsibility, although her children never became her single purpose in life. As with other aspects of her marriage, raising children for Dorothy Dushkin came as part of a varied life full of many commitments. During her second pregnancy they engaged a full-time nurse who lived with them through the following year. They also had a live-in maid. When the nurse had her regular day off, Dorothy took care of the children. She found this exhausting: "Tuesdays, Lena's day out, are hardest for me— Children are nerve-wracking & exhausting even when they're good. . . .

It is particularly difficult in our household with so much going on that they mustn't interfere with."[72]

Although she deeply appreciated the satisfactions of her home and vocation, Dorothy also recognized that to be happy she needed an emotionally intimate friend. She didn't believe that such a friendship would threaten or interfere with her marriage; in fact she mentions David's preoccupation with work as the reason that he himself could not fulfill her need to talk freely to someone who would listen. "Why shouldn't I be able to speak clearly & unembarrassed to my friends?" she wrote in the early years of her marriage. Dorothy accepted without self-doubt her need for emotional intimacy. She didn't take for granted that her husband would meet this need, and she didn't experience her longing for attention and companionship exclusively as a longing for David's attention and companionship. She considered her husband an intimate friend but not an exclusive one. They sustained a companionable relationship but not one that fully matched the companionate marriage model of romantic love, shared fun, and emotional intimacy.[73]

The distance that Dorothy Dushkin's experience of married love maintained from the popular ideal of companionate marriage also suggests the role that sex played in her marriage. Although she wrote little about sex in her journal, she approached sex with the same realistic expectations and optimism that she approached her emotional life with David and with her friends. Their love-making, at first, proved unsuccessful. Unlike Winifred and Tommy, whose first attempts at love-making presaged an unsatisfying sex life for the couple, Dorothy and David found help and reason to expect satisfying passion. Their honeymoon trip was to Europe. On board ship, after they experienced "the exhausting pain & thwarted effort of unripe intercourse" Dorothy feared that she might be "misformed in some way, or a coward." Once in London, however, she and David visited the clinic of the well-known sex adviser, Dr. Marie Stopes. Someone at the clinic sent them to "a sympathetic & informed doctor" who advised them that "in some cases the vagina does not yield readily" and gave them advice about massaging and exercising the muscles. "Since then," she wrote, still on her honeymoon, "things have been easier although as yet I've had no enjoyment— I am confident that that will come in good time for now I know there's nothing misformed & rather better in the long run."[74] Sex contributed to the satisfaction that Dorothy Dushkin felt in her marriage, yet it does not seem to have played the glorious role that it often appeared to hold in modern marriage.

Even after several years of marriage, Dorothy could write, "Every year has been a happy one since our marriage, but I think this has been perhaps the most eventful so far."[75] Yet the happiness that Dorothy found had not come from matching her life to the ideal of modern marriage. In a perceptive passage in 1934 Dorothy examined her life by comparing it with the life of the Victorian spinster. "I often wonder if I wouldn't have become like 'so & so' if I hadn't married or had the full life I've had. The old-maid prudishness could have easily developed in me. Intolerances, nervous self-justification, rigidity of various kinds & emotional giddiness. I have great sympathy for girls left unmarried. I so easily might have been such." Dorothy knew that her upbringing had allowed her to achieve an interior and creative life, but it also made it difficult for her to embrace an active life. Marriage made it possible for her to make a place for herself in the world, have a family, and accept the pleasures the world had to offer. She continued, reflecting on her debt to marriage, "The very being loved person is noticeably more attractive. I find less & less need to justify myself before others. I think I am as well adjusted emotionally & mentally as I can be—granted certain tendencies to homo-sexuality." Dorothy accepted her homoerotic urges even if she put them into the therapeutic language she learned at Smith College and in psychoanalysis. In most respects she embraced her desire for other women and claimed it as part of a full emotional life.[76]

Whereas the marriages of Winifred Willis and Dorothy Smith Dushkin contrast rather sharply, the reasons for the differences are hard to discern. Both women wanted creative professional lives—Winifred as a writer, Dorothy as a musician—and both achieved a degree of success in their chosen fields. Both women were introspective and considered themselves somewhat somber. Neither seemed destined for a conventional marriage. In the end, however, it seems that Winifred Willis's attempt to claim a conventional life worked badly for her whereas Dorothy Smith's difficulties as a young woman in forming relationships with men proved valuable to her in the long run.

As we have seen, Winifred Willis embraced the romantic ideal of marriage as a fulfillment of life. Her parents had broken off their marriage years earlier, and both of them lived outside middle-class norms—her mother attracted young lovers, her father drank.[77] Perhaps this added to

Winifred's desire to find a solid, nonartistic man, someone from a well-established family who could give her a sane and normal life. Yet the marriage she learned to expect from her culture, with warm companionship and comfortable surroundings, failed her. Tommy was not prepared to return the emotional closeness that she expected and craved. Financial crisis dashed their hopes. With so little in their lives that matched the companionate ideal, they found marriage unworkable.

Dorothy Smith, on the other hand, had been much more tentative about romance. She wanted love and companionship, yet she never seemed convinced that an overpowering emotional experience would change her life. Instead, Dorothy made a life with the materials at hand. She and David shared their love of music and their music school. If her role as wife and mother tended to take more of her time than her professional pursuits, at least she could feel a connection to her artistic calling and to her husband through her teaching and composition. Perhaps David Dushkin was better able to give emotional warmth than Tommy Thompson. It is also important to note, however, that Dorothy seems to have had either lower or more realistic expectations about the warmth she could expect from her husband. As we have seen, she expected at least some of her emotional needs to be met through relations with women.

From this comparison, it seems that Winifred's marriage suffered from her reliance on both the romantic and the companionate ideal, from a lack of emotional satisfaction for her, and from a lack of encouragement for her creative work. In her second marriage, to John Speakes, Winifred found both warmth and encouragement for her work as a writer. She also found sexual pleasure in her later marriage. Perhaps her relationship with John was also more realistic. Certainly, her reflections on her marriage to Tommy years afterward seem to indicate that Winifred had gained new insights about her emotional life—that she had expected too much of Tommy.[78] Although the single example of Winifred Willis can only be suggestive, it does seem to support Judge Ben Lindsey's call for trial marriages. Divorce, with all its trauma, seems to have given women experiences to make better marriages and to modify the companionate ideal to the needs and realities of their own lives.

# 5

## *The Silver Cord*

"One of my favorite fancies is that during my college years I have been training for parenthood," Martha Lavell reflected during her senior year at the University of Minnesota. Although in some sense Lavell's fancy held true for many women who expected to marry during or shortly after their college years, she did not have husband hunting in mind when she wrote about parenthood. She referred, instead, to her training in psychology and sociology. Martha Lavell drew her ideals of marriage and family from her reading in the social sciences of the late 1920s and from the discussions on these subjects held in her classes and among her friends. "My idea of marriage is a union primarily for the purpose of having children," she wrote. Reflecting both a theoretical radicalism about sex and her faith in eugenics, she continued that "Any other relation should be sanctioned *outside* of marriage, but only the physically and mentally fit with definite wish for children should be allowed to marry."

Lavell's speculations gave a large measure of responsibility to society and even the state for the proper rearing of children. Prospective parents would receive "special training in the art of caring for, teaching, and bringing up children." She looked forward to an idyllic setting for her own family, "somewhere in the country, in a large house with *sleeping porches*, surrounded by acres of wild land." The family would be large: "half a dozen children of our own, plus half a dozen more belonging to other people, orphans perhaps." The children would study at home, where Lavell would encourage their curiosity. "Cultivate a taste for scientific research, an interest in man and this world he lives in, a love of beauty and an ideal of service to humanity, and you have created an individual who will find the world good and life worth living. Such a home, preparing such citizens for the world, is my vision of the good life." Martha Lavell obviously idealized motherhood, yet her vision includes few of the traditional activities of the mother, and her home seems more like a social welfare agency than a typical family. She wrote later that she recognized that many of her ideas "are wild and impractical, and perhaps impossible," although she still longed for a husband and children. Behind Lavell's ideal lies a growing reliance on expertise in decisions about child rearing in the 1920s, and a related distrust of the family, and especially of motherhood.[1]

In 1927 the term "silver cord" entered American speech as a reference to the tight and sometimes unbreakable connections that mothers had for their children. The pejorative reference came from the title of Sidney Howard's play in which Mrs. Phelps entertains her two adult sons and the wife of one son and the fiancé of the other. Dave, the older son, has brought his new wife home to meet his mother. He and Christina met and married while abroad and planned a short visit with Mrs. Phelps before continuing on to New York City where both planned to pursue their professions, his architecture, hers research biology. The younger son, Robert, has invited his fiancé, Hester, to spend the weekend. Within minutes of the play's opening, it is clear that Mrs. Phelps approves of neither young woman. Hester she despises for her flapper ways, Christina for her modern ambitions. Although she employs a range of manipulative tactics to break up both couples, she succeeds only in ending Robert's engagement to Hester. Her nearly successful attempts to destroy Dave's marriage are thwarted by the intelligent, articulate and psychologically savvy Christina, whose insight into Mrs. Phelps's shortcomings provides the play's pointed criticism of overly affectionate mothers. After a disastrous first evening, Christina desperately urges Dave to cut their visit short and leave, afraid that if they linger she will lose him to his mother. At the play's climax she confronts Mrs. Phelps: "You belong to a type that's very common in these days, Mrs. Phelps—a type of self-centered, self-pitying, son devouring tigress." She ignores the family's protests and continues, "You and your kind beat any cannibals I've ever heard of! And what makes you doubly deadly and dangerous is that people admire you and your kind. They actually admire you! You professional mothers!"

Christina's most pointed criticism of professional mothers is that they use their sons to fulfill their romantic desires. She vows that she will love her own baby within bounds: "unpossessively—above all, unromantically." And she shocks the family by describing how far out of bounds the love of professional mothers may go as she explains to Dave that his mother wanted to separate them "because she couldn't bear the thought of our loving one another as we do. . . . And that's because down, down in the depths of her, grown man that you are, she still wants to suckle you at her breast!" As the play closes Dave realizes that he must break completely with his mother to find happiness with his wife. As he leaves he admits that he and his brother had been trapped in their mother's home, and he walks out the door as Mrs. Phelps implores him, "For God's sake, Dave, don't go with her! Not with that awful woman, Dave! That wicked woman! For God's sake don't leave me for her, Dave!" He escapes strangulation by the silver cord and presumably finds fulfillment in companionate marriage with a modern woman. His brother is not so lucky, and as the curtain falls Robert, cradled in his mother's arms, is engulfed forever.[2]

Motherhood, and the problems inherent in the overabundant affection mothers carry for their children, had become a pressing issue even before the 1920s. In her diary, Clara Savage's first mention of her future husband, Howard Littledale, who worked with her at the *New York Evening Post*, records that he escorted her to a train. On the way he confided to her that he had begun writing plays. "One was on 'Motherhood' but he could tell me no more for fear of shocking me!!!" Savage, who lived with her mother in an apartment in New York at the time, probably would have understood the potential for conflict in the relationship. Her later writings, as we shall see, warned against the potential dangers of the "mother instinct."[3]

The problem that middle-class Americans discovered in motherhood in the early decades of the twentieth century went hand in hand with new views on how to raise children. Sidney Howard contrasted the pathological, prudish, infantilizing mother represented by Mrs. Phelps with

mothers who *want* their children to be men and women and take care of themselves; mothers who are people, too, and don't have to be afraid of loneliness after they've outlived their motherhood; mothers who can look on their children as people and enjoy them as people and not be forever holding on to them and pawing them and fussing about their health and singing them lullabies and tucking them up as though they were everlasting babies.[4]

Although Howard referred to these as normal mothers, they seemed rare enough in the cultural reflections on motherhood of the period. And even though the daughter-in-law's speech to Mrs. Phelps refers to mothering of adult children, the same problems of overly affectionate attention appeared as problems in the literature on the care of infants and young children.

In the year following the opening of the play, a popular guide to child care by psychologist and advertising executive John B. Watson (with the assistance of his wife Rosalie Rayner Watson) went even further in attacking the problem mother by questioning the value of individual homes for children. "There are undoubtedly more scientific ways of bringing up children," Watson asserted, "which will probably mean finer and happier children." But if he questioned whether a child should know its parents, it was mainly its acquaintance with the mother that presented the problem. Throughout their work, the Watsons refer to the child as "him," while the only parent to appear in the work (except for the father's daily "half hour") was the mother. The book warned women to "remember when you are tempted to pet your child that mother love is a dangerous instrument." Rather than the coddling and affection that would surely cause serious damage, the work urged women to leave children with nurses, or if this was impractical, leave them in the back-yard for most of the day. "Never hug and kiss them, never let them sit on your lap." By the 1920s, much of what the Watsons offered seemed like common sense. Their book went through several editions, and John Watson actively spread his views in popular magazine articles during the last half of the 1920s. Popular author Floyd Dell, who criticized Watson on many points, nevertheless found "many fine things in this book."[5]

Young mothers in the 1920s often shared their culture's suspicion of motherhood. The relations that women had with their own mothers shaped their assimilation of the cultural norms. Although many women recalled warm relations with their mothers, their recollections also often included powerful conflicts with parents, especially mothers. Middle-class women wanted to raise their children differently from the ways they had been raised, to provide modern versions of nurture, and they looked to the expertise available in books and periodicals to give them the wisdom that their own mothers lacked. Yet, as in the case of romance and marriage, the feelings that women bore toward their children often failed to fit the culture's prescriptions. Although they may have worried about the implications of their actions, women still paid close and loving attention to their children. If they assimilated the notion that they must shape independent young men and women at an early age, they nevertheless resisted advice that contradicted their inclinations toward affectionate nurture.

### Mother as Villain

Middle-class Americans in the nineteenth century seem never to have dreamed that a mother's love might become a source of ill. Although Victorian Americans believed all emotions required self-restraint, mother love appeared in the advice literature of the era as the purest emotion and the one most likely to bless all who experienced it. A mother's love could keep her son on the straight and narrow even though temptations surrounded him as he grew older and entered the world.[6] A late Victorian novella, *Laddie*, offers a fully developed ideal of mother love. It is the story of a young physician whose mother visits him after years of separation. When she arrives in his offices he initially feels shame at her shabby appearance. Realizing this, the old woman leaves. Her son repents almost immediately and begins a search for her through the city. Only eighteen months later does he find her, in a hospital taking her last breaths. The mother has forgotten the son's shame, and as he comes to her side again, she blesses him and his fiancé. A mother's love is indestructible, the story tells us, even when it is rejected by its most cherished object. And in the heart of the loved one, the mother's love will always win out over more worldly sentiments.[7]

The nineteenth-century vision of mother love survived into the early decades of the twentieth century. Winfield Scott Hall, a professor of medicine in the 1920s, still maintained that the young child will become impressed with the "sacredness of life and of motherhood, and will be held to the mother by a bond of confidence and love." Best-selling author Gene Stratton-Porter endorsed motherhood through a character who tells her neighbor that her "highest aspiration is to be a clean, thrifty housekeeper, a bountiful cook, a faithful wife, a sympathetic mother."[8]

We catch a glimpse of mother love in the diary of Edna Claire Ferris, whose first son was born in 1905 shortly after the death of her husband in a train accident. Although Ferris had to work to support herself, she nevertheless stayed close to home and spent time with her son every day. It was more than a year after William's birth before she left him alone for an entire day. In her diary Ferris referred to her son as "Lover" and "Lover Boy," and she recorded every new development in her young son's life. For instance, she recorded his birthdays and every gift that he received. Ferris noted the beginning of William's formal schooling in 1910. "Dear little boy, it makes mother feel bad to have him strike out for himself."[9]

Middle-class women who came of age in the generation following Ferris conceived of motherhood far differently than Ferris did. The new opportunities available to young women born after 1880 inspired writers around 1900 with visions of mother/daughter conflicts as daughters left their mothers (and motherhood) for college and career. There appears to have been relatively little conflict between the first generation of college and professional women and their mothers. By 1900, however, the peer culture of the high school had become widespread among middle-class youth, and the generation that grew up after 1900 experienced competing pulls from the peer culture and the home. Edna Ferris worried that her son, William, was "restless and wild to do all sorts of impossible things." On his sixteenth birthday she wondered if she had been "too proud of him" in the past and fretted that she could not reconcile herself to his smoking cigarettes. The conflict that many teen-agers of the 1910s experienced with their parents led them to accept the new characterization of motherhood as stifling, undermining initiative and self-reliance.[10]

Social scientists and popular writers of the 1920s conceived of motherhood, like sex, as a biological fact. But, although the sex drive seemed more and more like a valuable asset in human life, a broad range of writers agreed that there was "something dangerous about the maternal instinct." Watson, who had no room for instincts in his system of psychology, believed that the sexual stimulation that women received from nursing made the child "a kind of attenuated surrogate for the husband. 'Mother love' is basically a positive sex reaction which rarely becomes overt." The natural satisfaction that women found in caring for their children could turn into a dangerous habit, with mothers providing more care than necessary and so making their children more and more dependent on them.[11] "A wonderfully sweet feeling to have your children turning to you for wisdom and guidance and protection," reflected a housewife in 1930s Long Island. "Sweet for the mother but deadly for the children as they struggle to grow up and become individuals. The mother in *The Silver Cord* always haunts me—what martyred selfishness!"[12]

Journalist Samuel Schmalhausen believed that the typical mother treated her child as "a sort of wonderful scapegoat for her frustrated human nature." According to Schmalhausen, Freud's Oedipus complex missed the most important pathology of family life—it was the mother who had the primary responsibility for shaping, and misshaping, the child. "How can the child attain to self dependence," he asked, "when a fond (i.e., foolish, selfish, blind, hysterical, unimaginative, unfulfilled, infantile!) parent is always on the scene to prevent it from developing a self to be dependent upon?" In exploring the family problems that "fill our courts and hospitals," reform school superintendent Miriam Van Waters included "mothers whose desire is not to nourish life and feeling in children, but to absorb it." Child psychologist Winnifred Richmond warned parents against too many restrictions on their adolescent daughters, but when she turned to the problem of overindulgence and ruling the girl by appeals to her love and sympathy, she addressed only mothers. Another child psychologist, Ada Hart Arlitt, also pointed to the problem of mothers who "bribe the child to continue to love her 'best in the world.' "[13]

The women who raised children in the early decades of the century bore the brunt of the ideological repudiation of Victorian sexual morality. John Watson portrayed these women as harpies of sexual prudery, "who have got nothing out of sex—who implant the view that there is nothing in sex." Another writer believed that the mothers of the 1920s had lacked adequate sexual thrills in their youth "so that they must now try to even up the count by means of vicarious thrills." A study of the sex lives of college women found that a few girls remained inhibited in spite of the liberating effects of college life. The writers referred to one girl whose mother drew "the silver cord tightly around her neck" by scolding her daughter even for kissing the girl's fiancé. A physician, writing a guide to the new morality, spent much of his introduction lamenting the survival of narrow-mindedness that handicapped many young women in finding happiness. "To me one of the saddest things about the somewhat odd, old-maidish, cold, and reserved type of girl is that commonly she is brought up by a psychopathic, reserved, over-religious, or sexually anaesthetic mother." He went on to lament the "misery these mothers now hand on to their daughters through their evil and wrong-headed and vicious training!" Wilhelm Stekel, who had made frigidity one of the most widely discussed psychic disorders of the 1920s, claimed that frigid women *"are not fit to be mothers."* Repressing their own sexual impulses, they "also struggle against every sexual expression of their children."[14]

Because sexual pleasure had become by the 1920s a fundamental element of married love, blighting the free play of sexual desire harmed marriage. But the 1920s abounded in images of mothers interfering directly in the lives and marriages of adult children. *Good Housekeeping*'s Clara Savage Littledale wrote of mothers who gave their daughters little preparation for married life and then encouraged continued dependence on them even after marriage. "She may believe that mother-love is her guiding principle. But actually, deep in her love for her daughter, is an unsuspected element of selfishness. She wants to keep her daughter a baby, *her* baby." Dorothy Dix regretted mothers who taught daughters "by precept and example to evade every duty of wifehood and motherhood." The relation of mothers to their sons, as in the Howard play, could become even more infantilizing and deadly to the growth of independence and individuality. A man with a fixed ideal of a wife similar to his mother would almost never be happy with his flesh and blood bride. One marriage guide for women offered a whole chapter on dealing with husbands who were attached to their mothers. G. V. Hamilton's study of married men and women found that visits from the mother of a spouse inevitably created problems for the marriage. Hamilton suspected the source of this interference was in the unsatisfactory sex lives of the older women. He wished he could make mothers realize "how stupid and selfish it is to defer the psychological weaning of their offspring until it is automatically effected by death or extreme old age."[15]

The mother who undermined the independence of adult children became a stock figure in the fiction of the period. When one of the wealthy young men in an Elinor Glyn novel proposes to the heroine, Ava, she suggests his mother might interfere. "Why, my mother will just eat you up," the wealthy suitor replies. "We've never been parted—She and I—and she's always said that she'll welcome the girl I marry, if she really loves me, and wouldn't come between us—and you wouldn't, Ava, I'm sure. I think a man is no man unless his mother takes the first place." Glyn, of course, leaves us with the implication that any man who allows his mother to interfere with his adult life is much less than a man should be. For readers in the Freud-savvy 1920s, the oedipal subtext appeared obvious and unanswerable. One college woman who saw *The Silver*

*Cord* wondered how many in the audience understood the scene at the end of the play when the son who could not bear to leave his mother sank his head onto her breast and agreed to go away with her. Probably most of them did.[16]

The image of stifling mothers that became so common in the early decades of the century shaped the ways that young men and women understood their own experiences. In reflecting on her love affair with author John Marquand, the Boston-bred actress Helen Howe noted that she and John, and John's wife Christina, "were extremely close to our mothers. A psychiatrist would have diagnosed that 'the mother bond' was unusually close." Although Howe, writing decades after her relationship with Marquand had ended, identified no problems resulting from these close mother bonds, her ability to place the mother–child relationship into a therapeutic framework reveals a common conception of how these relationships worked. Jane Sherman, on tour in the Far East, wrote home regularly to her mother telling her "if you only knew how much I needed you." Yet she noted that another of the dancers, whose mother came along for part of the trip, went into hysterics over conflicts with the mother. Photographer Margaret Bourke-White recalled that she married Everett Chapman in 1923 "with the sun in my eyes," but she faced "a silver-cord entanglement" before their honeymoon ended. "You got him away from me," her new mother-in-law told her. "I congratulate you. I never want to see you again." The opposition of her husband's mother proved ruinous for the couple who divorced just two years later.[17]

Although we know at least a little about the mother–daughter relation of virtually every woman whose personal papers form the basis for this study, it is impossible to offer a general characterization of the relations between these modern, middle-class women and their mothers. Expressions of affection are quite common. Although persistent conflict rarely appears in these documents, sporadic conflicts often appear. Like any long-term relationship, mother–daughter relations in our group had layers of experiences and reactions that called out a wide range of emotions and judgments. With the widespread questioning of the Victorian ideal of mother love current by the 1920s, daughters tended to understand conflicts with their mothers as part of a larger conflict of generations—that modern children had to throw off the bondage of inhibition and repression and embrace honesty and liberation. Even when women wrote loving letters to their mothers or recalled them with affection, virtually all of them occasionally acted in ways that contradicted their expressions of affection.

Autobiographies, such as those by Sally Carrighar and Olive Ewing Clapper, contain interpretations of mother–daughter conflict from the perspective of decades. Few accounts contain sharper divisions between mother and child than Sally Carrighar's, whose mother had suffered so severely in delivery that she could hardly bear the presence of her daughter. Even at six, Sally knew that if she moved too close or accidentally touched her mother she would shudder, "as if she had been touched by a snake or lizard." If they brushed in the corridor, her mother would "involuntarily shiver." Sally drew much closer to her father. Her mother, meanwhile, "managed everything, money, the household, the committee work at her church, so well." Years later, the adult Sally discussed her mother with a psychiatrist who gave the opinion that her mother must have been psychotic.[18]

Olive Ewing Clapper also provided a retrospective diagnosis of her mother, although one based on her mother's ignorance of psychology and the need for sex education. The mother of four daughters, Jennie Ewing "pounded into our ears, as she combed our hair" her hopes for their professional careers. She nevertheless also insisted that her daughters master domestic skills, even keeping Olive out of high school for six months so she could learn to cook and sew. Jennie Ewing also treated each daughter differently, creating the basis for later "complexes" in her daughter's opinion. Taken as a whole, Olive's description of her mother was warmly affectionate. But when Olive began to date Ray Clapper in high school, Olive found herself in conflict with her parents who worried that she and Ray were becoming too intimate too quickly. When they finally decided to send Olive to Indiana to let the romance cool off, Ray and Olive eloped. Although this offers a very dramatic instance of the competing attractions of family and romance, it also shows that affectionate families could harbor strong conflicts over the values of the peer culture.[19]

Accounts produced during the youth and adulthood of women in the 1920s offer portraits of attraction and conflict more complex than the retrospective diagnoses. Beth Twiggar noted her mother's birthday in 1930 and added, "I love her tremendously. And I'm not half nice enough to her." As we have already seen, Twiggar embraced the youth culture and heterosexual experimentation of the 1920s with the self-conscious recognition that youth must cast off all of the old standards. In an argument a few years earlier, Twiggar had called her mother "an old fool." She recorded her regret and remorse in her diary but also her commitment to new values. "I want to do things and be things, she can't understand. I want to be modern and whicked [*sic*] and sophisticated, and she thinks it is either naturel [*sic*] preverseness [*sic*] or the fault of my upbringing."[20]

Although Beth Twiggar may have expressed the conflict over new standards more directly than most diarists, the conflicts appear in a variety of papers. Gladys Hasty, for instance, expressed only affection for her family in her published journal, but she also recognized how much lighter and happier her parents' lives seemed after her grandfather, who had lived with the family, died. Ann Marie Low felt closer to her father and brother than to her mother and sister. Although committed to her rural life, she also wanted recognition as someone capable of taking on the family property. Jane Sherman had warm relations with both of her parents, and her mother in particular seems to have supported her artistic ambitions. As she departed for the Orient, she wrote of feeling "cruel and selfish" at leaving her family. In the Far East, however, she found herself confronting experiences on her own that she had to deal with and then explain to her parents as best she could. Both college and her social work seemed to distance Martha Lavell from her mother. At times they could enjoy open discussions on controversial topics such as sex and religion, but tension seems to have replaced warmer feelings by Martha's early adult years. Elizabeth Yates's diary recounts her struggle to claim self and independence in spite of her parents' insistence on the demands of class and family.[21]

Some young women embraced the modern world. Some confronted it. Some, apparently, tried to ignore it. Anne Morrow expressed only affection and admiration for her mother. Although she expressed a desire to attend Vassar College instead of her mother's alma mater, Smith College, this attempt to strike out on her own disappears in later entries without comment. Yet Morrow became thoroughly modern, dating during her college years, bobbing her hair, wearing short skirts. Her marriage to Charles Lindbergh was supported by her family, yet Lindbergh's background was strikingly different from Morrow's. Lindbergh read little and had little patience for the literary interests of Anne Morrow and her mother. After the couple married, they lived a life quite different from the comfortable world of law and banking that the Morrows inhabited. During her first year of marriage Anne Morrow Lindbergh traveled almost constantly with her husband as he surveyed air travel routes, worked to advance aviation, and did business for his airline company.[22] Anne Morrow's rebellion, if it can be called that, was muted and probably unconscious.

Ione Robinson left home at age sixteen to study art at the Pennsylvania Academy of Art in Philadelphia. On the train from Los Angeles she discovered a letter from her mother "so full of love and kindness, it made me feel that to be like you is my real goal." She hoped to be successful "so that we may be together soon again." On her trip she frequently wrote loving letters to her mother and told her everything about her life in the East. Yet in spite of an unbroken stream of affectionate correspondence, Robinson would only return home two years later. She studied in New York, France, and Mexico. Her newly acquired politics became a source of irritation when she hung a hammer and sickle in her mother's apartment during her one brief visit home. Her engagement, to a Communist activist, also upset her relations with her mother. Robinson's first marriage ended in divorce and her living situation in New York continued on the tenuous edges of the art world in which she longed to succeed. When presented with a marriage proposal from a melancholy but wealthy young man, her mother urged her to accept the proposal. In spite of the distance and conflict of the relationship, Robinson felt that her connection to her mother was the primary one in her life and so felt completely at a loss when her mother died in an auto accident soon after Robinson's second marriage.[23]

If daughters could maintain affectionate feelings toward their mothers even in the midst of rebellion against some of what the mothers stood for, feeling affection for mothers-in-law could be difficult even in the best circumstances. Marjorie Kinnan wrote to her fiancé about the prospect of living with his parents: "it isn't that we want to be selfish, or ungrateful, or don't care for the older generation. But you know as well as I do what a mess that situation ALWAYS makes." Gladys Bell Penrod lived in her mother-in-law's house for the first two years of her marriage. She frequently recounted feelings of frustration and irritation toward Sarah Penrod. Several months after moving in with her she wrote, "Three times I resolved to keep my tho'ts on agreeable subjects and as often I soon found myself on the old theme mother-in-law."[24]

## Modern Child Rearing

Forming the new generation still rested in the hands of mothers, and this at a time when motherhood seemed fundamentally flawed. Experts and advice literature, claiming the authority of science, attempted to mend the care of children with schedules, psychology, and expanded schooling, taking some roles from the mother and attempting to take many decisions out of the hands of parents. Psychologists and reformers alike brought motherhood under new, and sometimes unfavorable, scrutiny. Feminists, striving to broaden the sphere of opportunity available to women, often denigrated motherhood in favor of a career or a life in reform work.[25] The new stress on efficiency in housekeeping, including regulating the baby's feeding time, probably received ready acceptance from middle-class women who could expect to have fewer, if any, servants as the twentieth century continued. Beginning in the mid-1890s, child advice literature began to urge regimentation, schedule, and time discipline upon American mothers. Writers such as Luther Holt, reacting to the success of American industry and technology (and encouraged by producers of infant milk formulas), advised mothers to set fixed times for feeding, sleeping, and elimination.[26] By the early twentieth century, industrial time and motion studies would enter into housekeeping literature as devices for making wives and mothers more efficient.[27]

The psychology of William James also shaped the new child-rearing literature. James had presented habit as the "enormous fly-wheel of society," keeping each of us at our duty in spite of pain or other disincentives. Habit would become a fundamental explanation of human character in the "functional" phase of American psychology and a basic term in the behaviorist psychology of John Watson that emerged by 1920. Mrs. Max West, whose pamphlet for the Children's Bureau became one of the best sellers of child-rearing advice literature in the early decades of the century, described education of the infant using the same metaphor that James did, of deepening pathways in the brain. Like James, the new child-rearing literature insisted that parents not deviate from scheduled reinforcement of the new habit. Holt repeatedly warned that "Bad habits [whether eating too frequently or masturbating] are readily acquired but difficult to break." A 1931 manual included chapters outlining how good habits could be formed for sleeping, eating, and eliminating. The habit of "willing obedience" would become the foundation on which the adult could train the child in initiative and independence.

If good character remained the goal of child-rearing advice, that character, like the Jamesian self, would be built upon the basis of good habits.[28]

The emotional life of children also received attention from the new child-rearing experts. Nervousness, recognized as an affliction that struck mainly the middle class, also threatened infants and children according to Holt and those who followed him. Like the rest-cure therapists of the late nineteenth century, Holt urged mothers to keep babies in quiet and peaceful surroundings. "Infants who are naturally nervous should be left much alone," he warned, "should see but few people, should be played with very little, and should never be quieted with soothing sirrups or the 'pacifier.' " Many of the writers who followed Holt reproduced his proscription of play. Although some authors, such as Mrs. Max West, stressed the effect on the child's nerves, West and others also worried that showering children with kisses and other attention would "make him more dependent upon these attentions." Ada Hart Arlitt, writing five years after Watson, praised the "present-day method of leaving the baby in the crib without any unnecessary handling." Child-rearing experts reflected the growing cultural suspicion of motherhood and embodied this in warnings against "over-coddling" and in the goal of early individuation for children.[29]

Modern, scientific child rearing looked forward to a new generation of fully independent adults. Although it is unlikely that many women subscribed to Watson's ideal that children by age three "should begin to dress and act like youthful men and women," authorities agreed that parents should give their children the examples and experiences that would help them grow in "body, intelligence, personality and social relationships." If parents, especially mothers, could work against their selfish desires to overprotect children, then they might give them the ability to stand on their own feet and make their own way in the world.[30]

Modern mothers wanted the best for their children, including modern child rearing. Mildred Brewster recalled that she always treated her son "as if he were my age and could understand everything." Olive Clapper at least claimed familiarity with child advice literature.[31] Anne Morrow Lindbergh read a number of current books on child rearing just after her first child, Charles Jr., was born. "They all seem frightfully hipped on the overfondled child and its hard life," she wrote. Lindbergh took the warnings of experts to heart, trying not to coddle the baby. "He is allowed to get bumps on his head and let cry when he has a temper." Perhaps taking a leaf from Watson's advice, she left Charles Jr. with family members when she and Charles Sr. scouted a route to the Orient via the Arctic. "Don't let Betty give him too many toys at once," she wrote in her instructions, "just one or two, and change them about and don't let people fuss over him or pay attention to his little falls or mistakes, will you?"[32]

Caroline Gordon also faced the necessity of leaving her baby, Nancy, with her mother during her husband's year in France as a Guggenheim fellow and later during her own Guggenheim fellowship year. For Gordon, however, separation from Nancy brought her to recognize her own confusion over the place of her daughter in her life. When her mother came to take the baby, grandmother and infant took to one another quickly. "I never saw anybody as mad over a child," Gordon wrote to a friend. "She could hardly put her down a moment. All our modern ideas of not handling them were swept aside." Later, however, when Gordon had returned from her year in France, she determined to take her daughter back. "Mother is—indescribable. She is medieval in spirit." Although she did not specify the problems she found, Caroline Gordon obviously believed that Nancy's upbringing suffered without the benefit of modern expertise. Gordon's own mother had given her up to her mother to raise, so Gordon had to face personal conflicts over her own childhood in her relations with her mother and daughter. When she first left Nancy with her mother, she wrote that it was "doing all sorts of things to me, though. I've felt paralyzed for weeks."[33]

Like Caroline Gordon, many women by the 1920s had to face conflicts between their own upbringing and their ideas for rearing their children. They sought to cast off old methods of raising their children, to shape characters that could uphold social conventions but also become independent individuals. Dorothy Dushkin wrote of her "horror of having [her] child's initiative & mentality oppressed into any apprehensive or watchful regard for the average social convention waiting to take his or her cue from what the group does."[34]

To the extent that middle-class women accepted the authority of the child-rearing literature, they faced a serious contradiction. Child-rearing literature in the early decades of the century used the authority of science to focus the attention of mothers on the details of their children's development and then insisted that mothers not pay so much attention to their children. Whether it was Anne Morrow Lindbergh worrying that Charles Jr. should take his bumps, or Gladys Bell Penrod wondering how she could empathize with her children, women paid attention to the psychological component of their children's lives and added it to their list of concerns and, in doing so, violated the child-rearing tenets of the 1920s. "Your children do not appreciate your over-anxiety," wrote one expert. "They resent it." Anxiety or even concern could become a kind of mental fondling, leading to the interfering adult mother with her silver cord strangling at the independence of her young.[35]

While women found contradictions within the most authoritative child-rearing literature they also had to sort through messages within popular culture that contradicted the trend toward devaluing motherhood and reducing the emotional warmth of mothering. Americans often held to the values of the previous century while admitting some change in the circumstances or role of those values. For instance, Gloria Gregory's mother-in-law in *The Flapper Wife* might have been the sister of the infantilizing mother in *The Silver Cord*. Mrs. Gregory freely expresses her opinion and even appears on the scene at inopportune moments for Gloria, making it impossible for the flapper's free ways to continue. When Dick becomes ill and must go away for a rest, his mother goes with him. Yet Mrs. Gregory emerges from the work as a steadfast and righteous (if not quite sympathetic) figure, urging on Gloria the necessity of frugality and skill as a homemaker. As the book ends, Gloria expresses her enthusiasm for the companionate marriage she and Dick will have and also for the prospect of motherhood.[36]

There were, of course, groups within American society actively resisting the cultural trends of the 1920s. After 1915, a re-created Ku Klux Klan offered a vision of American women transcendent in their roles of wife and mother. At least one of the women in this study was attracted to the Klan's idealism. Gladys Bell, several months before her marriage, found a temporary refuge in Klan rhetoric from her feelings of ambivalence about the impending change in her life. "I believe it is woman's duty to use the God given impulse of Motherhood," she wrote. Only the exercise of the "sacred duty of child bearing and conscientious child training" could reverse the "swiftly deteriorating racial purity" of the nation. The Klan rhetoric called women back to an older notion of motherhood that held strong appeal for many women.[37]

If Beatrice Burton's book, like the Klan, called American women back to an older system of values, some trends within child rearing literature even in the 1920s, and more prominently in the 1930s, urged mothers and fathers alike to create a warm family environment.[38] In her popular novel *The Homemaker*, author and advice columnist Dorothy Canfield

Fisher created the character of overprotective Evangeline Knapp whose entire life energy she poured into housekeeping. A model of the new efficient housekeeper, Mrs. Knapp hated her life and work and resented her children and husband. When circumstances forced her husband into convalescence Mrs. Knapp took work as a department store sales clerk and soon found her purpose in life. As the months passed both Knapps realized their inner desires and needs. As the homemaker, Lester Knapp respected the humanity and individuality of his children and provided the nurturing that his overworked wife never could.[39]

Fisher believed that the fundamental insight of the "modern books and the scientists who wrote them" was to put oneself in the child's place, to understand the needs expressed by the child's actions, and to give some healthy encouragement for the development of those needs. In her novel Fisher shows the warmth and affection that flow between the understanding father and the three children he nurtured. Yet Fisher retained a suspicion of motherhood and of emotional intensity. When Lester Knapp's youngest son first went to him with a heartfelt request that Lester gladly granted, the boy was overcome with gratitude that Lester realized emerged from "a fathomless blackness of uncertainty." Lester spoke almost roughly to the boy to make him understand that the decision belonged to him as a right and to eliminate the emotional turmoil of the moment. "What a ghastly thing to have sensitive, helpless human beings absolutely in the power of other human beings!" Lester reflected, deciding that it must lead to sadism. "That's what it is to be a parent," he concluded. By substituting mother for parent in his insight we can see that Fisher retained the cultural concern about the role of mothers. This concern was not new to her; she had articulated it as early as 1916, pointing out in a work on "self-reliance" that the young child "is straining every nerve to learn how to 'do for himself' and his mother is straining every nerve to prevent him." Over a decade later Fisher continued to urge caution and common sense on parents, so that they might avoid the extremes of "steam-roller discipline" on the one hand, and hysterical indulgence on the other.[40]

Dorothy Blake, a Depression-era Long Island housewife, summed up the modern mother's dilemma when she wrote, "The Victorian mother knew she knew best—we only hope so." As someone who had grown up in the decades when modern child rearing had become widely accepted, Blake fully recognized the dangers of the silver cord and the goal of raising children for independence. "I wonder if these mothers, who say so devotedly, 'I simply lived for my children,' ever stop to think that, in the back of their minds, is the unspoken thought, 'My children will live for me.' " Blake reflected with satisfaction on her children's development as they grew up and out of rompers and kiddie cars and went beyond "total dependence on Jim and me to the desire to make their own decisions and mistakes." Blake believed that parents should provide the best physical care for children and good examples, but beyond that parents should allow children the freedom to adjust to their environment and to learn from their own mistakes.

By the 1930s, psychology had become a not-always-welcome tool for bringing up the kids. Blake frequently mentions I.Q. exams and child psychology. The mother's growing sophistication made her much more aware of nuances in the children's development. Although her husband told her that too much analysis " 'isn't good for anybody,' " Blake still wondered. On the one hand, she knew enough about Watson's ideas to recognize that too much closeness to a child could make the child "emotionally dependent on the parent," but Blake rejected this and tucked her children into bed anyway. On the other hand, she agreed to let her son go on an outing that she believed too far away because she wanted to give him an experience of independence. When Artie didn't return with the other boys, she became frightened for him, and all her good intentions dissolved into tears when Artie finally returned with a police officer. She also met the challenge of the new child-rearing trends that urged on parents methods of persuasion rather than authority. Blake told a speaker at a P.T.A. meeting that she thought cajoling children did not prepare them "for a life which requires that you do what you have to do and be pleasant about it." Blake lived through a transition in the common sense of child rearing. She had grown up with modern methods and knew them well even if she had doubts about some of their tenets. But she also accepted the underlying values of modern child rearing and questioned the emerging standards of the 1930s.[41]

Modern child rearing, then, as represented by Holt and Watson, grew up in competition with a Victorian notion of mother love and superseded it only briefly; by the 1930s an ideal of a much warmer family life became prominent. Even so, modern child rearing had a strong influence on the child-rearing beliefs and practices of the 1920s and 1930s. Raising independent children—that is, children who would cast off reliance on mothers—continued as a widely held goal. At the same time though, ambivalence about motherhood seems to have had no impact on women's eagerness to become mothers. The shape that motherhood assumed for any individual woman was determined by a mixture of child-rearing theory and assumptions, their own affectionate responses to their children's lives, and the practical limitations on the time and resources available to women.

### Embracing Motherhood

Whatever their feelings toward their own mothers, middle-class women in the 1920s held few reservations about becoming mothers themselves. Winifred Willis looked forward to having a child early in her marriage to Tommy. "I want one so much," she wrote, "that I am not going to do anything at all to prevent, poor as we are." Even though having children may sometimes have brought women into collision with financial problems, and face to face with other changes in their lives, middle-class women generally looked forward to starting families. Dorothy Smith Dushkin wrote that she was "overjoyed because of the event, and filled with wonderings as to how '*this*' will be *when*.'" Middle-class women in America had taken the lead in limiting their fertility. By the 1920s the average woman bore only about two children. The smaller number of children allowed parents to provide more material resources to each child and, in spite of the warnings of child-rearing literature, to give more attention to the development of each child.[42]

Although women, on the whole, looked forward to motherhood, they frequently expressed concerns about delivery. Edna Claire Ferris, from an earlier generation, made no mention of her second pregnancy in her diary until April 5, 1913, when she wrote, "I think I am going to be sick." Her son was born April 9. She wrote, simply, "It was a hard birth." Modern medicine, which had taken the pain away from many areas of life and reduced the danger of many medical procedures, may have heightened the dread of pain. Illness accompanied Lella Secor's pregnancy in 1918, for which her doctor gave her morphine. Isabelle McNelis Sickler expected both medicine and beer to help her through the sickness of the early months of her first pregnancy.[43]

The prospect of motherhood also brought women face to face with mortality. Anne Morrow Lindbergh felt an "overpowering sense of time, and people changing and going and other people taking their place." Fear for the health of the newborn and for the life of the mother appears occasionally in the personal papers of women. Dorothy Thompson, although delighted to have a child, worried that her advanced age might make for complications in the delivery. Thompson's delivery went very smoothly, although her concern over the dangers of delivery were appropriate to the obstetrics of the period. Caroline Gordon, in the hospital for an appendectomy, heard the "gay voices of young people" arriving for the birth of a child. Just as the Caesarian delivery ended, however, the mother died.[44]

Winifred Willis seems to have had little concern about her life, although she feared that she might lose control of herself in delivery, "calm & natural one moment, & a screaming, selfless thing the next. . . . Childbirth has no terror for me, save only that I might scream." When she had her delivery, however, the doctor used analgesic for the first stages of labor. "Of course, I had ether for the grande finale." Like a growing number of urban women, Willis had chosen to sidestep the pain of delivery through the use of scopolamine. Dorothy Smith Dushkin also remembered "no great pain only a series of curious, awesome & exciting sensations. Dr. Kelly gave me gas immediately for every pain as it came on."[45]

For middle-class women in the 1920s and 1930s who wished to continue their careers, children brought special difficulties. Although Dorothy Canfield Fisher might raise the issue of which spouse was better suited to the role of keeping house and nurturing children, even her pathbreaking work left a division of labor between work at home and work outside the home. College women like Martha Lavell and her friends might debate the issue of who should stay home, but most Americans took for granted that married mothers would keep house. Wealthy women, like Jessie Lloyd's mother, who could afford servants, could afford a career. Less prosperous families had to struggle to make two careers a possibility. Lella Secor, in the months following her first child's birth, searched in vain for reliable servants at the modest wages she and her husband could afford to pay. Caroline Gordon complained repeatedly of having too little time for her writing. Anticipating leaving her daughter behind a second time as she and her husband traveled to France, Gordon wrote, "God, I'd love to get out of the cares of a menage for a year!" Although Dorothy Thompson and Sinclair Lewis wanted the best for their son, Michael, Lewis had little to do with the boy. Thompson, still active as a journalist, had to hire servants for most housekeeping and made special efforts to hire servants with children to become Michael's playmates.[46]

Balancing the demands of household and career became especially difficult in the face of the presumption that married women should not work. Clara Savage, press secretary for the National American Women's Suffrage Association and then *Good Housekeeping* correspondent during World War I, married Pulitzer Prize-winning journalist Harold Littledale in 1920. After marriage Clara Savage Littledale ended her full-time career for several years while she raised their daughter and wrote freelance pieces for *Good Housekeeping* and other periodicals. In 1927, however, she became editor of the new *Parents* magazine and an influential guide to modern child rearing. About 1930 she apparently wrote a third-person sketch about herself entitled "A Mother Who Guides the Rearing of 500,000 Children." The typescript originals of the piece shows the efforts that Littledale made to meet any questions that might arise around her status as working mother. In version one she tells the putative interviewer, " 'I often think that the happiest women in the world may be those who love to do nothing but keep house and take care of children—and have curly hair! But, of course, it all depends on what you're used to.' " The draft ends with the assurance that her "husband and children show no bad effects from the fact that Mrs. Littledale has a job." The second version of the article goes even further in embracing (although subtly altering) the culture's preference for nonworking mothers. Instead of the quote ending with "curly hair," that sentence is crossed out and replaced by a handwritten insertion: "Homemaking itself is the most important job and unless a woman is specially trained and qualified for other work or unless economic necessity makes it imperative for her to have a paid position she will probably find her greatest usefulness and happiness as a homemaker—especially while her children are growing up." Special circumstances, including a clear talent for a profession, might alter a woman's natural vocation. Only so far did the editor of *Parents* encourage mothers to work.

As editor of *Parents* magazine, Clara Savage Littledale would help modern mothers understand the trends within child raising as these came to prominence. As we have seen above, Littledale warned against the dangers of the silver cord in her *Good Housekeeping* articles during the early 1920s. Even before this, in her days as a single woman professional, she had reflected on the demands of raising children. She did not embrace a particular approach in her journal in 1916; rather, she recognized the potential value of older conventions for children but added, "I couldn't teach my children arbitrary standards of right and wrong. Because it is too external." Instead, she hoped to give them understanding and emotional responses that would help them "to love other people, to dread to hurt anyone, to be always generous." Like Dorothy Canfield Fisher, Clara Savage Littledale believed that parents could help children develop social skills and emotional strategies for successful living.[47]

Perhaps more important than the specific goals of child raising in Littledale's reflection is her attitude that "old ideas" and "conventions" had only limited value. Modern women wanted modern approaches to raising their children. They believed that they lived in an era that had more to offer children and they wanted to free themselves and their children from the limitations of older values. Dorothy Smith Dushkin, who resented the oppressiveness of her own "Puritan" upbringing, felt "horror" at the prospect that her children's "initiative & mentality" might be suppressed into "watchful regard for the average social convention." In her career as a teacher she hoped to bring to her students feelings first of confidence and then of independence. Martha Lavell believed that children should have so much contact with other children that they would have no hesitation about their relations with other children and that they would also learn about sex without worries and misunderstandings. Like Martha Lavell, modern women wanted to raise children who would understand "the whole unvarnished truth," who would live without the repressive attitudes of earlier generations and so lead healthier lives. They also believed that the advances of human knowledge would make child rearing more scientific and give children better opportunities in life. Gladys Bell Penrod, for instance, wanted to include in her prenatal care "the theory of mental influence" to help the child's development.[48]

Yet although women took up modern child-rearing ideas with a ready belief in Watson's call for *better brought up babies,* they seem to have rejected, virtually unanimously, one of the central tenets of Watson's approach. Watson recommended that mothers limit emotional involvement with children so as to forestall repeated and damaging "love reactions." Watson seems to have placed his theory at odds with fundamental forces in women's lives. Mothers found children a source of unlimited emotional experience. "They can give you such thrills of pride, such hopeless discouragement, such terror and worry, such relief and happiness," wrote Dorothy Blake. Winifred Willis could hardly contain the joy she felt over her first child. She could not imagine a complete and fulfilling life without children. "My child," she wrote, "melts my being to a pure & exquisite emotion of tenderness." Three weeks later she wrote that her baby "enraptures me, ravishes me." Dorothy Thompson, separated from her son due to the demands of career and problems in her marriage, wrote that she ached "with loneliness and loss. He is dearer to me than my life." Anne Morrow Lindbergh tried earnestly to follow advice that warned against coddling and overmothering that she found in Watson's book and other sources. Yet when her husband's business or other demands kept her away from the baby, she yearned for more time with her child and regretted when she arrived home too late to spend time with Charles Jr.[49]

Child-rearing theories seem to have fallen by the wayside in the face of the minute-to-minute demands of motherhood. Dorothy Blake, as we have seen, held to a few important ideas and seemed to have a ready evaluation of child-rearing advice that came her way. Still, she found the reality of child rearing a constant challenge. Mothers, especially those of younger children, found little time to reflect on the theory of child care and many had to give up keeping regular diaries altogether. Gladys Bell Penrod wrote after one month of motherhood, "Nearly half of June gone and I never wrote a line. I do not know whether the advent of a baby is occupying my time and interest to the extent of causing this neglect, or whether I am merely lazy about it." As the months passed her situation changed little: "For reasons 'wise' or 'otherwise' I am neglecting my journal," she wrote when her baby was four months old. "Weir seems to monopolize every spare moment and weariness gets the better of me."[50]

"My Son is a bad little Bolshevik," Lella Secor wrote in a letter, noting that he cried whenever she turned away from him. "I have picked him up a dozen times this afternoon, only to have his tears turn like magic to smiles. . . . He has slept only a half hour since lunch. . . . I continue to have a strenuous time." Dorothy Smith Dushkin had a nurse helping with the children so that she, in turn, could work with her husband in their music school. When the nurse went away on her day off, or on vacation, all the responsibility fell to Dushkin. "Children are nerve-wracking & exhausting even when they're good." She seems to have worked toward her goal of giving the children an upbringing that would allow them to grow into independent and self-reliant adults, yet she found the work impossible without help. "There is so much physical energy & resourcefulness required in inventing pleasant occupations, avoiding quarrels & arguments & just providing adequate supervision."

Even so, she wanted to recognize their integrity and individuality. "I have no plans or ideas for them. They will show me what they need as they develop."[51]

Caroline Gordon's letters reveal the ambiguity of modern nurture. Like Dushkin, Gordon wanted her daughter Nancy to achieve independence, for instance by choosing her own clothes for school. Yet Nancy selected clothes so that her classmates would approve. Gordon also followed the precept of modern mothering that urged mothers to leave children with nurses and forego constant anxiety. When she could, Gordon left Nancy in the care of a maid so she could continue her writing. The maid told the girl that she might write a book too when she grew up. " 'Don't mention no books to me,' Nancy said, 'Mama has nearly drove me crazy, locking herself up every morning.' "[52]

### Motherhood's Demands on Self: Two Illustrations

A close examination of the child-rearing experiences of two women can suggest the range of emotional experiences that middle-class women discovered as mothers. Gladys Bell Penrod and Miriam Van Waters raised children during the early 1930s, and both struggled with the goals of instilling discipline and fostering independent personalities. Both women, whether they attempted to hold to the current of child-rearing literature or to ignore it, found their children endless sources of emotional intensity. Yet the differences between the concerns expressed by the two women illustrate that different individuals bring unique meanings to common cultural materials.

As we saw in an earlier chapter, Gladys Bell Penrod experienced romantic love and the prospect of marriage as a crisis of the self. Motherhood rarely appeared in her journal as a motive for marriage, and when it did appear she treated motherhood as a "great Heritage" or mission of women rather than as a desire for children. She and Marlin Penrod planned to practice some form of contraception, although they seem to have had only limited knowledge about birth control. In fact, all of her pregnancies were unplanned and seemed at least superficially unwanted. Less than six months after their marriage, Gladys Penrod learned that she was pregnant. She responded to the news with a mixture of concern for the future and happiness at the prospect of a child. Unlike her experience with marriage, however, Gladys reconciled herself to motherhood relatively quickly, in the space of one journal entry. "Of course, I re-

5.1 The Penrod family: Gladys and Marlin (Red) are standing. Seated are DeLane, Sarah (Red's mother), and Weir. Courtesy of Mr. and Mrs. DeLane Penrod.

belled at first, cried a little and fretted a lot," she wrote in the same entry where she first recorded her pregnancy. She went on: "but I think I am over that now, for a while at least. I'd rather have known more about it, given a better heritage etc. but for once I didn't have my way. . . . I want to live now for my baby."[53]

Gladys could take up the role and identity of motherhood with little hesitation in spite of her ambivalent feelings toward her own mother. She saw her mother as having lived for her children. On the one hand, Gladys wrote repeatedly of her feelings of tenderness and regard for her mother. For instance, in a letter to her mother she told her, "I don't have any friends that I'm sure of except *you* and my husband." On the other hand, Gladys seemed to struggle in her own mind over her mother's approach to raising her. Her mother left her "to sink or swim or stand on my own feet. . . . She didn't nag, or pry, or give advice or blame or expect gratitude or whine or—anything. She was just Mother, one of the best psychologists the world has had for she just was naturally right in her training." Gladys could affirm her mother's care of her in terms that make perfect sense in the context of modern child rearing. She went on to express an interesting caveat. "I know there were a few things left out of my life—as love & kisses and confidences, but perhaps I'm a better person today." Gladys resolved the ambivalence she felt toward her mother by ignoring the unappealing aspect of her relation to her mother and also by affirming a generalized ideal of motherhood.[54]

Although Gladys unhesitatingly affirmed the ideal of motherhood, she looked forward to childbirth with some apprehension. Ill during the early months of the pregnancy, she prayed for strength to "fight the poisons of my body and conquer." She also feared that childbirth might bring unbearable pain and perhaps even be fatal. "I don't want to die," she wrote in her first entry about the pregnancy. She could deal with some of this anxiety by assimilating it to the larger experience of motherhood—" 'Down thru' the valley of the shadow,' is the sacrifice a life makes for a life." Even in the hours just before giving birth Gladys found time to reflect on her "vague suspense and dread [of] the ordeal. . . . Tho' I love my freedom, I cannot have it always and since I am to be one of the 'Mother's of Men,' I may just as well begin the significant task, now as later."

Pregnancy also affected her relationship with her husband. "My lover husband seems more tender and loving than before," she wrote just after discovering that she was pregnant. "He simply doesn't know how to love me enough to satisfy himself for a few hours he's absent. He looks at me as one who worships—he is simply powerless to resist any look or touch of mine." The prospect of fatherhood made Marlin Penrod more attentive, more loving, and more pliable—more like the man Gladys always wanted him to be. At least during her first pregnancy, Red took on fatherhood with even less ambivalence than Gladys took on motherhood.[55]

Over the years, Gladys's ideas about raising her children became a complicated mix of pragmatic responses to situations, ideas gleaned from contemporary literature, and a continued belief in positive thinking and emotional management. "If I were wealthy," she wrote in 1929, "I'd buy all the books that were or are published on 'Child Training' and 'psychology of Childhood' and 'Mental Hygiene.'" In a 1930 notebook she listed eleven books on these topics, including works by Dorothy Canfield Fisher, Ada Hart Arlitt, and Michael V. O'Shea. The relative importance of heredity and environment, one of the great questions of social science during the 1920s, also struck Gladys as a crucial issue for her children. Although she believed that their father would give them "honor and upstanding manhood" as their birthright, she came down on the side of environment as having the most weight.[56] "I hope the Lord will spare me to an age where I shall have had opportunity to do all in my power to make environment count most in my sons' lives." She referred to a Dr. Crane as her authority when she reflected that "the mother teaches from love" so that she should "stand first in example and in influence." Children who imitated mothers with good character would themselves become more refined as they grew up. "Therefore what a responsibility we have. Beautiful for children's sakes. Learned and patient for their benefit."[57]

In apparent agreement with the reading she had done, Gladys believed that emotional responses to the actions of children must be measured and appropriate. Arlitt and other writers warned that parents should spare children undue stimulation, irritability, and other emotional turmoil. Gladys, who in addition to having read Arlitt also read some of the current literature on the nervous problems of children, took these warnings seriously. In her one concession to the widespread emphasis on regularity and schedule, she wondered if she could spare the infant Weir from colic if she stopped feeding him "every time he squirms." Gladys also readily accepted the connection made in advice literature between her moods and those of her child—"when I'm irritable, he is, when I'm angry, he is angry." She adopted a series of approaches meant to limit her negative influence, such as keeping her voice low, saying very little, and adopting consistent approaches to bad behavior. Just as Arlitt urged "willing obedience," other writers of the period believed that parents could gain the cooperation of children through creative and consistent approaches. Gladys seems to have taken for granted that her son's resistance to cooperation turned on her own shortcomings. "Poor little chap," she wrote, "he responds so well to patience and rebels so well to impatience that it seems that I should try a little harder to conquer my temper and remember that I'm only a 'big human' trying to domineer a little human by my size rather than by strategic leadership." Gladys persistently held up a notion of affection that differed from the one current with Watson, Arlitt, and other influential advice writers of the day. Gladys expressed little ambivalence over her affection for her children and apparently disregarded advice that ran contrary to her vision of motherly love.[58]

While Gladys drew freely, if selectively, from the child-rearing literature available to her, she persistently applied her long-held beliefs about emotional management and positive thinking to her children's behavior. She hoped her own moods would serve as a model to her sons, and she believed that a "psychological connection" existed between her mind and her children. During pregnancy, for instance, Gladys had attempted to influence the developing child through her own moods and behaviors. Because of the importance she gave to her role as model, guide, and teacher to her children, her child-rearing theory demanded that she possess consistent and virtually unattainable character traits, including "strength, courage, and patience" and bountiful affection. When these failed her, Gladys punished herself with her own sense of failure. A few months after her second son's birth she wrote, "I don't believe I've gained in grace during the week. I was terribly mean yesterday and I don't think much of my ability to 'train up a child in the way he should go.' I think I'm a failure."[59]

Just as Gladys seemingly ignored the advice literature's guidance on tenderness and affection, she also missed the encouragement that Arlitt and Dorothy Canfield Fisher offered mothers. Both advised that mothers should not become overly self-conscious. They should recognize that both too much discipline or too much indulgence work against the child's best interests. And mothers should free themselves from self-condemnation for the occasional mistake. Gladys could not forgive herself in this way. She embraced standards of conduct that demanded that she always think positively and take the most healthy-minded attitude toward her sons' behaviors. When she inevitably failed to do this, she saw herself as a failure and suffered bitter self-recriminations.[60]

While Gladys Penrod frequently found fault with herself as a mother, motherhood remained the role that gave her the greatest satisfaction. She addressed her occasional sense of inadequacy by looking for a source of emotional uplift. She reflected in one diary entry that her life was much better than the lives of most people. Gladys often employed this version of looking on the bright side; that is, by noting how bad things were for others, one's own lot may appear suddenly more desirable. Not only did she have a hardworking and sober husband instead of "a drunken or 'no-good' lout," she also saw the many people hurt by the Depression that had taken hold of the country. There were also clear satisfactions to motherhood. Her husband appreciated her hard work with the children. And she also had frequent experiences of overpowering affection for her children. Although she chided herself for "grouching" about the constant demands of child care, she also recalled how precious her son had seemed to her when he was sick and seemed in danger. She brought her reflection to a close with a prayer for "strength, courage, patience, and wisdom." Her desire for strength, courage, and patience were not new. Five years before she had hoped for the same three qualities as she looked forward to the birth of her first baby. In the earlier passage, however, she also hoped for health and beauty. After five years she had substituted wisdom. The needs of the young wife had remained constant in some respects, but now the mother of two could give up her earlier desire for feminine attractiveness and hope for clearer ideas of how to raise her two sons.[61]

Miriam Van Waters came from the first generation of college-educated women reformers. Although she was born in Greensburg, Pennsylvania, only about forty miles from Gladys Penrod's home in Elderton, Van Waters grew up in Portland, Oregon, and attended the University of Oregon. She went on to study psychology and anthropology at Clark University in Massachusetts, where she earned a Ph.D. with a dissertation on adolescent girls. By 1913, when she was granted the Ph.D., Van Waters had already become active in reforming the care of juvenile girls in the Massachusetts court system. From 1914 onward she worked with juvenile adolescent girls, as head of reformatories in Oregon, California, and, finally, Massachusetts. During her work in Cal-

5.2 Miriam Van Waters. Schlesinger Library, Radcliffe College.

ifornia, as both a reformatory administrator and court referee, she wrote *Youth in Conflict* (1925) and *Parents on Probation* (1927). With a growing national reputation, Van Waters was invited to work on the juvenile sections of the Harvard Crime Survey in 1927, and in 1932 she was appointed superintendent of the Women's Reformatory at Framingham. She would continue as superintendent until 1957, earning praise for the success of her institution and her leadership in the field of juvenile justice.[62]

Van Waters never married, but in 1932 she adopted a ten-year-old girl whom she had come to know through the California court system. Sarah would bring Van Waters both joy and frustration. For Van Waters, child rearing became a project of the self that required both shaping the personality of the child in her care and making demands on her own inner resources. Whenever Van Waters reflected on Sarah's conduct, she also connected her observations to a wider theory of conduct and to her personal struggles to achieve the ideal of the theory that she called vital conduct.

Culturally, Van Waters lived in both the Progressive and the modern eras at the same time. Like many women in Progressive reform, she maintained close ties to other women. In her attitude toward pain she seemed to embody Victorian reserve and stoicism. After a horse riding accident in the early 1930s she suffered "stab after stab" of pain in the hospital. But when asked if she wanted a drink or ether she refused both: "above all else you want *clearness*." Van Waters believed that when pain threatened to engulf, the "mature and competent" individual had recourse to awareness of others, among whom she included her daughter Sarah. Like the mother in labor, she would not allow pain to conquer her. Van Waters's reliance on calm, altruistic suffering reflects the values of an earlier period when the ideal of service held greater importance and when medicine offered fewer alternatives for avoiding pain.[63]

Van Waters's relation to her mother seems to have drawn no clear shape from either the Victorian or modern period. She clearly cared deeply for her mother, bringing her elderly mother to live with her in Framingham after her father's death. Yet Van Waters's mother had frequently left her alone in Oregon while she returned to visit family in Pennsylvania. This may have attenuated the closeness of the two women. Van Waters seems to have had few moments of mother worship. She traced her ideals to her father and considered him the model for her life.[64]

The superintendent's day at Framingham often began before breakfast, and Van Waters extended her work schedule until midnight to give her time for writing. Care for Sarah had to come, in part, from staff, servants, family, and friends. On her lists of activities for the day, time with Sarah could appear as one more scheduled activity: "8:15–9:45 Sarah: Bathe & care for boil: Read Stally & Co[.]" In a list of actions she needed to take before leaving on vacation she included "Household—: Sarah and responsibility," followed by the training of interns, articles and a speech she needed to write, meetings to attend, and departments to attend to. In her journals and commonplace books, Van Waters included child rearing as one more task in a busy and demanding life.

But if raising a child required careful scheduling, it also drew from Van Waters feelings of delight, tenderness, and frustration. Although she never simply wrote of generalized feelings for her daughter, Van Waters frequently commented on Sarah's behavior. Sarah's acts seem always to have had some emotional valence. "Sarah goes to bed on time: she is an angel." "The new day starts beautifully. Sarah is an angel—her eagerness for school shows growth." "Sarah: Bed ½ hr. late but a lovely 'going concern'—new consideration for her Mummie." Far more often bedtimes, mornings, and school turned into times of frustration for Miriam Van Waters. Although she tried to give Sarah a carefully planned routine, the little girl did not always appreciate the developmental advantage this gave her. One morning Van Waters reported that Sarah's face was "full of purpose—but it was (naturally) Her Purpose.—did not drink orange juice till 3rd request—left Dr. Chace waiting 5 min. No clearing off of downstairs." When Van Waters confronted Sarah with her failings, both of them went away feeling unhappy over the incident. Discussions with teachers often dealt with Sarah's laziness and irresponsibility.[65]

For Van Waters, child rearing came within her broader reflections on self and the nurturing of full humanity. "We posit a 'child,' " she began an abbreviated discussion of child development. Rather than clear stages, Van Waters assumed a process of growing consciousness of self and "non-self," with the acquisition of emotional responses such as "wonder, worship, amusement, compassion" followed by "deepening awareness of the self being adequate." This development of self applied not only to children but to any individual, child or adult. As self-awareness grows, Van Waters believed, it would entail new relations with others and new actions connecting the individual to the world. Many people achieve character, "a deposit of habits of right living." They follow routines, build homes and institutions, and live according to "fixed mores." But although these people have overcome the worst dangers of chaotic living, they miss fuller communion with the world around them and " 'whispers of the infinite.' " Yet these individuals held within themselves a life force that Van Waters referred to as vital conduct. Living in a disciplined manner opened the possibility of finding within oneself a source of life-transforming power.[66]

Whereas Van Waters described vital conduct in several different ways, the concept always included the exercise of the will to shape one's own life and also an ideal of service. In vital conduct one would live more fully each moment and live in some sense for others. Several strands of early-twentieth-century thinking met in vital conduct. The progressive ideal of service appeared there in full force, as did a kind of abundance therapy that called for the individual to discover greater powers within and so give the individual a more authentic life. Mind cure probably made its contribution, as did the Episcopalian spirituality of Van Waters's minister father. Vital conduct also fit comfortably with the child-rearing advice of modern experts.[67]

Van Waters measured her own conduct against this ideal of vital conduct and often found herself wanting. Each day demanded planning from beginning to end "to avoid senseless repetition, and to capture— channels for vital conduct." The day must include stability and routine but also had to leave room for spontaneity and novelty. Like Gladys Penrod, Van Waters often complained of losing control. At 10:30, after a demanding day, she found herself "over-stimulated, under disciplined, had lost the thread of conscious control, and the *meaning* of the day."

The limits of self-control, of course, appeared even more frequently in Sarah's behavior. Van Waters worried that Sarah did not fully use her possessions, such as her bicycle or oil paints. She didn't take proper care of the horses and went from wanting roller skates to wanting to learn to play the banjo. "There simply are no abiding interests, but rather an absorption in the fast flowing ones." Such lack of concentrated interest directly opposed the central value of vital conduct of making disciplined use of every moment. For Van Waters, there was a direct link between her own discipline and her daughter's. After reflecting on Sarah's lack of prudence with her allowance, she went on: "I suppose the indirect method of influence (controling [*sic*] my own short comings) is the only effective one." In an incident that Van Waters recounted two months later, she offered an example of how her loss of connection to the immediate situation turned out badly when she came home late to find Sarah going to bed twenty minutes late and scolded her for it. But Sarah had been singing with her uncle and grandmother, so her lateness had a good excuse. Van Waters took for granted that "all I have to do to have an efficient household and a loyal and happy staff is to discipline my own day, control my own expenditures, direct my attention." As with Gladys Penrod, the interior world of emotion and the external world of others should bend to the fully disciplined will.[68]

Although Van Waters's philosophy of child rearing and personal development were more sophisticated and coherent than Gladys Penrod's, both held similar understandings of the role of the mother in cultivating personal development. Mothers should become models of correct behavior and also work persistently to support good habits. Both women also espoused unattainable ideals for motherly behavior and experienced a sense of failure when they fell short of their own expectations. Yet both found enormous emotional gratification from their relationships with their children. Although Gladys Penrod and Miriam Van Waters had sharply different educations, lifestyles, and career accomplishments, both women found motherhood near the center of their emotional lives. In this respect, they represent the emotional experiences of virtually all of the mothers whose diaries and letters are included in this study. Just as these women fashioned individual compromises to integrate the era's varied, and often conflicting, images of romance and of marriage with their personal experiences, they worked to integrate the culture's various theories and models of motherhood with their experiences as mothers. For many, this role defined their emotional lives for years, providing the most intense joys as well as the most significant pains they would experience.

## 6

# *The Fountain*

In 1930 twenty-year-old Ruth Raymond entered a period of emotional difficulty that would last for over five years. Her suffering centered around feelings of inadequacy and anxiety which surfaced in relation to her college work, first at Mt. Holyoke and later at Radcliffe. After withdrawing from college Ruth continued in a downward spiral marked by increasing distress, inactivity, and alcohol use. Through her period of deepest depression Ruth considered entertainer Harry Richman to be her one friend, even though she never met him, and she found her greatest consolation in the sound of his voice. On one particularly bad day in 1935 she wrote, "I got drunk, I've been drunk ever since I got home, I've lost myself, I've lost work, I've lost everything, and played all my Harry Richman victrola records, which are real. I shall be very vulgar if I am ever ashamed of the solace those disks have been to me."[1]

About this time, Ruth's parents sought to console her and possibly cajole her out of what they may have considered self-destructive gloom, by purchasing tickets for a Harry Richman performance. Ruth saw this as her salvation and as incentive to hold herself together. A week before the concert she wrote, "Next Saturday Harry Richman. I didn't ask for help, after all, in vain. . . . If I am very good and very brave and don't bang my brains out against too many walls, I may have Harry Richman." The concert lived up to her expectations: "The real magnificence— I felt as if my spirit hadn't had a square meal, as if I hadn't been happy in my bones, since last January when I last heard him sing." One day shortly after the concert Ruth took advantage of her mother's absence to post secretly a letter to Harry. His response, two months later, pulled her through another period of emotional crisis. She wrote in her diary, "Dear Harry, I knew you'd come through again. You do drop in at the opportunist times, . . . now I flower, briefly it may be, into happiness, because of 'a humble, stupid, ordinary letter.' " Ruth copied Harry's letter into her diary, and over the years would take seriously his closing invitation: "Please feel free to write to me at any time, because I always enjoy hearing from my friends." Ruth wrote her final letter to Harry Richman nearly forty years after her first, just before his death in 1972. In it she thanked him again for the gift of his music.[2]

Ruth's diary entries suggest that through the music of Harry Richman and his contemporaries she found access to her interior world. At times she chose music to reflect her mood. During one period of loneliness she indulged in "the delicious misery of playing 'Moanin' Low' on the vic." After copying the words from the song in her diary, Ruth wrote, "All of a sudden I am very lonely, with a special kind of loneliness for a man who would say 'If I die where'll she be?' " Later the same year she wrote, "One of my bad days. Played ballads on the vic during all possible hours, much comforted by my newest gem, *Women Down in Memphis*, which has very fine qualities indeed." Other kinds of music took Ruth beyond her unhappiness. The songs Harry Richman sang at his 1935 concert apparently allowed Ruth to experience vicariously the lilting pleasure of "Putting on the Ritz" and the defiant optimism of "I Love a Parade." Fine performances of both the blues and the upbeat tunes stirred Ruth and satisfied her emotionally.[3]

Ruth's idiosyncratic emotional style remained consistent throughout the decade following her high school graduation. National events, including the Depression, had surprisingly little impact on her life. Her feelings of hopelessness and despair seemed unrelated to the country's economic crisis, which in fact she never mentioned in her diary of late 1929 or early 1930. Although she noticed and wrote about poverty and organized charities, she experienced no economic stress and seemed inconvenienced, but not deeply affected, by the financial problems of others.[4]

Although Ruth Raymond's personal crisis of the early 1930s has sources in her personal development, it also shows a number of themes that would hold true for many middle-class women. The Depression appears to have had little effect on emotional culture, and although it changed the fortunes and circumstances of middle-class families, it often appears to have had little impact on the emotional experience of middle-class women. Feelings of depression and dejection become very common among women as they approached their middle years. Women who fit well into the emotional culture of the time, as we have seen, often found their hopes for romance or companionship in marriage disappointed. Their counterparts who never found romance or marriage may have faced loneliness unbroken by the supportive network of female friends and relations on which an earlier generation of American women relied.

The economic crisis that settled on the country in 1929 and 1930 forced itself into the awareness of middle-class women. Photographer Margaret Bourke-White learned of the stock market crash from the bankers who kept crossing in front of her camera during a night shoot of a bank lobby for the nascent *Fortune* magazine. *Fortune*'s publishers considered closing down the magazine before its first issue. Martha La-vell, just entering her career as a social worker in Chicago as the Depression began, noted at the beginning of 1931 that the United Charities received one hundred new cases every day. She considered communism a possible solution. "Anything is better than an economic system based on greed and disregard of human life." "It seems that the bottom has fallen out of the world," wrote Ione Robinson early in the Depression. "As I view the economic chaos," wrote Viola White, "I bless my stars that I have no child to worry about."[5]

The experience of the Depression could vary greatly, depending on the region and economic class that a woman called home. Ann Marie Low, growing up in North Dakota during the 1920s, considered farming an "everlasting struggle." The miseries of the dust bowl years and the continued decline of crop and cattle prices that forced her family to give up farming by the mid-thirties seemed a part of the chronic depression that farming had entered in the early 1920s. In a college course on "rural sociology" in 1933 Low's instructor "asked how many of us expect to spend our lives in rural areas. I was the only one."[6]

Harriet Louise Hardy, from a comfortable middle-class family and about to embark on a career in medicine, could write briskly in 1933, "The world is full of interest these days . . . each looks himself over seriously to see what he has that can stand the shock of these times." She managed to stand the shock by working summers at a girl's camp to help pay for medical school, and in her fourth year she became doctor-in-residence at a Salvation Army hospital for foundlings. Her picture of the economic situation changed as her parents suffered financial reverses. Her father's air-conditioning business went bankrupt, and only her mother's inheritance saved the family's furniture. Her mother and father were eventually forced to rent out their summer home in Vermont as a guest house, with father working as cook and mother as housekeeper. Hardy sadly reflected a year after her earlier statement that "it is difficult to realize the economic world is near disaster again; that the ridiculous tempo of our times is about to throw us off the track to chaos & change; that dramatic problems are torturing men's lives and peace as never before—it has even reached my home."[7]

For some, the 1930s offered little anxiety. Dorothy Dushkin wrote in 1932 that the music school she ran with her husband continued to prosper "in spite of hard times all about us." Six months later she reflected on her family and the school and considered it "a very full & exciting life we lead & I'm lucky to be a part of it." Beth Twiggar, who began college in 1931, wrote virtually nothing about the Depression in her diary. In an annotation written in 1992, she wrote that she was shocked that her "own emotional circus took precedence" over the economic crisis. She recognized at the time that various friends faced problems and she learned of suffering from "newspapers and from train windows, in my debating group and Sociology classes." She also recalled that even though her parents, through stringent economy and hard work, protected her from the losses of the Depression, she and her friends made efforts to tone down their wardrobes and to make do with less. She believed that her father, who saw his "lifetime of work and prudence crumble away," died of the Depression in 1938, at age 68.[8]

Although from the retrospect of sixty years Beth Twiggar Goff could regret the indifference in her reflections on the Depression, diarists in general took note of the economic crisis only as it affected them personally. Diaries that dealt mainly with emotional experience treated national economic trends as incidental. Even Martha Lavell, whose social work activities had taken her into the homes of those most affected by the Depression, wrote in 1933, "Inertia is troubling me these days, for the same old reasons—no male companionship and no vocational success. The depression hasn't bothered me half as much as those two."[9] This may offer the most accurate guide to the impact of the Depression on emotionology in the 1930s. Women who came of age in the 1920s or earlier had little cause to give up their belief in romance, companionate marriage, and the need for emotional management. The experience of emotion as well as emotional culture may have shifted for younger middle-class women in the 1930s, although here the trends are ambiguous because of the ability of many middle-class households, like the Twig-gars, to maintain some modicum of their pre-Depression lifestyle. At the same time, trends that had begun in the 1920s apparently continued to shape emotional experience in the 1930s.

Adolescent conviviality seems, on balance, to have changed less as a result of the Depression than because of the continued spread of the adolescent peer culture. Dating, of course, required participation in the consumer culture and this suffered with the household stringencies of the 1930s. By the mid-1930s families spent proportionately less on adolescents than they had a decade before. The manager of one movie house in Muncie, Indiana, reported in 1935 that movies " 'have been hit just like jewelry and other luxury trades.' " The researchers who had returned to Muncie to study the impact of the Depression, however, tended to discount the manager's talk of woe and reported that movies held the "same large place in Middletown's leisure today that they did in 1925." As they had a decade earlier, movies gave adolescents a common vocabulary and a set of standards for behavior. "Joan Crawford has her amateur counterparts in the high-school girls who stroll with brittle confidence in and out of 'Barney's' soft-drink parlor, 'clicking' with the 'drugstore cowboys' at the tables."[10]

Dating and other emotional rituals of the youth culture probably continued to grow in acceptance with the growth in high school attendance. The Depression undermined incentives for young people to quit school. Even among families receiving relief in 1935–36, 58.5 percent of sixteen- to seventeen-year-olds attended school, with the percentage growing for every higher income group (almost 75 percent for families with income of $1,000 to $1,900 per year). Ann Marie Low, in the depressed farm belt, attended school dances and went to movies throughout the hard times of the late 1920s and early 1930s.[11]

With the expansion of adolescent heterosociality went a continued though slow decline of homosociality. Although no study of young women's sexuality as extensive as Katherine Bement Davis's came out of the Depression years, the social science literature of the period shaped a consensus on adolescent homoeroticism that saw a homosexual stage as a normal phase in development as long as it found expression only in idealized crushes.[12] One study from the late 1930s reported that homosexuals made up only a small portion of college women and that the commonplace passionate romances among women of an earlier era had largely passed from the scene at colleges.[13]

Marriage probably felt the impact of the Depression more directly than courtship. Leonard Rosenfeld proposed to Adele Siegel on April 6, 1936. She agreed, but only on the condition that they wait until circumstances would allow. This meant delaying their wedding until April 1, 1939. The Lynds recognized the reluctance to marry as a general trend in Muncie, although one that bottomed out by 1933. The marriage rate of 1935 had returned to the rate for the last half of the 1920s. The loss of assets undoubtedly created strains in marriages throughout the decade. The Lynds even speculated that the Depression may have brought wide-ranging emotional changes to men and women, as the role of breadwinner was lost to many men and taken up by some women. Outwardly, however, there appeared little change in gender roles in the mid-1930s. "The men were preoccupied with rebuilding the shaken fences of their job world, and the women were doing the familiar women's work of keeping house, rearing children, and going to clubs, with a modicum of church, charity, or civic work."[14]

The Lynds's general description would have served well for the life of Dorothy Blake whose published diary detailed a year of her life on Long Island during the Depression. Blake's husband had continued to work, although with a lower salary, and the family struggled to keep up house payments and maintain their middle-class lifestyle with less income. One of the themes that Blake returned to several times in her diary was that the Depression offered some residual benefits, among them the "intense mutual need" that she experienced with her husband: "all the time, our family getting closer and closer in understanding and love and partnership." For Blake, the Depression offered the opportunity for the realization of the emotional goals of companionate marriage.[15]

The economic crisis supported companionate marriage in other ways. During the Depression years most American men believed that wives should not work if their husbands were able to support them. This consensus entered into hiring decisions. From 1930 to 1940, women employed in the professions fell from 14.2 to 12.3 percent of the total. Viola White noted that the young men who had finished their Ph.D.s with her "are assured of jobs for next year, while I have no ghost of anything." White eventually found work as the librarian of Middlebury College. Gladys Bell Penrod looked for work during the early 1930s. Although she had ambivalent feelings about teaching again, she felt compelled to help move the family out of the tight financial condition it was in. She never found full-time work. One school board director, an old family friend, wrote her a letter in response to Gladys's letter of inquiry that reflected the policies of many school districts. "It is the intention of the Board to not employ any married teacher whose husband is working."[16]

Gladys Penrod's anxiety over her family's finances provides an illustration of ways that the Depression shaped emotional experience even if it made little change in emotional culture. Similarly, Miriam Van Waters worried that the Framingham Reformatory "cannot operate under the present budget, and I am assured there will be no increase. I cannot live on my salary—I spend most of it on [institutional] expenses and have reduced my standard of living."[17] But even though there are some clear effects of the Depression on individuals, it becomes very difficult to identify ways that the Depression shaped the emotional lives of women. We have only a handful of diaries that began in the 1920s and continued through the 1930s. These generally come from the most persistent diarists, women like Gladys Bell Penrod, Beth Twiggar Goff, Ruth Raymond, and Winifred Willis, whose ruminations became permanent features of their whole lives. As we pointed out in the previous chapter, diary-keeping dropped off sharply among women who had children, and this applies more generally to women as they moved beyond the early stages of marriage or career. By the time they reached their thirties, most women seemed to lose interest in writing about their lives.

The small number of diaries that go on through the entire adult lives of women offers the possibility of deeper analysis and suggests that mature adulthood presented women with anxiety, depression, and even health problems, and that this held true in spite of the personal style and outlook of individual women. Winifred Willis, for instance, saw herself as constitutionally melancholy, even during her early twenties. The breakdown of her marriage followed by nervous collapse seemingly consolidated this personal typing. Willis began to study the writings of Schopenhauer around the time of her nervous breakdown, and reflections on Schopenhauer would reappear in her journal for years to come. From 1928 her journal included fewer records of daily events and more responses to the writings of others, snatches from her memory, and self-reflection on past events. Harriet Louise Hardy, on the other hand, whose healthy-mindedness carried her through the sadness of unrequited love and would form a permanent feature of her approach to a challenging career, nevertheless suffered from the stresses of her work at Northfield Seminary combined with private practice. Although her autobiography does not mention her secret sorrow over losing "R," this may also have contributed to what she called a nervous breakdown that lasted from 1938 into 1939.[18]

Miriam Van Waters seems to have maintained a distinctive emotional style throughout her adult life. A recent biographer has pointed to Van Waters's efforts to provide the mothering that she missed during the prolonged absences of her own mother. Van Waters would become a reformatory superintendent, juvenile judge, and even an adoptive mother, all roles that allowed her to offer an idealized nurture to her charges and to her daughter. Yet the sense that Van Waters carried from childhood of never quite giving or doing enough also persisted. In spite of a full and successful career, Van Waters's diary reflects on her failures to properly care for her adopted daughter Sarah or to deal with staff in just the right way. She often slept poorly and many entries reflected her desire to find some standard of moral living that would allow her to find calm and confidence within herself.[19]

Beth Twiggar dealt with the problems of mature adulthood in ways that seemed to match cultural prescriptions yet clearly bent the culture's norms to her own needs. Although she lost much of the ebullience of her adolescent years after a broken engagement to a West Point cadet, she continued to hope for love and a full life. She found work, lived through a short and unsatisfactory marriage, and finally fell in love with the man she would be married to for ten years until his accidental death. Even if Beth Twiggar's life improved, her early adult years still gave her a full measure of questioning, anxiety, and feelings of incompleteness. In terms of the shape of her emotional life, the Depression appears to have made little difference. The same can be said for all of the persistent diarists.[20]

Persistent diarists, of course, may be more introspective, more sensitive to the nuance of their emotional lives than the great majority of people. Yet they do not appear to have differed in any other significant way from other middle-class women. The more casual diarists in our study, who kept diaries for one or only a few years, almost always turned to reflections on their emotional lives. Edythe Weiner's year-long diary at age fourteen covers many of the same themes that Beth Twiggar's diary did for that part of her life, although Twiggar wrote longer entries. Some psychological literature suggests that women deal with problems of relationship or other stresses of life more commonly by talking and pondering emotions than men do. If so, then the persistent diarists differed from other women only in their faithfulness to the written record.

If our diarists can serve as a guide to larger trends, then this points to important themes in the lives of mature women. The diarists found their emotional lives incomplete or unsatisfactory far more frequently than they experienced optimism and satisfaction. Clinical evidence is also suggestive. Whereas men have personality disorders and other mental health problems at a higher rate than women, from at least 1936 women have outnumbered men in cases of clinical depression by two to one. Recent psychological research has confirmed the prevalence of women who are both clinically and subclinically depressed. During the 1930s the term dejection would typically have been applied to individuals with what we now call mild depression, and the "discouraged or dispirited mood" that defines dejection certainly applies to many of the persistent diarists at some periods. However, all of the women who sensed incompleteness in their emotional lives also felt, from time to time, the hopelessness, inadequacy, or unworthiness that psychologists in the 1930s would have used to define pathological depression.[21]

A tentative conclusion that we may draw from these trends is that mature, middle-class women frequently found their emotional lives inadequate. Rather than the feelings of happiness promised in advertisements, or the sense of fullness and completeness offered by contemporary therapeutic strategies, middle-class women often fell into periods of self-doubt and self-blame. They missed something, whether it was romance or intensity or inner calm. Independence and career could leave women feeling they had failed in some important respects. Martha Lavell mourned the loss of her dream for a husband and children. "I don't know what I'll do with my life if I don't marry," she wrote in 1932 as she began her career in social work and research. Three years later she still longed for marriage: "it's all I want out of life, and as the years go by, my youth and vitality and potentialities for comradeship are being wasted."[22] Wealth seems to have made no difference. Anne Morrow Lindbergh could never rid herself of feelings of doubt about her life and adequacy, even after she married Charles Lindbergh in the late 1920s. Even though Lindbergh expressed herself more fluently than Gladys Penrod, who married a truck driver, the two women faced many of the same self-doubts.

The growing cultural preference for heterosexual and heterosocial relationships probably contributed more to the generalized dissatisfaction of mature women than the Depression. Twentieth-century women were less likely than women a century or fifty years previously to face the death of a child or husband (at least until old age), and they suffered less from childbirth or disease. Yet they were far more likely to lose a husband through divorce, and any grief or difficulty they encountered as they matured they had to face without the solace of passionate friendships or the supportive network of friends on which Victorian women relied. Organized feminism continued through the 1920s, but the number of women involved in feminist causes dropped sharply. The strong relationships among adult women that had characterized many of the Progressive-era organizations—settlement houses, women's colleges, social reform groups—declined as the twentieth century continued. Of the persistent diarists in this study, only Miriam Van Waters seems to have maintained a strong network of supportive women friends. Younger women joined the revolt against Victorianism by embracing life among men. Psychologist Lorinne Pruette claimed in 1930 that women had little interest in feminism because they believed it was "anti-man."[23]

The low estimate given to women's passionate attachments to other women meant that many women became wives and mothers or mature career women without the intimacy and support of other women. Gladys Penrod had depended on the loving attention of her friend Elsie during her early twenties. She received and valued "all kinds of love and confidence from Elsie" before her marriage. But after her marriage Penrod rarely mentioned Elsie, and when she did she often criticized her. Viola White lost all self-respect in her passion for an older friend, Beatrice, but the passion went largely unrequited. "The woman I love," she wrote in 1931, "the woman who is indispensable to me, regards me with gratitude when I let her alone." White's desire for intimacy remained individual. She never discovered the "community" that she idealized and that women of an earlier generation might have found in groups of likeminded women.[24]

Family continued to be important for young women, and the relations between daughters and mothers may have improved once the years of flaming youth had passed. But the cultural preference for seeing the mothering instinct as potentially dangerous, if not actively pernicious, weakened the ties of mothers and daughters.[25] Male mentors may have replaced older women friends for some women. Harriet Louise Hardy often mentions senior medical men who helped and encouraged her.

Male mentors, however, may have encouraged women to devote themselves more fully to career than to relationships and so aggravated the isolation they already experienced. During her first professional position at a girl's school and in her private practice, Hardy relied on the support of older male physicians and a professor at Cornell Medical School. The girls at the school chided her for being unmarried and gave her their wishes for a happier future.[26]

Modern marriage, of course, held out the most attractive alternative to intimate female friends. The companionship of husband and wife would become the basic relationship for women, the one around which all other relationships would turn. Yet as we have seen, companionate marriage promised women that it could fill their lives; for men, marriage continued to be only a part of life. Dorothy Dushkin, for whom modern marriage worked very well, nevertheless continued to search for and prize her close women friends. Children consumed much of Dorothy's time and thoughts. Her husband, David, who worked at home, illustrated the relation of most husbands to the home by popping in on the family several times during the day. Most of his time he gave to his teaching and to planning for their school.[27]

It was not a matter that women lost all contact with other women. They attended P.T.A. meetings and played bridge with friends. However, they rarely again experienced the close and often passionate bonds that many of them had enjoyed as adolescents. If they married, they invested their entire emotional capital in husband and family. This often failed to pay the dividends that American culture assured them it would. The relative isolation that women experienced as they established families and careers helps explain feelings of self-doubt and mild depression that appear so frequently in their diaries. The loss of supportive relationships also points toward the emotional strategies that women adopted in adulthood. Rather than relying on the help of other women and deriving emotional satisfactions from close friends, women looked inward for the resources to meet the crises of maturity.

A surprising number of our diarists found encouragement and hope from reading *The Fountain*, a novel by British author Charles Morgan that appeared in 1932. The emotional challenges that women faced in adulthood coinciding with the personal stress that many felt as a result of the Depression help to explain the popularity of Morgan's work. It is the story of Lewis Alison, a British soldier interned in Holland at the beginning of World War I, and of Julie von Narwitz, a young woman

Lewis had tutored many years before. They meet again when Lewis is released from a prison fortress into the keeping of Julie's stepfather, Baron van Leyden. Julie is married to a German officer, and both she and Lewis at first ignore and then struggle against their growing passion for one another.[28]

*The Fountain* became a bestseller on both sides of the Atlantic and received fulsome praise from critics. The *New York Times* reviewer described it as "literate as well as literary. . . . a novel of so delicate a flavor" that it could not be easily summarized. In the *Saturday Review of Literature*, reviewer and popular author Hendrik Willem Van Loon called *The Fountain* "a very civilized book . . . an interesting story interestingly told." It is tempting to read gender into Van Loon's review, which deals mainly with the captivity of the British soldiers in an old fortress, a phase of the story that takes up only a few chapters. The love story between Julie and Lewis, which takes shape over hundreds of pages, Van Loon refers to in one sentence. Even more central to the story are Lewis's reflections on a life of detachment and spiritual peace, of which Van Loon makes no mention at all. Emily Newell Blair, writing for *Good Housekeeping*, dealt not only with the spiritual significance of the love story but also with the possibility of human transcendence that the book presents. In her first sentences she conveyed the "deep spiritual experience" created by the book. "As I read it, there came to me a sense of detachment from the world about me. Again and again I found myself . . . drifting into utter stillness. It gave me not only a quiet desire to evoke this stillness, but mystically enabled me to do it."[29]

Blair's review pointed directly to the value that many women found in Morgan's book. Anne Morrow Lindbergh read *The Fountain* in the weeks following her son's kidnaping and murder. "This is what I want—*here*," she wrote. "This man knows!" She went on to quote a passage in which Morgan had described "stilling the soul" with the mind. Months later Lindbergh would again return in her reflections to a passage in *The Fountain* where Morgan had contrasted people who tried to lose themselves in a cause or pleasure or excitement with the saints who could retreat to islands of inner calm.[30]

Winifred Willis also read *The Fountain* at a time of personal trial, just after the breakup of her marriage and her own recovery from nervous distress. She wrote three years after the event: "I will never forget that day in the summer of 1932 when I first read 'The Fountain.' " In a new marriage and determined to make herself over, she felt the work "jolted me right back to earth. It gave myself to me, it gave me the world in a mingling of spiritual and earthy that defies description." Willis wanted a path toward spiritual self-reliance. An entry that recorded her reading of the book reflected that "the desire to be invulnerable is flawless."[31] Like Anne Morrow Lindbergh, she sought a calm within herself that would save her from the ravages of her emotions.

Harriet Louise Hardy approached life more optimistically than Lindbergh or Lockhart, and religion played a far larger role in her life than it did for either Lindbergh or Lockhart in their early adult years. Yet Hardy also felt drawn to Morgan's description of " 'the peace which is invulnerable. . . . ' I know I must become invulnerable," Hardy reflected, "and I am impregnable in proportion to the degree to which I develop my inner life."[32]

Martha Lavell found the book "puzzling in many ways. It concerned the contemplative life, and quietness of soul as a goal in life. To be beyond earthly things, pain and jealousy and ambitions, was the aim of two of the characters." Her pacifism and her career as a social worker colored her views of the book. So did her attraction to Norman Thomas and socialism. "They were fine men," she wrote of the characters. "But their philosophy seemed to me to be a rather egocentric one. They seemed to show no interest in social problems, in the question of evil. . . . Though they lived through the war, they gave no thought to its significance or to the suffering it caused." Alone among the diarists who commented on the work, Lavell dismissed the goal of inner peace as "rather a narrow goal."[33] Yet Lavell was also alone among these diarists in not suffering a crisis in her personal life during the early 1930s. She looked on the Depression as the great problem of the day and believed the work of the individual necessarily should turn to social goals.

Although not every woman who wrote a diary read *The Fountain* (or wrote about it if they did), the desire for an interior calm turns up repeatedly in the reflections of the diarists. We have already seen that Miriam Van Waters strived to achieve vital conduct, which she described as a natural power that individuals can tap within themselves. Dorothy Dushkin, who in the early thirties believed that she could calm her "emotional waywardness" by allowing herself to become absorbed in work and in the intensity of the moment, wrote a year later that she hoped to achieve a more meditative life, not giving herself up to mechanical tasks, petty conversations, gossip, or "mundane trivialities." Gladys Bell Penrod, who tried to manage away her emotional distress, expressed her

*6.1* Martha Lavell at Mills College in 1926. Photo by [Webster?]. Sophia Smith Collection, Smith College.

desire in terms that might have suited Morgan. "If there was a place where one could escape from thinking, I would be there now."[34]

Ruth Raymond also read *The Fountain*, perhaps as early as November 1932, and used a passage from it as the inscription for one of the volumes of her diary. In the passage Lewis Alison reflected that individuals "die to the instant" as time passes. Past selves become "strange ghosts . . . with whom they have no communication."[35] Although such a passage could have served as a commentary on the project of diary-keeping, Raymond offered no reflections on Morgan's book and so offers no help to psychologists or historians. The context provided by Raymond's diaries makes it clear that Ruth Raymond also wanted to find a place of repose as a respite or escape from the wearying realities she faced. For Raymond, however, the attempt to make a personal space meant drawing on a wide variety of materials from her culture, including, as the opening paragraphs of this chapter demonstrate, popular music. She dealt with her loneliness and personal pain in her diary, where she created an alternative world of virtual relationships to replace the real friendships and love relationships that eluded her. Even though Ruth Raymond was apparently more troubled than our other persistent diarists, she shared with many of the others a sense of dissatisfaction or incompleteness. Her writings also underline the pervasiveness and importance of popular culture in the emotional lives of young women.

Born in 1909, Ruth Raymond lived most of her life near Boston. Her father taught paleontology at Harvard, and Ruth attended Mt. Holyoke College and later Radcliffe College. She wanted to write, and she completed two novels which were never published. Ruth's precollege entries are energetic and feisty. "Read at your own risk," she defiantly commanded the curious who might look into her diary. Yet even as a teen-aged high school student, Ruth relied more on fantasy relationships than real ones for emotional gratification. She participated only tentatively in the youth culture. She went on most outings with her father or mother and spent much of her time alone, writing short stories, novels, and lengthy diary entries. One of the few high school romances she mentions took place mainly in her imagination. She wrote frequently about David, with whom she suggests she had some kind of understanding. After he became interested in another girl, she magnified even her slightest encounters with him, investing them with emotional meanings and depth. She even claimed that he was afraid her attraction was too strong, and that was why he sat with his back to her with another girl's initials scrawled on his desk.[36]

Ruth's friendships with young women, although in some cases sustained over many years, typically did not include either shared confidences or frequent socializing. Anna Napoli, Ruth's one close high school friend, married shortly after graduation, and Ruth's contact with her was limited thereafter to occasional visits at Anna's home. At college Ruth failed to win emotional intimacy from other young women, although she did make several friends and developed a crush on one young woman. Shortly after arriving at Mt. Holyoke in 1928 she wrote about a "slim girl, black hair cut boyish" with "tapering brown face dustily vivid at the cheekbone, long light eyes aslant; aquiline nose; mouth red, triangular and sullen." She obviously admired this girl, and also feared her a little bit, nicknaming her "Hell-Hath-No-Fury-Like." Even though she referred to this peer as "my mistress," Ruth's encounters with her remained tentative: "One night I spoke to her on the stair, but she merely looked baleful."[37] She also wrote of dancing with a different girl at a college social and looked forward to her sophomore year with yet another girl. None of these relationships seems to have been very strong, however, and none lasted after Ruth left Mt. Holyoke in 1929. Although Ruth Raymond continued to mention female friends, none of them except Anna seemed to have been very intimate with her.

During her college years, Ruth also dreamed of romance. "I know now what it is college doesn't give that I want. . . . Love. I have to love somebody or something to be happy. Love." She accurately reflected the culture's prescription for fulfillment and held on to it. At the end of 1928, she wished "to meet someone who will love me and whom I'll fall in love with this next year." Later she seems to have shifted away from a romantic picture of her love, desiring instead "to be loved as is—loved with all my sins on my head." She pictured a companionate ideal—"two people putting their feet on the table and saying 'Hell' and grinning at their private joke." Yet Ruth remained socially isolated. She participated in events that did not present the possibility of forming personal relationships. To her mother's dismay, Ruth once chose to attend a local football game rather than have a party for a young man who had expressed an interest in her.[38]

Her lack of any intimate relationship threw Ruth Raymond back onto her own resources—her reading, her diary, her hopes for the future. She left Radcliffe in the spring of 1930 after one year of study and then lived at home, attending town sporting events and high school alumni meetings. She pursued her dream of writing, yet her work remained unpublished, frustrating her hopes for a literary career. The years of the Great Depression turned into years of personal depression for Ruth. "Now today I am half crazy with depression," she wrote in early 1930. "One of my bad days," she wrote a few months later.[39]

Ruth's bad days increased in frequency throughout the early 1930s. In 1935 she pinned her hopes for emotional well-being on a trip to England and Scotland where she planned to conduct research for a book on the Duke of Perth. Although she made the trip, Ruth's hopes went unfulfilled. While in Great Britain she suffered several illnesses and a number of disappointments. She returned home months ahead of schedule, "mercilessly ill, Culloden of my spirit, broken, lost."[40]

Within weeks of her return home Ruth found herself hospitalized at Massachusetts General Hospital where she learned after "three days in the hospital and all manner of tests" that she was "merely suffering the punishment of having no young friends or new moon." The diary context of this somewhat cryptic remark shows that Ruth understood her problem as lack of romance. For treatment Ruth was referred to a psychoanalyst, Dr. Bauer, whom she described as "everything that is good and kind, tho he does tend to dismiss Perth and the book and genius as so many symptoms of frustration." Ruth secured a promise from her parents to send her back to Scotland the following spring, but agreed in exchange to fulfill the obligations of her gender and station: "Meanwhile, I am to have my 'coming out,' seek the joy I should have had ten years ago."

Ruth rarely mentioned her psychoanalytic treatment in her diary, except to wryly denigrate the process from time to time. Several weeks after beginning treatment with Dr. Bauer, for example, she followed a passage concerning the moral character of the recently deceased actor Jack Pickford by noting that her analyst "would probably think I was furtively sinning in imagination with a dead playboy." Ruth not only accused psychoanalysis of indecency, she attributed to it some responsibility for her ongoing alcohol abuse. She characterized the week after her discharge from the hospital as "One hopeless blank day and then another, when I am either harassed or stupid; harassed when I think of the liberating beauties of psychoanalysis, and stupid when I remedy the situation." By "remedy" she meant consuming enough brandy or stout to numb her pain and allow her to forget the insights offered by psycho-analysis.[41]

Ruth sought relief from her isolation and feelings of depression in a number of places other than Dr. Bauer's office. For years she took comfort from religion, praying at a Catholic church during her years at Mt. Holyoke, and after returning home she looked for a Catholic church in Boston. But Raymond never became Catholic and never seems to have felt much power in religious practice. She enjoyed the ritual of lighting candles and saying prayers, but when her grandfather died "words wouldn't come." Rather than pray that night she shared a bottle of wine with her father. "I drank—it was good—and so to bed." During periods of distress Ruth frequently turned to alcohol as a means of dealing with her depression. "The second day of crise on crise, getting drunk and then sobering up so I could sleep without passing out," she wrote. "Moments of wildly crying aloud for someone to help me—only brandy and Harry Richman do."[42]

As her reliance on the popular singer and actor Harry Richman indicates, Ruth pulled together elements from the popular culture to ease her depression. She attended movies several times a week. During one eight-month period she saw 102 movies, including some movies that she saw more than once. During the 1930s she followed popular music on the radio and collected albums of her favorite songs. She invested herself emotionally in the lives of movie and radio celebrities, reading about them, worrying over their lives, and occasionally writing letters to them or about them. In her diary Ruth frequently wrote of actors and entertainers as if they were her personal friends whose troubles she felt deeply. In an early diary entry she wrote, "Gloria is ill! Lovely, incomparable, glorious Gloria! I am praying for her recovery." Ten years later she felt distraught at the news that Will Rogers had been killed. "I can't believe it now; he was assumed, he was part of one's life, he was America, and more personal losses have shocked me less."[43]

In fact, Ruth had been fortunate in the years through early adulthood and suffered no intensely painful personal losses. What her life lacked in tragedy, though, she seemed to create through her vicarious involvement in the lives of home-town peers, especially the young men who played sports for area teams. After seeing one young athlete at the movie theater with his date, Ruth recorded at length her fears for him: "The boy's decent, and she, that lovely little thing, trim coat and smart hat and silken legs and pretty, powdered face, is corruption. . . . This is real to me—corruption with a winsome white face . . . corruption showing off, parading the conquest of health and strength and simplicity, smiling to right and left so that everyone shall see." The next day Ruth reflected on her fears for the young man: "This little game of mine of playing mother from a distance warns me that even dream children give pain. How much more children you do not choose yourself!"

Ruth's play at motherhood addressed an emptiness that seemed to grow more pointed as she moved through young adulthood. She wrote lengthy passages describing her pain for suffering children whose misfortunes radio broadcasters detailed, and shortly before her twenty-fifth birthday she considered her frustrated hopes for a family of her own: "I cry whenever I see children in the movies, cried tonight when Barbara Stanwyck in a radio playlet stole tin soldiers for her small brother. I had two lovely afternoons this fall, one when the little boys from up the street came to call and I showed them father's childhood collection of fossils and arrowheads, the other when the elder of them came alone and we talked geology of all things." Ruth considered this pain unique and realized that her usual strategies for self-comfort did not apply. "I was used to being bothered by other things, but not this," she wrote. "There are substitutes for the other things, after all."[44]

Ruth Raymond never married or had children and in that sense failed to fulfill the 1930s prescription for womanly happiness. Paradoxically, she relied more heavily than many of the diarists on cultural materials for emotional fulfillment, but she never achieved the life those materials celebrated. In place of the companionship of marriage or the intense love of motherhood, Ruth substituted devotion as a fan and self-conscious compassion for strangers. Films, music, popular literature, and sports provided Ruth with both the images and the relationships around which she built her emotional life.

Ruth eventually finished her college degree through the Harvard Extension program and worked for more than twenty years as a medical librarian. Although her career may not have seemed to her a fitting substitute for the family she wanted, her diary entries and correspondence into the 1970s indicate that she built satisfying friendships and moved beyond the depression she suffered as a young woman.[45]

Although Ruth Raymond seems lonelier than many of our diarists, her life recapitulates in its way themes that have appeared consistently in the diary writing of middle-class women in the early decades of the twentieth century. Popularity with peers, romance, and companionate marriage served as the culturally defined goals and measures of success for various stages in a woman's life, and these goals promised full emotional lives. Most middle-class women appropriated these goals and shaped an emotionology around them. Yet a tension persisted between emotional culture and emotional experience. Some women discovered feelings of confusion or emptiness instead of bliss in romance or companionate marriage; others, like Martha Lavell or Ruth Raymond, found romance impossible to achieve. Whereas their culture gave them the values, images, and even the scripts for their emotional lives, it also denigrated the warm relationships they might have found with other people, especially women, outside of marriage and so offered meager resources for living through the confusion and struggle of adult life.

# Notes

## Notes to the Preface

1. Cheryl Cline, *Women's Diaries, Journals and Letters: An Annotated Bibliography* (New York: Garland Press, 1989), xii; Margo Culley, *A Day at a Time: The Diary Literature of American Women from 1764 to the Present* (New York: The Feminist Press, 1985), 4–13; Marlene A. Schiwy, *A Voice of Her Own: Women and the Journal-Writing Journey* (New York: Simon and Schuster, 1996), 32, 34; Carolyn G. Heilbrun, *Writing a Woman's Life* (New York: Ballantine, 1988), 15, 37, 45–46.

2. For recent descriptions of these methods see Amadeo Giorgi, "Phenomenological Psychology," in Jonathan A. Smith, Rom Harré, and Luk Van Langenhove, eds., *Rethinking Psychology* (London: Sage, 1995), 24–42; Barney Glaser, *Emergence vs. Forcing: Basics of Grounded Theory Analysis* (Mill Valley, CA: Sociology Press, 1992); Kathy Charmaz, "Grounded Theory," in Jonathan A. Smith, Rom Harré, and Luk Van Langenhove, eds., *Rethinking Methods in Psychology* (London: Sage, 1995), 27–49.

3. The recent scholarship on women's development is vast. Among the most prominent works are Nancy Chodorow, *The Reproduction of Mothering: Psychoanalysis and the Sociology of Gender* (Berkeley: University of California Press, 1978) and Carol Gilligan, *In a Different Voice: Psychological Theory and Women's Development* (Cambridge, MA: Harvard University Press, 1982). Ellyn Kaschak, *Engendered Lives: A New Psychology of Women's Experiences* (New York: Basic Books, 1992) criticizes the reliance that Gilligan and Chodorow place on psychoanalytic theory. On women's ways of understanding and dealing with relationships, see Ruthellen Josselson, *The Spaces Between Us: Exploring the Dimensions of Human Relationship* (San Francisco: Jossey Bass, 1992), esp. 224–290.

4. The Papers of Beth Twiggar Goff, 90-M130, 90-M8, Schlesinger Library, Radcliffe College. The comment was written in February 1992 with reference to an entry written December 5, 1934, box 1, volume 34.

### Notes to Chapter 1

1. Viola C. White, *Partridge in a Swamp: The Journals of Viola C. White, 1918–1941* (Taftsville, VT: Countryman Press, 1979), (February 12, 1918), 11.
2. Ibid.; J. H. Denison, *Emotion as the Basis of Civilization* (New York: Charles Scribners Sons, 1928), vii, 6, 21.
3. Theodore R. Sarbin, "Emotion and Act: Roles and Rhetoric," in Rom Harré, ed., *The Social Construction of Emotions* (New York: Basil Blackwell, 1986), 83–90; James R. Averill, "A Constructivist View of Emotion," in Robert Plutchik and Henry Kellerman, eds., *Emotion: Theory, Research, and Experience* (New York, Academic Press, 1980), 308–316.
4. On Victorian emotional culture, see Peter N. Stearns, *American Cool: Constructing a Twentieth Century Emotional Style* (New York: New York University Press, 1994), chapter 2; Karen Lystra, *Searching the Heart: Women, Men and Romantic Love in Nineteenth-Century America* (New York: Oxford University Press, 1989), 3–11; Jan Lewis, "Mother's Love: The Construction of an Emotion in Nineteenth-Century America," in Andrew E. Barnes and Peter N. Stearns, eds., *Social History and Issues in Human Consciousness* (New York: New York University Press, 1989), 209–229.
5. Peter N. Stearns and Carol Z. Stearns, "Emotionology: Clarifying the History of Emotions and Emotional Standards," *American Historical Review* 90 (October 1985): 813–836; Stearns, *American Cool*; Paul C. Rosenblatt, *Bitter, Bitter Tears: Nineteenth-Century Diarists and Twentieth-Century Grief Theories* (Minneapolis: University of Minnesota Press, 1983), chapter 3; Charles Dickens, *A Christmas Carol* [1843] (Toronto: Bantam Books, 1986), 77–78; John B. Watson, *Psychology from the Standpoint of a Behaviorist* (Philadelphia: J. B. Lippincott, 1919), 199.
6. Roderick Nash, *The Nervous Generation: American Thought, 1917–1930* (Chicago: Rand McNally and Co., 1971), 136; Ann Douglas, *Terrible Honesty: Mongrel Manhattan in the 1920s* (New York: Noonday Press/ Farrar Straus and Giroux, 1995), 3–28; White, *Partridge in a Swamp* (October 2, 1921), 63.
7. Lewis, "Mother's Love", 209–229; Stanley Coben, *Rebellion Against Victorianism: The Impetus for Cultural Change in 1920s America* (New York: Oxford University Press, 1991), 3–27.
8. Gilbert H. Barnes and Dwight L. Dumond, eds., *Letters of Theodore*

*Dwight Weld, Angelina Grimké and Sarah Grimké, 1822–1844,* volume 2 (New York: D. Appleton-Century, 1934), 560; Peter N. Stearns, "Girls, Boys and Emotions: Redefinitions and Historical Change," *Journal of American History* 80 (June 1993): 39–53; John F. Kasson, *Rudeness & Civility: Manners in Nineteenth-Century Urban America* (New York: Hill and Wang, 1990), chapter 5; David S. Reynolds, *Walt Whitman's America: A Cultural Biography* (New York: Vintage Books, 1995), 249–251; Lewis, "Mother's Love," 218–219; Burton Raffel, *Poets & Con Men: Emotional History in Late Victorian America* (Hamden, CT: Archon, 1986), 9.

9. The quote is from William McDougall, "Should All Taboos be Abolished?" in V. F. Calverton and S. D. Schmalhausen, eds., *Sex in Civilization* (New York: The Macauley Co., 1929), 86; John C. Burnham, "The Progressive Era Revolution in American Attitudes toward Sex," *Journal of American History* 59 (March 1973): 885–908; Coben, *Rebellion Against Victorianism,* 43; Douglas, *Terrible Honesty,* 31–40; V. F. Calverton, *The Bankruptcy of Marriage* (New York: The Macauley Co., 1928), 12–14, 34; Floyd Dell, *Love in the Machine Age: A Psychological Study of the Transition from Patriarchal Society* (New York: Farrar and Rinehart, 1930), 6.

10. Viola Goode Liddell, *With a Southern Accent* (Norman: University of Oklahoma Press, 1948), 61–65; Ann Marie Low, *Dust Bowl Diary* (Lincoln: University of Nebraska Press, 1984), 4–5, 29.

11. The quote is from the Papers of Martha Lavell, Sophia Smith Collection, Smith College [hereafter cited as Lavell Papers] folder 2, February 25, 1932; Gilman M. Ostrander, *American Civilization in the First Machine Age* (New York: Harper and Row, 1970), 122–123; on advertising see Daniel Starch, *Principles of Advertising* (New York: McGraw-Hill, 1923); Edward K. Strong, Jr., *The Psychology of Selling and Advertising* (New York: McGraw-Hill, 1925), chapters 9 and 10; Albert T. Poffenberg, *Psychology in Advertising* (Chicago: A. W. Shaw, 1925), 40; "Consumptionism" was coined by Samuel Strauss in 1917, see William Leach, *Land of Desire: Merchants, Power, and the Rise of a New American Culture* (New York: Vintage Books, 1994), 267–268.

12. Melvin E. Haggerty, *Enrichment of the Common Life* (Minneapolis: University of Minnesota Press, 1938), 10–12, 17–18.

13. William R. Leach, "Transformations in a Culture of Consumption: Women and Department Stores, 1890–1925," *Journal of American History* 71 (September 1984): 320; see also Susan Porter Benson, *Counter Cultures: Saleswomen, Managers, and Customers in American Department Stores, 1890–1940* (Urbana: University of Illinois Press, 1986).

14. Jessamyn West, *Double Discovery: A Journey* (New York: Harcourt Brace

Jovanovich, 1980), 46, 75, 112; Vincent Sheehan, *Dorothy and Red* (Boston: Houghton Mifflin, 1963), 167–168.

15. Dorothy Canfield Fisher, *The Home-Maker* (New York: Harcourt Brace and Co., 1924), 259.

16. Liddell, *Southern Accent*, 230–231; The Papers of Dorothy Weiner First, 92-M10, Schlesinger Library, Radcliffe College [cited hereafter as First Papers; the diary, a bound volume, is in a folder by itself and will appear with dates only], March 28 and April 5, 1929.

17. The Papers of Clara Savage Littledale, A-157, Schlesinger Library, Radcliffe College [hereafter cited as Littledale Papers], box 1, volume 16, March 14, 1914; volume 17, May 15, 1915.

18. The Papers of Ruth Raymond, 81-M18, Schlesinger Library, Radcliffe College [hereafter cited as Raymond Papers], box 1, volume 3, November 2, 1927; box 1, volume 13, October 3, 1935.

19. Emily Tapscott Clark, *Ingenue Among the Lions: The Letters of Emily Clark to Joseph Hergesheimer*, Gerald Langford, ed. (Austin: University of Texas Press, 1965), (July 4, 1921), 11–12.

20. Lavell Papers, folder 1, February 29, 1928.

21. The Papers of Winifred Lockhart Willis, MC369, Schlesinger Library, Radcliffe College [hereafter cited as Willis Papers], box 1, volume 2, December 2, 1924 and July 22, 1923.

22. Kasson, *Rudeness & Civility,* chapters 2 and 5; Karen Haltunnen, *Confidence Men and Painted Women: A Study of Middle-Class Culture in America, 1830–1870* (New Haven, CT: Yale University Press, 1982), chapter 1.

23. Stearns, *American Cool,* 274; John Dewey, "Individualism, Old and New," *New Republic* 61 (February 5, 1930): 295.

24. William McDougall, *Outline of Psychology* (New York: Charles Scribner's Sons, 1923), 436; John B. Watson, *Psychology from the Standpoint of a Behaviorist,* 397; John B. Watson, *Behaviorism* (Chicago: University of Chicago Press, 1924, 1930), 199, 274; Warren I. Sussman, " 'Personality' and the Making of Twentieth-Century Culture," in *Culture as History: The Transformation of American Society in the Twentieth Century* (New York: Pantheon Books, 1973, 1984), 271–285.

25. Lavell Papers, box 1, folder 2, July 27, 1930.

26. Anne Morrow Lindbergh, *Bring Me a Unicorn: Diaries and Letters of Anne Morrow Lindbergh* (New York: Harcourt Brace Jovanovich, 1971), (November 1928), 240.

27. John Dewey, *Human Nature and Conduct: An Introduction to Social Psychology* (New York: Henry Holt and Co., 1922), 138.

28. Anne Morrow Lindbergh, *Hour of Gold, Hour of Lead: Diaries and Let-*

*ters of Anne Morrow Lindbergh, 1929–1932* (New York: Harcourt Brace Jovanovich, 1973), (January 13–14, 1930), 120.

29. The Papers of Dorothy Smith Dushkin, Sophia Smith Collection, Smith College [hereafter cited as Dushkin Papers], box 3, volume 2, February 10, 1930.

30. Gladys Hasty Carroll, *To Remember Forever: The Journal of a College Girl, 1922–1923* (Boston: Little, Brown and Co., 1963), 19–20.

31. The Papers of Gladys Bell Penrod, Indiana Country Historical and Genealogical Society, Indiana, PA [hereafter cited as Penrod Papers. The papers consist mainly of diaries in bound volumes and the citation will furnish the date. When an item other than a diary is used, we provide a brief description of the item.], November 1, 1925.

32. Alice Miller Mitchell, *Children and Movies* (Chicago: University of Chicago Press, 1929), 4–5; Edgar Dale, *The Content of Motion Pictures* (New York: MacMillan, 1935), 1.

33. West, *Double Discovery*, 47, 170.

34. Dushkin Papers, box 3, folder 2, January 16, 1935.

35. Sumiko Higashi, *Cecil B. DeMille and American Culture: The Silent Era* (Berkeley: University of California Press, 1994), 8–20.

36. Dushkin Papers, box 3, folder 1, February 20, 1926; Martha Lavell found "the chariot-race was the most exciting thing I've ever seen," Lavell Papers, box 1, folder 1, January 2, 1927.

37. Katharine Du Pre Lumpkin, *The Making of a Southerner* (New York: Knopf, 1946), 200.

38. Penrod Papers, September 27, 1919; on the impact of movies in the 1920s see Lary May, *Screening Out the Past: The Birth of Mass Culture and the Motion Picture Industry* (New York: Oxford University Press, 1980), 109–146. Roderick Nash's thesis in *Nervous Generation* is that Americans in the 1920s tended to hold onto earlier truths to help them deal with the clamor of the new culture.

39. Raymond Papers, box 1, volume 12, August 1934–June, 1935, 255–261; it is not clear if this was her movie attendance for five months or for one month. Lawrence Levine discusses the appropriation of mass culture materials in "The Folklore of Industrial Society: Popular Culture and Its Audience," *American Historical Review* 97 (December 1992): 1380–1392.

40. Emile Coué, *Self-Mastery through Conscious Autosuggestion* (New York: American Library Service, 1922); Lillian Roth, *I'll Cry Tomorrow* (New York: Frederick Fell, 1954), 42–43; Jane Sherman, *Soaring: The Diary and Letters of a Denishawn Dancer in the Far East, 1925–1926* (Middletown, CT: Wesleyan University Press, 1976), (December 29, 1925), 84; on the therapeutic culture see Donald Meyer, *The Positive Thinkers: Religion as*

*Pop Psychology from Mary Baker Eddy to Oral Roberts* (New York: Pantheon Books, 1965, 1980), 23–45; T. J. Jackson Lears, "From Salvation to Self-Realization: Advertising and the Therapeutic Roots of the Consumer Culture, 1880–1930," in Richard Wrightman Fox and T. J. Jackson Lears, eds., *The Culture of Consumption: Critical Essays in American History, 1880–1890* (New York: Pantheon, 1983), 1–38.

41.  Marjorie Kinnan Rawlings, *Selected Letters of Marjorie Kinnan Rawlings,* Gordon E. Bigelow and Laura V. Monti, eds. (Gainesville: University of Florida Press, 1983), (October 1918), 19–20.

42.  The Papers of Helen Howe, 77-M218, 78-M104, Schlesinger Library, Radcliffe College, box 1, folder 292, 14–15. [This memoir of Helen Howe's affair with John Marquand, the only item used from her papers, will hereafter appear as Howe Memoir.]

43.  Ione Robinson, *A Wall to Paint On* (New York: E. P. Dutton, 1946), (November 25, 1927), 26.

44.  Lavell Papers, box 1, volume 2, July 23, 1930.

45.  Raymond Papers, box 1, volume 1, June 30, 1925.

46.  First Papers, January 31, 1929.

47.  Dale Carnegie, *How to Win Friends and Influence People* (New York: Simon and Schuster, [1936] 1964), chapter 2, parts 3–6.

48.  George Herbert Mead, *Mind, Self, and Society: From the Standpoint of a Social Behaviorist*, Charles W. Morris, ed. (Chicago: University of Chicago Press, 1934, 1962), 135–144; Arthur Wallace Calhoun, "The Child as a Social Product," in V. F. Calverton and Samuel D. Schmalhausen, *The New Generation: The Intimate Problems of Modern Parents and Children* (New York: The Macauley Co., 1930), 74; Margaret Mead, *Letters from the Field, 1925–1975* (New York: Harper & Row, 1977), (December 11, 1925), 40.

49.  Sarbin, "Emotion and Act," 88–91, distinguishes between dramatistic rhetorical acts, in which the individual draws upon a wide range of cultural scripts for emotion, and dramaturgical acts, in which the individual shapes the script as demanded by the situation. Although we do not use these terms in our text, we take for granted that in recording their emotional experiences women engaged in both kinds of rhetorical acts.

50.  White, *Partridge in a Swamp*, 11; Sally Wood, ed., *The Southern Mandarins: Letters of Caroline Gordon to Sally Wood, 1924–1937* (Baton Rouge: Louisiana State University Press, 1984), 63, 81–82.

51.  Penrod papers, November 20, 1925.

52.  Clara Savage Littledale, "You and Your Worries," *Good Housekeeping* 75 (December 1922): 153–154; on emotional management see Arlie Russell Hochschild, *The Managed Heart: Commercialization of Human Feel-*

*ings* (Berkeley: University of California Press, 1983), 35–55 and Stearns, *American Cool*, chapter 8.

53. Dushkin Papers, box 3, folder 2, July 1929; Penrod Papers, September 24, 1927.

## Notes to Chapter 2

1. The Papers of Beth Twiggar Goff, 90-M130, 90-M8, Schlesinger Library, Radcliffe College [hereafter cited as Goff Papers], box 1, volume 1, February 19, 1928, February 24, 1928.

2. Warner Fabian, *Flaming Youth* (New York: Boni Liveright, 1923), 321. Fiction concerned with the new youth culture spanned the literary spectrum, including works as different as F. Scott Fitzgerald, *This Side of Paradise* (New York: Scribner, 1920) and Carman Barnes, *Schoolgirl* (New York: Horace Liveright, 1929).

3. Goff Papers, box 1, volume 1, March 1, 1928.

4. The gendered spheres of youth are discussed in Joseph F. Kett, *Rites of Passage: Adolescence in America 1790 to the Present* (New York: Basic Books, 1977), chapter 5; E. Anthony Rotundo, *American Manhood: Transformations in Masculinity from the Revolution to the Modern Era* (New York: Basic Books, 1993), 247–283; Carroll Smith-Rosenberg, "The Female World of Love and Ritual: Relations Between Women in Nineteenth-Century America," *Signs: Journal of Women in Culture and Society* 1 (Autumn 1975): 1–29; Ellen K. Rothman, *Hands and Hearts: A History of Courtship in America* (Cambridge, MA: Harvard University Press, 1987), 119–122.

5. Reed Ueda, *Avenues to Adulthood: The Origins of the High School and Social Mobility in an American Suburb* (Cambridge: Cambridge University Press, 1987), chapter 5, and 119–151; John Modell, *Into One's Own: From Youth to Adulthood in the United States, 1920–1975* (Berkeley: University of California Press, 1989), 79, points out that only 6.4 percent of seventeen-year-olds graduated from high school in 1900, but 50.8 percent by 1940; Kett, *Adolescence*, 245.

6. The Papers of Adele Siegel Rosenfeld, 90-M109, Schlesinger Library, Radcliffe College [hereafter cited as Rosenfeld Papers; all of the diaries are in box 2, so citations will include only the volume and date], volume 1, January 10, 1931; Ueda, *Avenues to Adulthood*, 119.

7. Kett, *Adolescence,* 215, 218–219, 235; Modell, *Into One's Own,* 119; Ueda, *Avenues to Adulthood,* 150–151.

8. Miriam Van Waters, *Youth in Conflict* (New York: Republic Publishing Co., 1925), 83; The Papers of Miriam Van Waters, Schlesinger Library,

Radcliffe College [hereafter cited as Van Waters Papers], box 1, volume 3, August 30, 1935.

9. M. V. O'Shea, *The Trend of the Teens* (Chicago: Frederick J. Drake and Co., 1920), 17.

10. Penrod Papers, May 11, 1926; Lavell Papers, box 1, volume 1, December 1927 undated.

11. Ann Marie Low, *Dust Bowl Diary* (Lincoln: University of Nebraska Press, 1984), 1.

12. The Papers of Harriet Louise Hardy, Schlesinger Library, Radcliffe College [hereafter cited as Hardy Papers], box 1, volume 3, June 15, 1933.

13. Ben B. Lindsey and Wainwright Evans, *The Revolt of Modern Youth* (New York: Boni and Liveright, 1925), 33; Robert Lynd, "Family Members as Consumers," *Annals of the American Academy of Political and Social Science* 160 (March 1932): 86–93; Gilman Ostrander, *American Civilization in the First Machine Age* (New York: Harper and Row, 1970), 21; Kenneth Kenniston, "Social Change and Youth in America," *Daedalus* (Winter 1962): 145–171; Stuart Ewen, *Captains of Consciousness: Advertising and the Social Roots of the Consumer Culture* (New York: McGraw-Hill, 1976), 139–143.

14. Pearl Buck, *My Several Worlds: A Personal Record* (New York: John Day Co., 1954), 92; Paula S. Fass, *The Damned and the Beautiful: American Youth in the 1920s* (New York: Oxford University Press, 1977), 220–233; Ostrander, *American Civilization,* 21.

15. Margaret Mead, *Blackberry Winter: My Earlier Years* (New York: William Morrow and Co., 1972), 95, 102–103.

16. Ilka Chase, *Past Imperfect* (Garden City, NY: Doubleday, Doran and Co., 1941), 51.

17. Viola C. White, *Partridge in a Swamp: The Journals of Viola C. White, 1918–1941* (Taftsville, VT: Countryman Press, 1979), (September 22, 1931), 126.

18. Fabian, *Flaming Youth*, 92; Viola White, *Partridge in a Swamp*, (December 3, 1922), 126; Peter N. Stearns, "Girls, Boys and Emotions: Redefinitions and Historical Change," *Journal of American History* 80 (June 1993): 28–32; Modell, *Into One's Own*, 112–113.

19. Caroline Gordon, *The Southern Mandarins: Letters of Caroline Gordon to Sally Wood, 1924-1937*, Sally Wood, ed. (Baton Rouge: Louisiana State University Press, 1984), Spring 1926, 25; Emily Tapscott Clark, *Ingenue Among the Lions: The Letters of Emily Clark to Joseph Hergesheimer*, Gerald Langford, ed. (Austin: University of Texas Press, 1965), April 1923, 136.

20. Dushkin Paper, box 3, folder 2, September 9, 1926.

21. Jane Sherman, *Soaring: The Diary and Letters of a Denishawn Dancer in*

*the Far East, 1925–1926* (Middletown, CT: Wesleyan University Press, 1976), April 19, 1926, 123.

22. Raymond Papers, box 1, volume 7, September 23, 1929, volume 4, January 12, 1929, volume 5, July 23, 1929.

23. Lavell Papers, box 1, volume 1, March 14, 1928, August 6, 1930.

24. Elizabeth Yates, *My Diary — My World* (Philadelphia: Westminster Press, 1981), (December 6, 1919), 55; Sherman, *Soaring*, (July 28, 1926), 181.

25. Mead, *Blackberry Winter*, 112; Penrod Papers, May 11, 1925; Raymond Papers, box 1, volume 4, January 4, 1928.

26. William I. Thomas, *The Unadjusted Girl: With Cases and Standpoint for Behavior Analysis* (Boston: Little, Brown and Co., 1923), 72; Linda W. Rosenzweig, *The Anchor of My Life: Middle-Class American Mothers and Daughters, 1880–1920* (New York: New York University Press, 1993), 22–23; Ruth M. Alexander, *The "Girl Problem": Female Sexual Delinquency in New York, 1900–1930* (Ithaca: Cornell University Press, 1995), 1–2; Carolyn Strange, *Toronto's Girl Problem: The Perils and Pleasures of the City, 1880–1930* (Toronto: University of Toronto Press, 1995), 9; Mary E. Odem, *Delinquent Daughters: Protecting and Policing Adolescent Female Sexuality in the United States, 1885–1920* (Chapel Hill: University of North Carolina, 1995), chapter 1.

27. Dorothy Dix (pseudonym), *Dorothy Dix — Her Book: Every-day Help for Every-day People* (New York: Funk and Wagnalls Co., 1926), 303; Louis Berman, *The Glands Regulating Personality: A Study of the Glands of Internal Secretion in Relation to the Types of Human Nature* (New York: MacMillan, 1922), 212; Hutchins Hapgood, *A Victorian in the Modern World* (New York: Harcourt Brace and Company, 1939), 501.

28. Lavell Papers, box 1, volume 1, January 8, 1928.

29. Jessamyn West, *Double Discovery: A Journey* (New York: Harcourt Brace Jovanovich, 1980), 271; Gordon, *Southern Mandarins*, (1925), 18.

30. Kett, *Adolescence*, 261, points out that necking and petting are in the youth vocabulary before 1920; Modell, *Into One's Own*, 89.

31. Ueda, *Avenues to Adulthood*, 147; Ellen K. Rothman, *Hands and Hearts: A History of Courtship in America* (Cambridge, MA: Harvard University Press, 1984), 205, points to the use of bicycles by the 1890s as a means for young couples to escape their homes. She gives the period of 1870 to 1920 as the time when Victorian courtship practices changed toward the modern version. The Papers of Hallie Ferguson Davis, Special Collections, Vassar College, personal memoir, p. 8.

32. Littledale Papers, box 1, volume 15, April 25, 1907.

33. The Papers of Doris Stevens, 76–246, Schlesinger Library, Radcliffe College [hereafter cited as Stevens Papers], box 6, "Chap Book". The "Chap Book" is not paginated.

34. Stevens Papers, box 6, volume 181, April 14, 1908, May 21, 1908, May 22, 1908.

35. Malcolm Cowley, *Exile's Return: A Literary Odyssey of the 1920s* (New York: Viking Press, 1934), 22; Cornelia Stratton Parker, "An American Idyll, I: Episodes in the Life of Carleton H. Parker," *Atlantic* (March 1919): 300.

36. Marjorie Kinnan Rawlings, *Selected Letters of Marjorie Kinnan Rawlings,* Gordon E. Bigelow and Laura V. Monti, eds. (Gainesville: University of Florida Press, 1983), (September 15, 1918), 18.

37. O'Shea, *The Trend of the Teens,* 105; Penrod Papers, diary for 1919.

38. Beth L. Bailey, *From Front Porch to Back Seat: Courtship in Twentieth-Century America* (Baltimore: Johns Hopkins University Press, 1988), 13–24, describes the date as it came into common practice among middle-class youth; Lindsey, *Revolt of Youth,* 25–26; Pamela Haag, "In Search of 'The Real Thing': Ideologies of Love, Modern Romance and Women's Sexual Subjectivity in the United States, 1920–1940," *Journal of the History of Sexuality* 2 (1992): 547–577.

39. Strange, *Toronto's Girl Problem,* 119–120; David Nasaw, *Going Out: The Rise and Fall of Public Amusements* (New York: Basic Books, 1993), 85; The Papers of Marion Taylor, A-86, Schlesinger Library, Radcliffe College [hereafter cited as Taylor Papers], box 1, volume 14, January 18 and 31, 1920.

40. Ione Robinson, *A Wall to Paint On* (New York: E. P. Dutton, 1946), (September 20, 1928), 46; Papers of Sarah Merry Bradley Gamble, MC368, Schlesinger Library, Radcliffe College [hereafter cited as Gamble Papers], box 8, volume 164, March 19, 1915; Modell, *Into One's Own,* 71–72; Lois Banner, *American Beauty* (New York: Knopf, 1983), 176.

41. Yates, *My Diary — My World* (December 31, 1921), 95; Dushkin Papers, box 3, folder 1, June 20, 1924; Rosenfeld Papers, volume 1, February 6, 1931; Low, *Dust Bowl Diary* (May 14, 1936), 145.

42. Herbert Blumer, *Movies and Conduct* (New York: MacMillan, 1933); Hedda Hopper, *From Under My Hat* (New York: Doubleday, 1952), 45.

43. Sherman, *Soaring,* (December 9 and 10, 1925), 66–67.

44. The Diary of Isabelle McNelis Sickler, Tyrone Historical Society, Tyrone, PA [hereafter cited as Sickler Diary], August 10, 1922.

45. Dushkin Papers, box 3, folder 1, June 20, 1924.

46. First Papers, March 6, 1929, April 22, 1929, December 16, 1929.

47. Rosenfeld Papers, volume 1, June 5, 1931, February 14, 1931.

48. First Papers, January 8 and 16, 1929, February 3 and 10, 1929, May 11, 1929.

49. Raymond Papers, box 1, volume 4, November 27 and 28, 1927.

50. Dushkin Papers, box 3, folder 1, August 21, 1924.

51. Anne Morrow Lindbergh, *Bring Me a Unicorn: Diaries and Letters of Anne Morrow Lindbergh* (New York: Harcourt Brace Jovanovich, 1971), (April 1928), 160–161.

52. Taylor Papers, box 1, volume 14, June 19 and 30, 1920.

53. Lavell Papers, volume 1, January 18, 1928, July 7, 1928; Taylor Papers, box 1, volume 14, January 9, 1925.

54. Taylor Papers, box 1, volume 14, January 9, 1925, February 21, 1924.

55. Dorothy Bromley and Florence Haxton Britten, *Youth and Sex: A Study of 1300 College Students* (New York: Harper and Brothers, 1938), 3; Ernest W. Burgess, "Sociological Aspects of the Sex Life of the Unmarried Adult," in Ira S. Wile, *The Sex Life of the Unmarried Adult: An Inquiry into and an Interpretation of Current Sex Practices* (New York: Vanguard, 1934), 138.

56. V. F. Calverton, *The Bankruptcy of Marriage* (New York: The Macauley Co., 1928), 92, quoting from *The New Student*.

57. Grace Elliott Loucks and Harry Bone, *The Sex Life of Youth* (New York: Association Press, 1929), 67–72; *Nation* remark from Burgess, "Sociological Aspects," 125.

58. Sherman, *Soaring*, (December 20, 1925), 78, (May 21, 1926), 148.

59. Lavell Papers, volume 2, February 12, 1930; Penrod Papers, April 9, 1925.

60. First Papers, February 17, 1929.

61. Rosenfeld Papers, volume 1, April 18, 1931, November 8, 1931 but on page for January 15, 1931.

62. Rosenfeld Papers, volume 1, May 1930, May 14, 1931.

63. Rosenfeld Papers, volume 1, November 2, 1931, December 4, 1931, August 1, 1931 but on page for July 6, 1931.

64. Karen Lystra, *Searching the Heart: Women, Men and Romantic Love in Nineteenth-Century America* (New York: Oxford University Press, 1989), 27, 42; Warren I. Sussman, " 'Personality' and the Making of Twentieth-Century Culture," in *Culture as History: The Transformation of American Society in the Twentieth Century* (New York: Pantheon Books, 1973, 1984), 271–285; T. J. Jackson Lears, *No Place of Grace: Antimodernism and the Transformation of American Culture, 1880–1929* (New York: Pantheon Books, 1981), 39; Philip Cushman, "Why the Self is Empty: Toward a Historically Situated Psychology," *American Psychologist* 45 (May 1990): 599–611; William H. Sheldon, "Social Traits and Morphologic Types," *Journal of Personnel Research* 6 (1927): 47–55; Ueda, *Avenues to Adulthood*, 132–136); Clark, *Ingenue Among the Lions*, (April 1923), 138; Robinson, *A Wall to Paint On*, (September 20, 1928), 45.

65. Vincent Sheehan, *Dorothy and Red* (Boston: Houghton Mifflin, 1963), 229.

66. Yates, *My Diary — My World*, (April 26, 1918), 27; Ueda, *Avenues to*

*Adulthood*, 129; Rosenfeld Papers, volume 1, April 7, 1936, 35; Gamble Papers, box 8, volume 163, May 3 and 30, 1912.

67. Ueda, *Avenues to Adulthood*, 129; Penrod Papers, October 21, 1922.

68. Gamble Papers, box 8, volume 163, May 3, 1912.

69. Raymond Papers, box 1, volume 3, May–September 1927; volume 8, May–August 1930, August 8, 1930.

70. Penrod Papers, January 14, 1924; compare Robert Latou Dickinson and Lura Ella Beam, *A Thousand Marriages: A Medical Study of Sex Adjustment* (Baltimore: Williams and Wilkins Co., 1931), 21; T. J. Jackson Lears, *Fables of Abundance: A Cultural History of Advertising in America* (New York: Basic Books, 1994), 69.

71. Raymond Papers, box 1, volume 3, October 16, 1927.

72. Elinor Glyn, *The Philosophy of Love* (New York: Authors' Press, 1923), 146; Lavell Papers, volume 1, July 7, 1928; Banner, *American Beauty*, 206–207.

73. I. M. Hotep (pseudonym), *Love and Happiness: Intimate Problems of the Modern Woman* (New York: Knopf, 1938), 133.

74. Sherman, *Soaring*, (May 10, 1926), 138; Dushkin Papers, box 3, folder 1, March 1, 1920; Gordon, *Southern Mandarins*, (Spring 1932), 101.

75. Gladys Hasty Carroll, *To Remember Forever: The Journal of a College Girl, 1922–1923* (Boston: Little Brown and Co., 1963), 254.

76. Phyllis Blanchard, *The Adolescent Girl: A Study from the Psychoanalytic Viewpoint* (New York: Moffat Yard and Co., 1920), 50.

77. Clara Savage Littledale, "You and Your Worries," *Good Housekeeping* 75 (December 1922): 152; Harvey Green, *The Uncertainty of Everyday Life, 1915–1945* (New York: Harper Collins, 1992), 176.

78. Elinor Glyn, "*It*" (New York: The Macauley Co., 1927), 46.

79. Green, *Uncertainty*, 176; T. J. Jackson Lears, *Fables of Abundance: A Cultural History of Advertising in America* (New York: Basic Books, 1994), 171–172; Margaret Sanger, *Happiness in Marriage* [1926] (Elmsford, NY: Maxwell Reprint Co., 1969), 55.

80. First Papers, January 17, 1929; Taylor Papers, box 1, volume 14, May 6, 1920; Yates, *My Diary — My World*, (January 5, 1921), 81.

81. Goff Papers, box 1, volume 1, June 25, 1926, volume 10, September 19, 1928.

82. Viola Goode Liddell, *With a Southern Accent* (Norman: University of Oklahoma Press, 1948), 80–81.

83. Goff Papers, box 1, volume 1, February 25, 1928.

84. H. D. Hill, "Wanted: Personality," *Atlantic Monthly* 143 (March 1929): 352; "*It*" (1927); A. A. Roback, "Personality: The Very Crux of Human Relationships," *The Century* 119 (October 1929): 98.

85. Hotep, *Love and Happiness,* 74.
86. First Papers, January 17, 1929.
87. Lillian Roth, *I'll Cry Tomorrow* (New York: Frederick Fell, 1954), 53; Raymond Papers, box 1, volume 5, June 21, 1929.
88. Blumer, *Movies and Conduct,* 154.
89. Martha Lavell read this in a column by Dorothy Dix, Lavell Papers, volume 1, April 2, 1928.
90. Raymond Papers, box 1, volume 7, February 28, 1929.
91. Taylor Papers, box 1, volume 5, July 26, 1915; volume 12, September 1918 undated.
92. First Papers, February 26, 1929.
93. First Papers, February 23, 1929.
94. Modell, *Into One's Own,* 104; Jessie Lloyd O'Conner, Harvey O'Conner, and Susan M. Bowler, *Harvey and Jessie: A Couple of Radicals* (Philadelphia: Temple University Press, 1988), 79; Raymond Papers, box 1, volume 4, June 17, 1928.
95. Chase, *Past Imperfect,* 47–49.
96. First Papers, April 4, 1929.
97. First Papers, February 1 and 21, 1929.
98. Floyd Dell, *Love in the Machine Age: A Psychological Study of the Transition from Patriarchal Society* (New York: Farrar and Rinehart, 1930), 405; Fass, *Damned and Beautiful,* 56–57.
99. Goff Papers, box 1, volume 10, September 20, 1928.
100. Goff Papers, box 1, volume 5, June 12, 1928, February 27, 1928; volume 24, October 11, 1930; volume 24, September 22, 1929.
101. Goff Papers, box 1, volume 1, February 23, 1928; volume 11, September 21, 1928; volume 2, Late March 1928, March 16, 1928, volume 12, October 21, 1928.
102. Goff Papers, box 1, volume 2, March 15, 1928; volume 11, September 16, 1928; volume 13, January 1, 1929; volume 12, November 2 and 3, 1928,; volume 16, February 2, 1929.
103. Goff Papers box 1, volume 2, November 2, 1928; volume 1, February 19, 1928; volume 24, September 23, 1929; volume 12, August 10, 1928; In a personal communication to the authors, Mrs. Goff emphasized the social and personal satisfactions of necking, as opposed to sexual desire. "When a boy 'necked' me what I enjoyed was his intense interest." She became genuinely sensually alive only much later in life.
104. Fabian, *Flaming Youth,* 99; Kevin White, *The First Sexual Revolution: The Emergence of Male Heterosexuality in Modern America* (New York: New York University Press, 1993), chapter 1.
105. Goff Papers, box 1, volume 24, September 18, 1929.

106. Goff Papers, box 1, volume 14, December 19, 1928; volume 24, October 11, 1930; volume 1, February 25, 1928; Haag, "In Search of 'The Real Thing,' " 547–577.

107. Taylor Papers, box 1, volume 14, February 20, 1923; Modell, *Into One's Own,* 95–96.

108. Katherine Bement Davis, *Factors in the Sex Life of Twenty-Two Hundred Women* (New York: Harper and Brothers, 1929), 247–250; Thomas, *Unadjusted Girl,* 95.

109. Steven Seidman, *Romantic Longings: Love in America, 1830–1980* (New York: Routledge, 1991); Lillian Faderman, *Odd Girls and Twilight Lovers: A History of Lesbian Life in Twentieth-Century America* (New York: Columbia University Press, 1991), 52, 88–90, 99; Bromley and Britten, *Youth and Sex,* 118, but 120–121 makes this ambiguous; George Chauncey Jr., "From Sexual Inversion to Homosexuality: The Changing Medical Conceptualization of Female Deviance," in Kathy Peiss and Christina Simmons, eds., *Passion and Power: Sexuality in History* (Philadelphia: Temple University Press, 1989), 107.

110. Blanchard, *The Adolescent Girl,* 169; Mead, *Blackberry Winter,* 112–113.

111. Lavell Papers, volume 1, April 2, 1928, August 16, 1929; volume 2, May 1, 1931.

112. Dushkin Papers, box 3, folder 2, November 14, 1929, January 15, 1930, May 10, 1933, April 14, 1935.

113. The Papers of Azalia Peet, Sophia Smith Collection, Smith College [hereafter cited as Peet Papers], December 14, 1913.

114. Rosenfeld Papers, volume 1, January 8, 1931.

115. Raymond Papers, box 1, volume 4, March 30, 1928.

116. Goff Papers, box 1, volume 24, November 1, 1929. In a personal communication to the authors, Mrs. Goff has written that she and Peggy were sophisticated; they knew about female homosexuality and Beth had read Radclyffe Hall's *The Well of Loneliness* (1928). But they never thought of themselves as lesbians or believed that anything regarding homosexuality applied to them.

117. Davis, *Factors in the Sex Life,* 251; Loucks and Bone, *Sex Life of Youth,* 49–51; Blanchard, *Adolescent Girl,* 54.

118. Goff Papers, box 1, volume 28, October 3, 1930.

119. Loucks and Bone, *Sex Life of Youth,* 50–51.

120. Taylor Papers, box 1, volume 5, March 15, 1915; volume 4, April 13, 1915.

121. Taylor Papers, box 1, March 22, 1915; volume 9 typescript, February 1918 undated.

122. Blanchard, *Adolescent Girl,* 54; Goff Papers, box 1, volume 12, October 21, 1928; Taylor Papers, box 1, volume 7, April 28, 1916.

123. Taylor Papers, box 1, volume 4, April 6, 1915; volume 9, February 1918, January 26, 1918, March 1918.

124. Taylor Papers, box 1, volume 12, May 1919 undated; volume 9, September 19, 1917, January 2, 1918, April 1918.

125. Taylor Papers, box 1, volume 14, October 6, 1919, January 1922; volume 15, January 9, 1925.

126. Taylor Papers, box 1, volume 14, January 4, 1921, January 16, 1922.

127. Taylor Papers, box 1, volume 14, January 4, 1921.

128. Taylor Papers, box 1, volume 5, April 22, 1915.

*Notes to Chapter 3*

1. Penrod Papers, September 27, 1919, November 17, 1919.

2. James Reed, *The Birth Control Movement and American Society: From Private Vice to Public Virtue* (Princeton: Princeton University Press, 1984), 165; Robert Latou Dickinson and Lura Ella Beam, *The Single Woman: A Medical Study in Sex Education* (Baltimore: Williams and Wilkins, 1934), chapter 16, 405, 432; *see also* Robert Latou Dickinson and Lura Ella Beam, *A Thousand Marriages: A Medical Study of Sex Adjustment* (Baltimore: Williams and Wilkins Co., 1931).

3. Dickinson and Beam, *Single Woman*, 128, 204–205, 211.

4. John Modell, *Into One's Own: From Youth to Adulthood in the United States, 1920–1975* (Berkeley: University of California Press, 1989), 83. Only 14 percent of women who graduated from high school married by age eighteen; only 15 percent of high school graduates did *not* work before marriage.

5. Zelda Fitzgerald, "Eulogy on the Flapper," *The Collected Writings,* Matthew J. Bruccoli, ed. (New York: Collier Books, 1991), 391.

6. Phyllis Blanchard, "The Flapper and Social Evolution," *Journal of Applied Sociology* 10 (1926–1927): 440–445. Historians today distinguish between the flapper and the new woman. Commentators in the 1920s did not always make this distinction. June B. West, "The 'New Woman,' " *Twentieth Century Literature* 1 (July 1955): 55–68.

7. Ilka Chase, *Past Imperfect* (Garden City, NY: Doubleday, Doran and Co., 1941), 51; Gamble Papers, box 8, folder 160, 22; Linda W. Rosenzweig, *The Anchor of My Life: Middle-Class American Mothers and Daughters, 1880–1920* (New York: New York University Press, 1993), 92; Elizabeth Yates, *My Diary — My World* (Philadelphia: Westminster Press, 1981), 102–103.

8. Stanley Coben, *Rebellion Against Victorianism: The Impetus for Cultural Change in 1920s America* (New York: Oxford University Press, 1991), 49; Dorothy Bromley and Florence Haxton Britten, *Youth and Sex: A*

*Study of 1300 College Students* (New York: Harper and Brothers, 1938), 8; Steven Seidman, *Romantic Longings: Love in America, 1830–1980* (New York: Routledge, 1991), 68; Anne Morrow Lindbergh, *Bring Me a Unicorn: Diaries and Letters of Anne Morrow Lindbergh* (New York: Harcourt Brace Jovanovich, 1971), 6–7.

9. Gladys Hasty Carroll, *To Remember Forever: The Journal of a College Girl, 1922–1923* (Boston: Little Brown and Co., 1963), 72–73.

10. Lavell Papers, volume 1, October 3, 1927, December 1927 undated.

11. Carroll, *To Remember Forever*, 80, 82; William H. Chafe, *The Paradox of Change: American Women in the 20th Century* (New York: Oxford University Press, 1991), 70, 101.

12. "Clara Savage Littledale," in Barbara Sicherman and Carol Hurd Green, eds., *Notable American Women: The Modern Period* (Cambridge, MA: Harvard University Press, 1980), 421–423; Littledale Papers, box 1, volume 16, January 6, 1914; March 23, 1914, May 22, 1914, December 4, 1914.

13. Littledale Papers, box 1, volume 16, January 10, 1914.

14. Bromley and Britten, *Youth and Sex*, 51; Carroll Smith-Rosenberg, "The New Woman as Androgyne: Social Disorder and Gender Crisis, 1870–1936," in *Disorderly Conduct: Visions of Gender in Victorian America* (New York: Oxford University Press, 1985), 253; Rosalind Rosenberg, *Beyond Separate Spheres: Intellectual Roots of Modern Feminism* (New Haven, CT: Yale University Press, 1982), 189–197; William H. Chafe, *The American Woman: Her Changing Social, Economic, and Political Roles, 1920–1970* (London: Oxford University Press, 1972), 102, 111–115; William I. Thomas, *The Unadjusted Girl: With Cases and Standpoint for Behavior Analysis* (Boston: Little Brown and Co., 1923), 325–326, 328; Paula S. Fass, *The Damned and the Beautiful: American Youth in the 1920s* (New York: Oxford University Press, 1977); Sheila Rothman, *Woman's Proper Place: A History of Changing Ideals and Practices, 1870 to the Present* (New York: Basic Books, 1978), 180–184; Pearl Buck, *My Several Worlds: A Personal Record* (New York: John Day Co., 1954), 91.

15. Elinor Glyn, *The Philosophy of Love* (New York: Authors' Press, 1923); Anne Hirst, *Get Your Man — and Hold Him* (New York: H. C. Kinsey, 1937), 5.

16. Paul Popenoe, *Modern Marriage: A Handbook for Men*, 2nd ed. (New York: MacMillan, 1925, 1940), 121–123, 135.

17. Herbert Blumer, *Movies and Conduct* (New York: MacMillan, 1933), 17, 88–89.

18. Glyn, *Philosophy*, 187; Elinor Glyn, *"It"* (New York: The Macauley Co., 1927), 10.

19. Roderick Nash, *The Nervous Generation: American Thought, 1917–1930*

(Chicago: Rand McNally and Co., 1971), 137; Roland Marchand, *Advertising the American Dream: Making Way for Modernity, 1920–1940* (Berkeley: University of California Press, 1985), 53–62.

20. Peet Papers, December 14, 1913, September 17, 1915.
21. Yates, *My Diary — My World,* June 28, 1919, 49–50; May 16, 1925, 175.
22. Lavell Papers, volume 1, January 8, 1928.
23. Jane Sherman, *Soaring: The Diary and Letters of a Denishawn Dancer in the Far East, 1925–1926* (Middletown, CT: Wesleyan University Press, 1976), July 9, 1926, 173; December 30, 1926, 245.
24. Raymond Papers, box 1, volume 3, October 12, 1927.
25. Howe Memoir, box 1, folder 292, 20.
26. Ione Robinson, *A Wall to Paint On* (New York: E. P. Dutton, 1946), July 30, 1929, 102; August 10, 1929, 104–105.
27. Carroll, *To Remember Forever,* 36–38, 193, 260.
28. Vincent Sheehan, *Dorothy and Red* (Boston: Houghton Mifflin, 1963), quote from September 9, 1927, 33, 15.
29. Dushkin Papers, box 3, folder 2, May 27, 1930; Emily Tapscott Clark, *Ingenue Among the Lions: The Letters of Emily Clark to Joseph Hergesheimer,* Gerald Langford, ed. (Austin: University of Texas Press, 1965) (February 1923), 118; Howe Memoir, box 1, folder 292, 57; Raymond Papers, box 1, volume 4, December 28, 1928; Ann Marie Low, *Dust Bowl Diary* (Lincoln: University of Nebraska Press, 1984), (July 9, 1934), 100.
30. Willis Papers, box 1, volume 2, July 15, 17, 18, 22, 1923, September 9, 1923.
31. Viola C. White, *Partridge in a Swamp: The Journals of Viola C. White, 1918–1941* (Taftsville, VT: Countryman Press, 1979), (August 21, 1918), 28; (March 11, 1932), 131; (January 4, 1931), 118; (January 11, 1931), 119; Zelda Fitzgerald to F. Scott Fitzgerald, "Late summer/early fall 1930" in *Collected Writings,* 456.
32. Littledale Papers, box 1, volume 18, October 3, 1916, October 10, 1917 on pages for January 19 and 20, 1916.
33. Hirst, *Get Your Man,* 42–52; Clara Savage Littledale, "If Your Heart is Broken," *Good Housekeeping* 75 (September 1922): 23, 168–172.
34. Modell, *Into One's Own,* 105–106; Grace Elliott Loucks and Harry Bone, *The Sex Life of Youth* (New York: Association Press, 1929), 34; Floyd Dell, *Love in the Machine Age: A Psychological Study of the Transition from Patriarchal Society* (New York: Farrar and Rinehart, 1930), 343.
35. Peet Papers, April 6, 1913.
36. "Island communities" comes from Robert H. Wiebe, *The Search for Order, 1877–1920* (New York: Hill and Wang, 1967); T. J. Jackson Lears has discussed the impact of modern culture on the self in various works, including "From Salvation to Self-Realization: Advertising and the Thera-

peutic Roots of the Consumer Culture, 1880–1930," in *The Culture of Consumption: Critical Essays in American History, 1880–1890* (New York: Pantheon, 1983), 1–38 and *Fables of Abundance: A Cultural History of Advertising in America* (New York: Basic Books, 1994), 161.

37. White, *Partridge in a Swamp* (June 26, 1926), 88. Social scientists, including historians, have characterized this loss of firm values and confidence in a single self-understanding as fragmented, mutable, saturated, or empty. Thom Verhave and Willen van Hoorn, "The Temporalization of the Self," in Kenneth J. Gergen and Mary M. Gergen, eds., *Historical Social Psychology* (Hillsdale, NJ: Lawrence Erlbaum Associates, 1984), 325–346; Kenneth J. Gergen, *The Saturated Self: Dilemmas of Identity in Contemporary Society* (New York: Basic Books, 1991), 44–49; Philip Cushman, "Why the Self Is Empty: Toward a Historically Situated Psychology," *American Psychologist* 45 (May 1990): 599–611.

38. Lindbergh, *Bring Me a Unicorn*, (September 1922), 6; (May 18, 1926), 30–31; (Spring 28 undated), 170–171; Yates, *My Diary — My World*, (June 11–15, 1920), 64–66.

39. Low, *Dust Bowl Diary*, (May 26, 1930), 37; Robinson, *Wall to Paint On*, (December 2, 1927), 27–28; (May 10, 1928), 33.

40. Lavell Papers, volume 2, July 12, 1930; Dushkin Papers, box 3, folder 2, August 12, 1926; Jessamyn West, *Double Discovery: A Journey* (New York: Harcourt Brace Jovanovich, 1980), 218, 247.

41. White, *Partridge in a Swamp*, (June 24, 1928), 101; Yates, *My Diary — My World*, (October 26, 1923), 134; Lella Secor, *Lella Secor: A Diary in Letters, 1915–1922*, Barbara Moench Florenz, ed. (New York: Burt Franklin and Co., 1978), (March 26, 1916), 61.

42. Lella Secor, *Lella Secor*, 140; Low, *Dust Bowl Diary*, (May 7, 1934), 95, (January 2, 1937), 174; William H. Chafe, *The Paradox of Change: American Women in the 20th Century* (New York: Oxford University Press, 1991), 109–111.

43. Littledale Papers, box 1, volume 16, April 13, 1914; Clara Savage Littledale, "Can a Girl Afford to Marry?" *Good Housekeeping* 73 (November 1921): 15ff; Dickinson and Beam, *Single Woman*, 133.

44. Ben B. Lindsey and Wainwright Evans, *The Revolt of Modern Youth* (New York: Boni and Liveright, 1925), 121; Loucks and Bone, *Sex Life of Youth*, 25.

45. Dorothy Dix (pseudonym), *Dorothy Dix — Her Book: Every-day Help for Every-day People* (New York: Funk and Wagnalls Co., 1926), 303; Louis Berman, *The Glands Regulating Personality: A Study of the Glands of Internal Secretion in Relation to the Types of Human Nature* (New York: MacMillan, 1922), 1–2; Don Cabot McCowan, *Love and Life: Sex Urge and Its Consequences* (Chicago: Pascal Covici, 1928), 171 on glands; Ed-

ward K. Strong Jr., *The Psychology of Selling and Advertising* (New York: McGraw-Hill), 1925, 145–158; Daniel Starch, *Principles of Advertising* (New York: McGraw-Hill, 1923) chapter 12; Albert T. Poffenberg, *Psychology in Advertising* (Chicago: A. W. Shaw, 1925), 25–26.

46. Joseph Jastrow, "The Implications of Sex," in V. F. Calverton and Samuel D. Schmalhausen, eds., *The Next Generation* (New York: The Macauley Co., 1930), 130; Glyn, *Philosophy*, 78, 107.

47. Joseph F. Kett, *Rites of Passage: Adolescence in America 1790 to the Present* (New York: Basic Books, 1977), 261; Dickinson and Beam, *Single Woman,* chapter 16; Bromley and Britten, *Youth and Sex,* 3–5.

48. Phyllis Blanchard, *The Adolescent Girl: A Study from the Psychoanalytic Viewpoint* (New York: Moffat Yard and Co., 1920), 178; Dickinson and Beam, *Thousand Marriages,* 76–77 and *Single Woman,* 405, 432; Elton Mayo, "Should Marriage be Monotonous?" *Harpers Monthly* 151 (September 1925): 425–426; McCowan, *Love and Life,* 118.

49. Lary May, *Screening Out the Past: The Birth of Mass Culture and the Motion Picture Industry* (New York: Oxford University Press, 1980), 142; Elaine Tyler May, *Great Expectations: Marriage and Divorce in Post-Victorian America* (Chicago: University of Chicago Press, 1980), 101; Pamela Haag, "In Search of 'The Real Thing': Ideologies of Love, Modern Romance and Women's Sexual Subjectivity in the United States, 1920–1940," *Journal of the History of Sexuality* 2 (1992): 547–577; First Papers, May 14, 1929; West, *Double Discovery,* 229.

50. Sherman, *Soaring,* (July, 16, 1926), 176; White, *Partridge in a Swamp,* (October 12, 1918), 29; West, *Double Discovery,* 102.

51. Willis Papers, box 1, volume 2, October 14, 1923, September 27, 1923.

52. Dushkin Papers, box 3, folder 1, July 1925; folder 2, December 31, 1926, March 14, 1930.

53. Littledale Papers, box 1, volume 18, October 8–9, 1916.

54. Quote from Edward Carpenter, *Love's Coming-of-Age: A Series of Papers on the Relation of the Sexes* (London: George Allen and Unwin Ltd., 1896), 16. The demand for Carpenter's work was apparently greatest during the 1910s, with five reprints of the work between 1909 and 1919. Littledale Papers, box 1, volume 17, November 30, 1915; volume 18, October 8–9, 1916.

55. Dickinson and Beam, *Thousand Marriages*, 93; Dushkin Papers, box 3, folder 2, October 22, 1929; Howe Memoir, box 1, folder 292, 54.

56. Willis Papers, box 1, volume 2, November 30, 1923, November 26, 1923, March 11, 1924.

57. Dickinson and Beam, *Single Woman,* 135; see Goff Papers, box 1, volume 24; Bromley and Britten, *Youth and Sex,* 70; Marjorie Kinnan Rawlings, *Selected Letters of Marjorie Kinnan Rawlings,* Gordon E. Bigelow and

Laura V. Monti, eds. (Gainesville: University of Florida Press, 1983), (December 15, 1918), 30, 27.

58. Penrod Papers, June 25, 1924, March 5 and 6, 1922.

59. Penrod Papers, April 29, 1922, May 13, 1922.

60. Dickinson and Beam, *Single Woman,* 130–131; Modell, *Into One's Own,* 144–146.

61. Penrod Papers, November 16, 1922, December 24, 1922, December 31, 1919, June 17, 1922. The decision between two lovers, one wealthy and one poor, was also the plot of a novel that Gladys read, though not until after she resolved her situation with Red and Junior.

62. Marie Corelli, *The Life Everlasting: A Reality of Romance* (New York: Grosset and Dunlap, 1911), 73.

63. Penrod Papers, July 13, 1922, March 26, 1922, May 13, 1922.

64. Penrod Papers, July 26, 1924, March 18, 1925, March 4, 1923. Clelia Duel Mosher, who conducted one of the earliest sex surveys, only managed to express her passion in letters to an imaginary friend. Rosenberg, *Beyond Separate Spheres,* 205.

65. Penrod Papers, November 16 and 20, 1924, December 1, 1924, April 1, 1925.

66. Penrod Papers, following April 22, 1924, January 11, 1921.

67. Penrod Papers, November 1922 undated.

68. Corelli, *Life Everlasting,* 21, 96–100, 135–137.

69. Penrod Papers, June 20, 1922, May 30, 1922; January–February 1924, notebook first page; October 27, 1925.

70. Penrod papers, May 18, 1924, February 11, 1925, March 1, 1925, April 21, 1925; Corelli, *Life Everlasting,* 378.

71. Penrod Papers, November 1922 undated, April 9, 1925, July 14, 18, and 21, 1922.

72. Penrod Papers, December 10 and 12, 1924.

73. Dickinson and Beam, *Single Woman,* 428, 166, 210–211.

74. I. M. Hotep (pseudonym), *Love and Happiness: Intimate Problems of the Modern Woman* (New York: Knopf, 1938), 46; Glyn, *Philosophy,* 44–45; McCowan, *Love and Life,* 128–133, says homosexuality is not a perversion, but he discusses it in a chapter on sexual perversions. He believed homosexuals were sexually unbalanced and could benefit from advances in the endocrine field. Jeffrey Weeks, "Movements of Affirmation: Sexual Meanings and Homosexual Identities," in Kathy Peiss and Christina Simmons, eds., *Passion and Power: Sexuality in History* (Philadelphia: Temple University Press, 1989), 70–86.

75. Harriet Louise Hardy obituary, *Boston Globe,* October 15, 1993.

76. Hardy Papers, box 1, volume 2, September 11 and 17, 1933, March 13, 1933, April 25, 1934.

77. Hardy Papers, box 1, December 4, 1934, March 30, 1932, September 24, 1931, April 25, 1934.

78. Hardy Papers, box 1, volume 2, December 30, 1931, October 22, 1931, October 17, 1932.

79. Hardy Papers, box 1, volume 2, February 12, 1932, October 18, 1931, April 24, 1932, February 27, 1933; Weeks, "Movements of Affirmation" deals with the male versus female characteristics of lesbians.

80. Hardy Papers, box 1, volume 2, January 11, 1932, October 17, 1932, April 24, 1932, December 11, 1931, February 27, 1933.

81. Hardy Papers, box 1, volume 2, April 17, 1932.

82. Hardy Papers, box 1, volume 6, October 22, 1935, December 4, 1934, February 23, 1935.

83. Hardy Papers, box 1, volume 4 November 2, 1934, May 29, 1935; volume 5, January 5 and 23, 1936.

84. Harriet Louise Hardy, *Challenging Man-Made Disease* (New York: Praeger, 1983), 24.

85. Hardy, *Challenging Man-Made Disease*, chapters 4, 10, 12.

### Notes to Chapter 4

Parts of this chapter appeared in a different form in *An Emotional History of the United States*, Peter N. Stearns and Jan Lewis, eds. (New York: New York University Press, 1998).

1. Willis Papers, box 1, volume 10, July 22, 1924.

2. Willis Papers, box 1, volume 10, February 24, 1926.

3. Beatrice Burton, *The Flapper Wife* (New York: Grosset and Dunlap, 1925), 8, 344.

4. V. F. Calverton, *The Bankruptcy of Marriage* (New York: The Macauley Co., 1928); Viola C. White, *Partridge in a Swamp: The Journals of Viola C. White, 1918–1941* (Taftsville, VT: Countryman Press, 1979), (June 26, 1926), 88; "The Rocky Road from the Altar," *Literary Digest* 77 (February 26, 1927): 31–32; Lary May, *Screening Out the Past: The Birth of Mass Culture and the Motion Picture Industry* (New York: Oxford University Press, 1980), 142.

5. Samuel D. Schmalhausen, "The Sexual Revolution," in V. F. Calverton and S. D. Schmalhausen, eds., *Sex in Civilization* (New York: The Macauley Co., 1929), 406 (discusses the "new morality" on page 401) and "Family Life: A Study in Pathology," in Calverton and Samuel D. Schmalhausen, eds. *The Next Generation* (New York: The Macauley Co., 1930), 276; G. V. Hamilton, *A Research in Marriage* (New York: Medical Research Press, 1929), 3.

6. Penrod Papers, January 12, 1926.
7. Sidney Howard, *The Silver Cord: A Comedy in Three Acts* (New York: Charles Scribners Sons, 1927), 194.
8. William A. Alcott, *The Moral Philosophy of Courtship and Marriage* (Boston: John P. Jewett, 1857), 43–44; Karen Lystra, *Searching the Heart: Women, Men and Romantic Love in Nineteenth-Century America* (New York: Oxford University Press, 1989), 192–194; James Reed, *The Birth Control Movement and American Society: From Private Vice to Public Virtue* (Princeton: Princeton University Press, 1984), 20–33; Kevin White, *The First Sexual Revolution: The Emergence of Male Heterosexuality in Modern America* (New York: New York University Press, 1993), 172–174.
9. Carroll Smith-Rosenberg, "The Female World of Love and Ritual: Relations Between Women in Nineteenth-Century America," *Signs: Journal of Women in Culture and Society* 1 (Autumn 1975): 1–29; E. Anthony Rotundo, *American Manhood: Transformation in Masculinity from the Revolution to the Modern Era* (New York: Basic Books, 1993), 239–240; Arthur W. Calhoun, *A Social History of the American Family*, volume 2, *From Independence through the Civil War* (New York: Barnes and Noble, 1918), 83.
10. Steven Mintz and Susan Kellogg, *Domestic Revolutions: A Social History of American Family Life* (New York: Free Press, 1988), 108–109; see also Reed, *Birth Control*, chapter 5; Peter N. Stearns, "Girls, Boys and Emotions: Redefinitions and Historical Change," *Journal of American History* 80 (June 1993): 39–53; Reed Ueda, *Avenues to Adulthood: The Origins of the High School and Social Mobility in an American Suburb* (Cambridge: Cambridge University Press, 1987); John Modell, *Into One's Own: From Youth to Adulthood in the United States, 1920–1975* (Berkeley: University of California Press, 1989), 105–106; Linda W. Rosenzweig, *The Anchor of My Life: Middle-Class American Mothers and Daughters, 1880–1920* (New York: New York University Press, 1993), 6.
11. John C. Burnham, "The Progressive Era Revolution in American Attitudes toward Sex," *Journal of American History* (March 1973): 885–908; Edward Carpenter, *Love's Coming-of-Age: A Series of Papers on the Relation of the Sexes* (London: George Allen and Unwin Ltd., 1896), 72–80; Ellen Key, *Love and Marriage*, Arthur G. Chater, trans. (New York: G. P. Putnam's Sons, 1911), 49–55; For recent evaluations of the sexual changes of the early twentieth century, see: Carl N. Degler, "What Ought To Be and What Was: Women's Sexuality in the Nineteenth Century," *American Historical Review* 79 (December 1974): 1467–1490 and Rosalind Rosenberg, *Beyond Separate Spheres: Intellectual Roots of Modern Feminism* (New Haven, CT: Yale University Press, 1982), 179, 185, 204.

12. Mary Ware Dennett, "Sex Enlightenment for Civilized Youth," in Calverton and Schmalhausen, *Sex in Civilization*, 101; Floyd Dell, *Love in the Machine Age: A Psychological Study of the Transition from Patriarchal Society* (New York: Farrar and Rinehart, 1930), 341, 403 132.

13. John B. Watson, "After the Family—What?" in Calverton and Schmalhausen, *Next Generation*, 56–60.

14. Sophonisba P. Breckinridge, *Women in the Twentieth Century: A Study of their Political, Social and Economic Activities* (New York: McGraw-Hill Book Co., 1933), 101; V. F. Calverton, *The Bankruptcy of Marriage* (New York: The Macauley Co., 1928), 61–62; Charlotte Perkins Gilman, "Sex and Race Progress," in Calverton and Schmalhausen, *Sex in Civilization*, 123; Margaret Sanger, "The Civilizing Force of Birth Control," in Calverton and Schmalhausen, *Sex in Civilization*, 529; Lorinne Pruette, "The Flapper," in Calverton and Schmalhausen, *Next Generation*, 587.

15. Ernest R. Groves, Edna L. Skinner, and Sadie J. Swenson, *The Family and Its Relationships* (Chicago: J. B. Lippincott, 1932), 165, 174.

16. Anne Morrow Lindbergh, *Hour of Gold, Hour of Lead: Diaries and Letters of Anne Morrow Lindbergh, 1929–1932* (New York: Harcourt Brace Jovanovich, 1973), (July 2, 1929), 53; (August 6, 1929), 64; Anne Morrow Lindbergh, *Bring Me a Unicorn: Diaries and Letters of Anne Morrow Lindbergh* (New York: Harcourt Brace Jovanovich, 1971), (March 1927), 69.

17. Sickler Diary, September 13, 1922; Lella Secor, *Lella Secor, A Diary in Letters, 1915–1922,* Barbara Moench Florenz, ed. (New York: Burt Franklin and Co., 1978), (October 1, 1917), 155; Ione Robinson, *A Wall to Paint On* (New York: E. P. Dutton, 1946), (December 2, 1929), 122–123.

18. Hedda Hopper, *From Under My Hat* (Garden City, NY: Doubleday and Co., 1952), 20.

19. Vincent Sheehan, *Dorothy and Red* (Boston: Houghton Mifflin, 1963), (March 12, 1928), 87.

20. William H. Chafe, *The Paradox of Change: American Women in the 20th Century* (New York: Oxford University Press, 1991), 68.

21. Robert S. Lynd and Helen Merrell Lynd, *Middletown: A Study in American Culture* (New York: Harcourt Brace and Co., 1929), 118–120; Hamilton, *Research in Marriage*, 82; Dorothy Dix (pseudonym), *Dorothy Dix—Her Book: Every-day Help for Every-day People* (New York: Funk and Wagnalls Co., 1926), 306.

22. Christina Simmons, "Modern Sexuality and the Myth of Victorian Repression," in Kathy Peiss and Christina Simmons, eds., *Passion and Power: Sexuality in History* (Philadelphia: Temple University Press, 1989), 165–166; Hannah M. Stone and Abraham Stone, *A Marriage Manual: A Prac-*

*tical Guide-Book to Sex and Marriage*, rev. ed. (New York: Simon and Schuster, 1935), 155; Paul Popenoe, *Modern Marriage: A Handbook for Men*, 2nd ed. (New York: MacMillan, 1925, 1940), 137–143; Elton Mayo, "Should Marriage be Monotonous?" *Harpers Monthly* 151 (September 1925): 422; Robert Lynd, "Family Members as Consumers," *Annals of the American Academy of Political and Social Science* 160 (March 1932): 87–89; Christine Frederick, *Selling Mrs. Consumer* (New York: Business Bourse, 1929), 12; Dorothy M. Brown, *Setting a Course: American Women in the 1920s* (Boston: Twayne, 1987), 106–108; Chafe, *Paradox*, 111–115.

23. Clara Savage Littledale, "Adam at Home," *Good Housekeeping* 75 (August 1922): 49ff; Anne Hirst, *Get Your Man — and Hold Him* (New York: H. C. Kinsey, 1937), 84–88; Frederick, *Selling Mrs. Consumer*, 29–31; Susan Strasser, *Never Done: A History of American Housework* (New York: Pantheon Books, 1982), 203, 244–248, 263–264.

24. Lynd, "Family Members as Consumers," 89; Grace Elliott Loucks and Harry Bone, *The Sex Life of Youth* (New York: Association Press, 1929) gave two examples of extravagant wives, one of a spendthrift husband, 94; Hearty Earl Brown, "The Vacation of Charlie French," *Atlantic Monthly* 124 (July 1919): 54; Clara Savage Littledale, "Living Happily Ever After," *Good Housekeeping* 74 (March 1922): 15, 154; Hirst, *Get Your Man*, 94.

25. Hamilton, *Research in Marriage*, 97, 101; Elaine Tyler May, *Great Expectations: Marriage and Divorce in Post-Victorian America* (Chicago: University of Chicago Press, 1980), 138; Christine Frederick, *The New Housekeeping: Efficiency Studies in Home Management* (Garden City, NY: Doubleday Page and Co., 1912), 103; Edna Claire Ferris, "Diary of Edna Claire Ferris, 1878–1931" in Eugene Hutchinson Mallory III, ed., *Good Life and Hard Times: A Mallory Family History*, published by editor, facsimile in Huntington Library, FAC 1083, [hereafter cited as Ferris Diary], November 6, 1929.

26. Penrod Papers, January 17, 1931, July 15, 1931.

27. Penrod Papers, April 14 and 15, 1931, May 3, 1931.

28. Frederick, *Selling Mrs. Consumer*, 45.

29. Schmalhausen, "Sexual Revolution,", 355; Watson, "After the Family," 68.

30. Stone and Stone, *Marriage Manual*, 155; Katherine Bement Davis, *Factors in the Sex Life of Twenty-Two Hundred Women* (New York: Harper and Brothers, 1929), 58, 76; Robert Latou Dickinson and Lura Ella Beam, *A Thousand Marriages: A Medical Study of Sex Adjustment* (Baltimore: Williams and Wilkins Co., 1931), 56; Hamilton, *Research in Marriage*, 233, 537; Sheila Rothman, *Woman's Proper Place: A History of Changing Ide-*

*als and Practices, 1870 to the Present* (New York: Basic Books, 1978), 179–180.

31. Hirst, *Get Your Man*, 116; Simmons, "Modern Sexuality," 169–170; Jeffrey Weeks, "Movements of Affirmation: Sexual Meanings and Homosexual Identities," in Peiss and Simmons, *Passion and Power*, 166; Ellen Key Trimberger, "Feminism, Men, and Modern Love: Greenwich Village, 1900–1925," *Powers of Desire: The Politics of Sexuality*, Ann Snitow, Christine Stansell, and Sharon Thompson, eds. (New York: Monthly Review Press, 1983), 134; Steven Seidman, *Romantic Longings: Love in America, 1830–1980* (New York: Routledge, 1991), 4; Burnham, "Progressive Era Revolution," 901.

32. Reed, *Birth Control Movement*, 143–193; Robert Latou Dickinson and Lura Ella Beam, *A Thousand Marriages: A Medical Study of Sex Adjustment* (Baltimore: Williams and Wilkins Co., 1931), 67.

33. Modell, *Into One's Own*, 115; Davis, *Factors in the Sex Life*, 12; Hamilton, *Research in Marriage*, 134; Marjorie Kinnan Rawlings, *Selected Letters of Marjorie Kinnan Rawlings*, Gordon E. Bigelow and Laura V. Monti, eds. (Gainesville: University of Florida Press, 1983), 27.

34. Hirst, *Get Your Man*, 12.

35. Lynd and Lynd, *Middletown*, 112; Ben B. Lindsey, "Wisdom for Parents," in Calverton and Schmalhausen, "Sex in Civilization," 189; Hamilton, *Research in Marriage*, 346–347; Watson, "After the Family," 65.

36. Lindsey, "Wisdom for Parents," 189; Phyllis Blanchard, "Sex in the Adolescent Girl," in Calverton and Schmalhausen, "Sex in Civilization," 540; Dennett, "Sex Enlightenment," 99.

37. Dennett, "Sex Enlightenment," 101; Hamilton, *Research in Marriage*, 204; Penrod Papers, April 28, 1925.

38. I. M. Hotep (pseudonym), *Love and Happiness: Intimate Problems of the Modern Woman* (New York: Knopf, 1938), 46; Penrod Papers, April 28, 1925; Wilhelm Stekel, "Frigidity in Mothers," in V. F. Calverton and Samuel Schmalhausen, eds. *The New Generation* (New York: The Macauley Co., 1930), 247; Weeks, "Movements of Affirmation," 169–170.

39. Hamilton, *Research in Marriage*, 543.

40. Peet Papers, August 23, 1914; Margaret Marsh, "Suburban Men and Masculine Domesticity, 1870–1915," *American Quarterly* 40 (June 1988): 165–188; Francesca M. Cancian and Steven L. Gordon, "Changing Emotion Norms in Marriage: Love and Anger in U.S. Women's Magazines since 1900," *Gender and Society* 2 (September 1988): 315, 309.

41. Popenoe, *Modern Marriage*, 137; Dorothy M. Brown, *Setting a Course: American Women in the 1920s* (Boston: Twayne Publishers, 1987), 102–103; Paula S. Fass, *The Damned and the Beautiful: American Youth in the 1920s* (New York: Oxford University Press, 1977), 93; Francesca Cancian,

*Love in America: Gender and Self-Development* (Cambridge: Cambridge University Press, 1987), 34; Mintz and Kellogg, *Domestic Revolutions*, 113–114.

42. Margaret Sanger, *Happiness in Marriage* [1926] (Elmsford, NY: Maxwell Reprint Co.), 30; Elinor Glyn, *The Philosophy of Love* (New York: Authors' Press,1923), 177; Littledale, "Adam at Home," 49, 128–131.

43. Sanger, *Happiness in Marriage,* 177; Hirst, *Get Your Man,* 104, 106; Dix, *Dorothy Dix,* 8–9, 39, 53–54; Cancian and Gordon, "Changing Emotion Norms," 317.

44. Kevin White, *The First Sexual Revolution: The Emergence of Male Heterosexuality in Modern America* (New York: New York University Press, 1993), 148, 173–179; Cancian, *Love in America,* 37.

45. Robinson, *A Wall to Paint On,* (December 12, 1929), 124; Sickler Diary, August 25 and 26, 1923; Sheehan, *Dorothy and Red,* (October 27, 1929), 167.

46. Hamilton, *Research in Marriage,* 79; Hirst, *Get Your Man,* 104; Mayo, "Should Marriage Be Monotonous?" 427; Don Cabot McCowan, *Love and Life: Sex Urge and Its Consequences* (Chicago: Pascal Covici, 1928), 172.

47. Ben B. Lindsey and Wainwright Evans, *The Revolt of Modern Youth* (New York: Boni and Liveright, 1925), 138–139; McCowan, *Love and Life,* 72–73; Lorinne Pruette referred to Watson's view in "Some Modern Portraits and Their Interpretations," in Ira S. Wile, ed., *The Sex Life of the Unmarried Adult: An Inquiry into and an Interpretation of Current Sex Practices* (New York: Vanguard, 1934), 296–297.

48. Ilka Chase, *Past Imperfect* (Garden City, NY: Doubleday Doran and Co., 1941), 146–147; Lavell Papers, volume 2, May 16, 1928, June 3, 1930.

49. Jessie Lloyd O'Conner, Harvey O'Conner, and Susan M. Bowler, *Harvey and Jessie: A Couple of Radicals* (Philadelphia: Temple University Press, 1988), 118–120.

50. Chase, *Past Imperfect,* 146; First Papers, February 10, 1929; V. F. Calverton, *The Bankruptcy of Marriage* (New York: The Macauley Co., 1928), 72, 150.

51. Chase, *Past Imperfect,* 89; O'Conner, *Couple of Radicals,* 126; Pearl Buck, *My Several Worlds: A Personal Record* (New York: John Day Co., 1954), 96; William L. O'Neill, *Divorce in the Progressive Era* (New Have, CT: Yale University Press, 1967), 67.

52. Penrod Papers, January 13, 1925.

53. Rawlings, *Selected Letters,* (November 11, 1933), 80; Robinson, *A Wall to Paint On,* (August 27, 1934), 239, (September 30, 1934), 240.

54. Willis Papers, Biographical sketch by Evelyn Harter Glick in box 4, folder 43; box 1, volume 2, November 26, 1923, March 11, 1924.

55. Willis Papers, box 1, volume 2, May 7, 1924, March 18, 1924, May 24, 1924.
56. Willis Papers, box 1, volume 2, September 5, 1924, July 24, 1924; box 2, volume 10, August 2, 1924, 56, July 22, 1924, 53.
57. Willis Papers, box 1, volume 2, August 2, 1924, January 27, 1925.
58. Willis Papers, box 1, volume 2, October 27, 1924, July 3, 1924; box 2, volume 10, January 11, 1925, 77.
59. Willis Papers, box 2, volume 10, September 5, 1924, 62, May 15, 1925, 94; box 1, volume 3, March 12, 1925.
60. Willis Papers, box 2, volume 10, May 1, 1928; Raymond Papers, box 1, volume 11, January 19, 1933.
61. Willis Papers, box 1, volume 3, February 23, 1925, May 15, 1925; box 1, volume 4, June 11, 1926; box 2, volume 10, November 13, 1927.
62. Willis Papers, box 1, volume 3, May 15, 1925; box 2, volume 10, November 2, 1929.
63. Willis Papers, box 2, folder 10, December 24, 1928.
64. Dushkin Papers, box 3, folder 2, March 20 and 23, 1930.
65. Dushkin Papers, box 3, folder 2, July 27, 1930.
66. Dushkin Papers, box 3, folder 2, February 11, 1931
67. Dushkin Papers, box 3, folder 2, November 11, 1931.
68. Dushkin Papers, box 3, folder 2, November 5, 1933, March 1, 1934.
69. Dushkin Papers, box 3, folder 2, November 5, 1933, October 15, 1935.
70. Dushkin Papers, box 3, folder 2, May 10, 1933.
71. Dushkin Papers, box 3, folder 2, August 16, 1930.
72. Dushkin Papers, box 3, folder 2, December 31, 1934.
73. Dushkin Papers, box 3, folder 2, November 23, 1934.
74. Dushkin Papers, box 3, folder 2, August 16, 1930.
75. Dushkin Papers, box 3, folder 2, December 31, 1934.
76. Dushkin Papers, box 3, folder 2, November 23, 1934.
77. Willis Papers, box 1, folder 2, October 14, 1923, February 15, 1924.
78. Willis Papers, box 2, folder 10, May 1937 undated, February 2, 1938.

## *Notes to Chapter 5*

1. Lavell Papers, folder 1, June 1, 1930, September 23, 1930.
2. Sidney Howard, *The Silver Cord: A Comedy in Three Acts,* (New York: Charles Scribners Sons, 1927), 87–88, 91–92.
3. Littledale Papers, box 1, volume 16, June 3, 1914.
4. Howard, *The Silver Cord,* 193.
5. John B. Watson and Rosalie Rayner Watson, *Psychological Care of Infant and Child* (New York: W. W. Norton and Co., 1928), 5–6, 87, 81, 84; Ben Harris, " 'Give me a dozen healthy infants . . .': John B. Watson's

Popular Advice on Childrearing, Women, and the Family," in Miriam Lewin, ed., *In the Shadow of the Past: Psychology Portrays the Sexes: A Social and Intellectual History*, (New York: Columbia University Press, 1984), 128; Floyd Dell, *Love in the Machine Age: A Psychological Study of the Transition from Patriarchal Society* (New York: Farrar and Rinehart, 1930), 137.

6. Peter N. Stearns, *American Cool: Constructing a Twentieth Century Emotional Style* (New York: New York University Press, 1994), 34–36; Jan Lewis, "Mother's Love: The Construction of an Emotion in Nineteenth-Century America," in Andrew E. Barnes and Peter N. Stearns, eds., *Social History and Issues in Human Consciousness* (New York: New York University Press, 1989), 209–224.

7. Evelyn Whitaker, *Laddie and Miss Toosey's Mission* (Philadelphia: Henry Altemus, 1897).

8. Winfield Scott Hall, "The Adolescent Period: Its Problems, Regimen and Hygiene," in M. V. O'Shea, ed., *The Child: His Nature and His Needs* (New York: The Children's Foundation, 1924), 314; Gene Stratton-Porter, *Laddie: A True Blue Story* (Garden City, NY: Doubleday Page and Co., 1913), 437.

9. Ferris Diary, June 21, 1906, August 22, 1910.

10. Linda Rosenzweig, *The Anchor of My Life: Middle-Class American Mothers and Daughters, 1880–1920* (New York: New York University Press, 1993), 112–113; Ferris Diary, July 19, 1920, March 5, 1921.

11. Clara Savage Littledale, "Adam at Home," *Good Housekeeping* 75 (August 1922): 128–131; John B. Watson, "After the Family—What?" in V. F. Calverton and Samuel Schmalhausen, eds., *The New Generation: The Intimate Problems of Modern Parents and Children*, (New York: The Macauley Co., 1930), 55–73.

12. Dorothy Blake, *The Diary of a Suburban Housewife* (New York: William Morrow, 1934), 99.

13. Samuel Schmalhausen, "Family Life: A Study in Pathology," in Calverton and Schmalhausen, *The New Generation*, 278–279, 287; Miriam Van Waters, *Youth in Conflict* (New York: Republic Publishing Co., 1925), 86; Winnifred Richmond, *The Adolescent Girl: A Book for Parents and Teachers* (New York: MacMillan, 1925), 56; Ada Hart Arlitt, *Adolescent Psychology* (New York: American Book Company, 1933), 89.

14. John B. Watson, "After the Family—What?" in Calverton and Schmalhausen, *The New Generation*, 65; Lorinne Pruette, "The Flapper," in Calverton and Schmalhausen, *The New Generation*, 572; Dorothy Dunbar Bromley and Florence Haxton Britten, *Youth and Sex: A Study of 1300 College Students* (New York: Harper and Brothers, 1938), 52; I. M. Hotep

(pseudonym), *Love and Happiness: Intimate Problems of the Modern Woman* (New York: Knopf, 1938), 46; Wilhelm Stekel, "Frigidity in Mothers," in Calverton and Schmalhausen, *The New Generation*, 254, 255.

15. Clara Savage Littledale, "Putting It Up to Mother," *Good Housekeeping*, 77 (September 1923): 156; Dorothy Dix (pseudonym), *Dorothy Dix — Her Book: Every-day Help for Every-day People* (New York: Funk and Wagnalls Co., 1926), 322; Grace Elliott Loucks and Harry Bone, *Sex Life of Youth* (New York: Association Press, 1929), 87–89; Don Cabot Mc-Cowan, *Love and Life: Sex Urge and Its Consequences* (Chicago: Pascal Covici, 1928), 136; Anne Hirst, *Get Your Man — and Hold Him* (New York: H. C. Kinsey and Co., 1937), 117–126; G. V. Hamilton, *A Research in Marriage* (New York: Medical Research Press, 1929), 116–117.

16. Elinor Glyn, *"It"* (New York: The Macauley Co., 1927), 69. Raymond Papers, box 1, volume 3, October 18, 1927.

17. Howe Memoir, box 1, file 292, 58–59; Jane Sherman, *Soaring: The Diary and Letters of a Denishawn Dancer in the Far East, 1925–1926* (Middletown, CT: Wesleyan University Press, 1976), (May 10, 1926), 137–138, (May 13, 1926), 143; Margaret Bourke-White, *Portrait of Myself* (New York: Simon and Schuster, 1963), 27.

18. Sally Carrighar, *Home to the Wilderness* (Boston: Houghton Mifflin, 1973), 8, 16, 9.

19. Olive Ewing Clapper, *One Lucky Woman* (Garden City, NY: Doubleday and Co., 1961), 21, 29, 35–40.

20. Goff Papers, box 1, volume 28, October 5, 1930; box 1, volume 1, February 27, 1928.

21. Gladys Hasty Carroll, *To Remember Forever: The Journal of a College Girl, 1922–1923* (Boston: Little Brown and Co., 1963), (December 2, 1922), 145; Ann Marie Low, *Dust Bowl Diary* (Lincoln: University of Nebraska Press, 1984) 36–37; Sherman, *Soaring*, (August 7, 1925), 34; Lavell Papers, box 1, volume 2, February 9, 1931, box 1, volume 3, January 22, 1933; Elizabeth Yates, *My Diary — My World* (Philadelphia: Westminster Press, 1981), (June 15, 1924), 145–146.

22. Anne Morrow Lindbergh, *Bring Me a Unicorn: Diaries and Letters of Anne Morrow Lindbergh* (New York: Harcourt Brace Jovanovich, Inc., 1971), (late 1928), 248; and *Hour of Gold, Hour of Lead: Diaries and Letters of Anne Morrow Lindbergh, 1929–1932* (New York: Harcourt Brace Jovanovich, 1973), 6, 15.

23. Ione Robinson, *A Wall to Paint On* (New York: E. P. Dutton, 1946), (June 18, 1927), 7; (November 20, 1929), 118.

24. Marjorie Kinnan Rawlings, *Selected Letters of Marjorie Kinnan Rawlings,*

Gordon E. Bigelow and Laura V. Monti, eds. (Gainesville: University of Florida Press, 1983), (November 15, 1918), 24; Penrod Papers, September 25, 1925.

25. Susan Strasser, *Never Done: A History of American Housework* (New York: Pantheon Books, 1982), 230, 240; Robert S. Lynd and Helen Merrell Lynd, *Middletown in Transition: A Study in Cultural Conflicts* (New York: Harcourt Brace Jovanovich, 1937, 1965) 151; Steven Mintz and Susan Kellogg, *Domestic Revolutions: A Social History of American Family Life* (New York: Free Press, 1988), 121; Sheila M. Rothman, *Woman's Proper Place: A History of Changing Ideals and Practices, 1870 to the Present* (New York: Basic Books, 1978), 210–212; Peter N. Stearns, "Girls, Boys and Emotions: Redefinitions and Historical Change," *Journal of American History* 80 (June 1993): 54; Stearns, *American Cool*, 165–168.

26. L. Emmett Holt, *The Care and Feeding of Children: A Catechism for the Use of Mothers and Children's Nurses,* 5th ed. (New York: D. Appleton and Co., 1909), 42–45; Daniel Beekman, *The Mechanical Baby: A Popular History of the Theory and Practice of Child Raising* (Westport, CT: Lawrence Hill and Co., 1977), 110–113.

27. Christine Frederick, *The New Housekeeping: Efficiency Studies in Home Management* (Garden City, NY: Doubleday Page and Co., 1912), chapters 1 and 2 on applications of efficiency and time and motion studies to housework; Strasser, *Never Done*, 263–264.

28. William James, *Psychology: Briefer Course* in *William James: Writings 1878–1899* (New York: Literary Classics of the United States, Inc., 1992) chapter 10, and pages 145, 139, 141, 161, 186; Mrs. Max West, *Infant Care* (Washington, D.C.: Government Printing Office [Care of Children Series No. 2], 1914) 63; Ada Hart Arlitt, *The Child from One to Twelve* (New York: Whittlesey House, McGraw-Hill Company, Inc. 1931), 22.

29. Holt, *Care and Feeding of Children,* 165; West, *Infant Care,* 60; Arlitt, *Child from One to Twelve,* 96.

30. Watson, *Psychological Care,* 111; Van Waters, *Youth in Conflict,* 66; Loucks and Bone, *Sex Life of Youth,* 32; E. Anthony Rotundo, *American Manhood* (New York: Basic Books, 1993), 116–117; Robert L. Griswold, *Fatherhood in America: A History* (New York: Basic Books, 1993), 88–94; Paula S. Fass, *The Damned and the Beautiful: American Youth in the 1920s* (New York: Oxford University Press, 1977), 89–90; Sheila Rothman, *Woman's Proper Place: A History of Changing Ideals and Practices, 1870 to the Present* (New York: Basic Books, 1978), 210–213. Historical literature is divided on the direction of child rearing, but appears to agree on the advice against overprotecting children.

31. Mildred Brewster, *Red Leaves* (New York: Pageant Press, 1959) 10; Clapper, *One Lucky Woman*, 131.

32. Lindbergh, *Hour of Gold* (July 30, 1930), 141; (March 1931), 156; (May 2, 1931), 163.

33. Sally Wood, ed., *The Southern Mandarins: Letters of Caroline Gordon to Sally Wood, 1924–1937* (Baton Rouge: Louisiana State University Press, 1984), (1925), 17; September 9, 1926, 27.

34. Dushkin Papers, box 3, folder 3, December 31, 1936.

35. Clara Savage Littledale, "You and Your Worries," *Good Housekeeping* 75 (December 1922): 151.

36. Beatrice Burton, *The Flapper Wife* (New York: Grosset and Dunlap, 1925), 344.

37. Penrod Papers, December 30, 1924; Kathleen M. Blee, *Women of the Klan: Racism and Gender in the 1920s* (Berkeley: University of California Press, 1991), 11–12, 46, 52.

38. Fass, *The Damned and The Beautiful*, 89–90; Griswold, *Fatherhood in America,* 93; Rotundo, *American Manhood*, 116–117.

39. Dorothy Canfield Fisher, *The Homemaker* (New York: Harcourt Brace and Co., 1924), 178 and *What Grandmother Did Not Know* (Boston: The Pilgrim Press, 1922), 12–13.

40. Dorothy Canfield Fisher, *Self-Reliance: A Practical and Informal Discussion of Methods of Teaching Self-Reliance, Initiative and Responsibility to Modern Children* (New York: Henry Holt Co., 1916, revised 1929), 19, 236; Fisher, *Grandmother Did Not Know*, 12–13; Fisher, *Homemaker*, 174.

41. Blake, *Diary of a Suburban Housewife*, 166, 219, 41, 39, 34, 133, 35.

42. Willis Papers, box 1, volume 2, September 25, 1924; Dushkin Papers, box 3, folder 1, October 15, 1931; James W. Reed, "The Birth Control Movement Before Roe v. Wade," *Journal of Policy History* 7 (1995): 22–52.

43. Ferris Diary, October 10, 1916; Adele Siegel Rosenfeld records two teeth filled "without pain, thanks to $N_2o$," Rosenfeld Papers, February 6, 1936; T. J. Jackson Lears discusses modern intolerance of pain in *Fables of Abundance: A Cultural History of Advertising in America* (New York: Basic books, 1994), 166–167; Lella Secor, *A Diary in Letters*, Barbara Moench Florence, ed. (New York: Burt Franklin and Co., 1978), (April 4, 1918), 170; Sickler Papers, January 16 and 28, 1923.

44. Lindbergh, *Hour of Gold,* (March 24, 1931), 158; Vincent Sheehan, *Dorothy and Red* (Boston: Houghton Mifflin, 1963) 170; Wood, *The Southern Mandarins,* (April 25, 1932), 106.

45. Willis Papers, box 1, volume 4, October 18, 1926, December 1926 undated; [Although scopolamine had become available by the 1914, many

American women believed that physicians were holding it back from them and actively campaigned for the use of the drug in delivery; see Judith Walzer Leavitt, *Brought to Bed: Birthing Women and Their Physicians in America, 1750 to 1950* (New York: Oxford University Press, 1986), chapter 5, 130*ff.*; Dushkin Papers, box 3, folder 2, October 8, 1932.

46. Lavell Papers, box 1, volume 1, October 3, 1927; Jessie Lloyd O'Conner, Harvey O'Conner, and Susan M. Bowler, *Harvey and Jessie: A Couple of Radicals* (Philadelphia: Temple University Press, 1988), 58–60; Secor, *Diary in Letters* (March 14, 1919), 187–188; Gordon, *Southern Mandarins* (June 15, 1932), 114; Sheehan, *Dorothy and Red*, 181–190.

47. Littledale Papers, box 1, volume 10, article drafts, undated; box 1, volume 18, October 18, 1916.

48. Dushkin Papers, box 3, folder 3, December 31, 1936; Lavell Papers, box 1, volume 1, April 15, 1928; Penrod Papers, March 28, 1926.

49. Watson, *Psychological Care,* 74–75; Blake, *Diary of a Suburban Housewife,* 103–104; Willis Papers, box 1, volume 4, December 2 and 22, 1926; Sheehan, *Dorothy and Red,* 309; Lindbergh, *Hour of Gold,* (January 28, 1931), 152; Carol Gilligan, *In a Different Voice: Psychological Theory and Women's Development* (Cambridge, MA: Harvard University Press, 1982), 62. Psychological theory today seems consistently to agree on the importance of relationship in the lives of women.

50. Penrod Papers, June 14, 1926, September 29, 1926.

51. Secor, *Lella Secor,* 189; Dushkin Papers, box 3, folder 2, October 15, 1935.

52. Gordon, *Southern Mandarins,* (Fall 1931), 88–89.

53. Penrod Papers, March 3, 1925, September 12, 1925, October 10, 1927, September 15, 1928.

54. Penrod Papers, October 30, 1926, January 30, 1930, January 17, 1931, April 19, 1926, May 19, 1926.

55. Penrod Papers, September 12, 1925, March 3, 1925, May 11, 1926.

56. Penrod Papers, September 12, 1929, January 17, 1928. During the 1920s social scientists generally moved toward explanations of behavior that emphasized environment over heredity. See Carl N. Degler, *In Search of Human Nature: The Decline and Revival of Darwinism in American Social Thought* (New York: Oxford University Press, 1991), chapter 4.

57. Penrod Papers, August 21, 1929.

58. Ada Hart Arlitt, *The Child from One to Twelve* (New York: Whittlesey House, 1931), 119–120; Wexberg is discussed in Beekman, *The Mechanical Baby,* 113–119; Penrod Papers, May 25, 1926, November 23, 1930, December 11, 1928.

59. Penrod Papers, November 23, 1930, May 25, 1926, September 12, 1925, December 11, 1928.

60. Arlitt, *Child from One to Twelve*, 214–215; Dorothy Canfield Fisher, *What Grandmother Did Not Know*, 245.

61. Penrod Papers, September 12, 1925, January 25, 1930.

62. Robert M. Mennel, "Miriam Van Waters," in Barbara Sicherman and Carol Hurd Green, eds., *Notable American Women: The Modern Period* (Cambridge, MA: Harvard University Press, 1980), 709–711.

63. Van Waters Papers, box 1, volume 1, April 27, 1933, February 9, 1933.

64. Van Waters Papers, box 1, volume 3, August 12, 1935, September 2, 1935; Estelle B. Freedman, *Maternal Justice: Miriam Van Waters and the Female Reform Tradition* (Chicago: University of Chicago Press, 1996), *Maternal Justice*, 13–17.

65. Van Waters Papers, box 1, volume 1, August 25, 1933; box 1, volume 3, October 13, 1935; box 1, volume 1, March 20, 1933, September 27, 1933, May 2, 1934, January 3, 1933; box 1, volume 2, May 10, 1934.

66. Van Waters Papers, box 1, volume 3, September 14, 1934; box 1, volume 2, February 27, 1934; box 1, volume 1, February 8, 1933.

67. Van Waters Papers, box 1, volume 2, January 30, 1934; box 1, volume 3, November 16, 1935.

68. Van Waters Papers, box 1, volume 1, September 4, 1933; box 1, volume 2, May 3 and 4, 1934, January 7, 1934, September 11, 1935; box 1, volume 3, September 3, 1935, 63, November 5, 1935.

### Notes to Chapter 6

1. Raymond Papers; summary of Ruth Raymond's life 1930–1935 is drawn from box 1, volumes 7–13; quote from box 1, volume 13, September 5, 1935.

2. Raymond Papers, box 1, volume 13, October 5 and 12, 1935, December 2, 1935; box 4, volume 44.

3. Raymond Papers, box 1, volume 7, January 2, 1930, April 17, 1930; box 1 volume 13, October 12, 1935.

4. Raymond Papers, box 1, volume 7, November 4, 1929.

5. Margaret Bourke-White, *Portrait of Myself* (New York: Simon and Schuster, 1963), 72; Lavell Papers, folder 2, January 1, 1931; Ione Robinson, *A Wall to Paint On* (New York: E. P. Dutton, 1946), 206; Viola White, *Partridge in a Swamp: The Journals of Viola C. White, 1918–1941* (Taftsville, VT: Countryman Press, 1979), (November 12, 1934), 164.

6. Ann Marie Low, *Dust Bowl Diary* (Lincoln: University of Nebraska Press), (May 12, 1933), 84.

7. Hardy Papers, first quote from box 1, volume 3, April 4, 1933; see also box 1, volume 2, April 14, 1932 and box 1, volume 4, August 2, 1934;

final quote from box 1, volume 3, July 26, 1933; Harriet Louise Hardy, *Challenging Man-Made Disease* (New York: Praeger, 1983), 9–10.

8. Dushkin Papers, box 3, volume 2, October 10, 1932, February 18, 1933; Goff Papers, box 1, annotations for 1992, 4–5.

9. Lavell Papers, folder 3, October 8, 1933.

10. John Modell, *Into One's Own: From Youth to Adulthood in the United States, 1920–1975* (Berkeley: University of California Press, 1989), 131; Robert S. Lynd and Helen Merrell Lynd, *Middletown in Transition: A Study in Cultural Conflicts* (New York: Harcourt Brace and Co., 1937, 1965), 260, 261.

11. Modell, *Into One's Own*, 128; Low, *Dust Bowl Diary*, 34, 66.

12. Douglas A. Thom, *Normal Youth and Its Everyday Problems* (New York: D. Appleton-Century Co., 1932), 60–61.

13. Dorothy Dunbar Bromley and Florence Haxton Britten, *Youth and Sex: A Study of 1300 College Students* (New York: Harper and Brothers, 1938), 13.

14. Rosenfeld Papers, folder 1, April 6, 1936, Wedding Invitation, Lynd and Lynd, *Middletown in Transition*, 149, 179.

15. Dorothy Blake, *The Diary of a Suburban Housewife* (New York: William Morrow, 1934), 40–41.

16. Modell, *Into One's Own*, 127; William H. Chafe, *The Paradox of Change: American Women in the Twentieth Century* (New York: Oxford University Press, 1991), 101; White, *Partridge in a Swamp*, 140; Penrod Papers, letter from James Nelson to Gladys Bell Penrod, July 20, 1933.

17. Van Waters Papers, box 1, volume 1, October 13, 1932.

18. Willis Papers, box 2, volume 10, 1928; Hardy, *Challenging Man-Made Disease*, 24–25.

19. Estelle B. Freedman, *Maternal Justice: Miriam Van Waters and the Female Reform Tradition* (Chicago: University of Chicago Press, 1996), 160, 213–214; mention of sleep problems also appears throughout notebooks, Van Waters Papers.

20. Goff papers, box 1, folder 1, background notes.

21. Karen Nolen-Hoeksma, "Sex Differences in Unipolar Depression: Evidence and Theory," *Psychological Bulletin* 101 (1987): 259–282; Jessie Bernard, "Homosociality and Female Depression," *Journal of Social Issues* 32 (1976): 213–235; E. Wexberg, "Zur Klinik und Pathogenese der leichten Depressionszugustände," *Zeitschrift für die gesamte Neurologie und Psychiatrie* 112 (1928): 549–574, reports the same ratio for admissions to a hospital in Germany in 1928; Frances M. Culbertson, "Depression and Gender: An International Review," *American Psychologist* 52 (January 1997): 25–31; Howard C. Warren, ed., *Dictionary of Psychology* (New York: Houghton Mifflin, 1934), 73.

22. Lavell Papers, folder 2, January 17, 1932; folder 3, June 28, 1935.

23. Stanley Coben, *Rebellion Against Victorianism: The Impetus for Cultural Change in 1920s America* (New York: Oxford University Press, 1991), 111; Chafe, *Paradox of Change*, 28–31; Freedman, *Maternal Justice,* chapter 12; V. F. Calverton and Samuel D. Schmalhausen, *The New Generation: The Intimate Problems of Modern Parents and Children* (New York: The Macauley Co., 1930), 587.

24. Penrod Papers, February 9, 1925, February 17, 1927; Viola White, *Partridge in a Swamp* (January 4, 1931), 118.

25. Linda Rosenzweig, *The Anchor of My Life: Middle-Class American Mothers and Daughters, 1880–1920* (New York: New York University Press, 1993), chapter 9.

26. Hardy, *Challenging Man-Made Disease*, 20, 23; Hardy Papers, box 1, volume 4, December 16, 1934.

27. Dushkin Papers, box 3, folder 2, October 9, 1932.

28. Charles Morgan, *The Fountain* (New York: Knopf, 1932), 12–83.

29. Eiluned Lewis, "Charles Lanbridge Morgan," *Dictionary of National Biography, 1951–1960*, E. T. Williams and Helen M. Palmer, eds. (Oxford: Oxford University Press, 1971), 748–749; Percy Hutchinson, "A Novel of Great Distinction," *New York Times*, June 5, 1932; Hendrik Willem Van Loon, "Prisoner's Love," *Saturday Review of Literature* (New York: Saturday Review Associates), June 4, 1932, 767–768; Emily Newell Blair, "Emily Newell Blair Names Some Notable Books You Should Read This Summer," *Good Housekeeping* 95 (August 1932): 144–145.

30. Anne Morrow Lindbergh, *Hour of Gold, Hour of Lead: Diaries and Letters of Anne Morrow Lindbergh, 1929–1932* (New York: Harcourt Brace Jovanovich, 1973), (June 21, 1932), 280; (August 21, 1932), 305–306.

31. Willis Papers, box 2, volume 10, June 1935 and August 26.

32. Hardy Papers, box 1, volume 2, September 6, 1932.

33. Lavell Papers, box 1, volume 3, December 25, 1932 and October 12, 1932.

34. Van Waters Papers, box 1, volume 1, February 8, 1933; Dushkin Papers, box 3, volume 2, January 26, 1931, February 11, 1931, February 23, 1932; Penrod Papers September 3, 1929.

35. Charles Morgan, *The Fountain,* 49; inscription in Raymond Papers, box 1, volume 13.

36. Raymond Papers, box 1, volume 1, February 22 and 18, 1925.

37. Raymond Papers, box 1, volume 3, September 28, 1927; box 1, volume 4, January 14, 1928, November 11, 1927.

38. Raymond Papers, box 1, volume 3, October 12, 1927; box 1, volume 4, December 30, 1928; box 1, volume 7, January 2, 1930, February 2, 1930.

39. Raymond Papers, box 1, volume 7, February 2, 1930, April 17, 1930.

40. Raymond Papers, box 1, volume 13, July 2, 1935; Culloden refers to the final defeat of the Highland Jacobites.
41. Raymond Papers, box 1, volume 13, August 26, 1935, September 12, 1935, August 31, 1935.
42. Raymond Papers, box 1, volume 6, July 1, 1929; box 1, volume 7, January 9, 1930; box 1, volume 13, October 5, 1935.
43. Raymond Papers, box 1, volumes 13, August 1935–March 1936; box 1, volume 7, April 17, 1930; box 1, volume 1, February 17, 1925; box 1, volume 13, August 17, 1935.
44. Raymond Papers, box 1, volume 8, October 13 and 14, 1930; box 1, volume 12, November 1, 1934.
45. Raymond Papers, box 4, volumes 42–44.

# *Index*